Strategy for Financial Mobility

Harvard Business School Classics

Strategy for Financial Mobility

Gordon Donaldson
Harvard Business School

Harvard Business School Press
Boston, Massachusetts

The paper used in this publication meets the requirements
of the American National Standard for Permanence of Paper
for Printed Library Materials Z39.48–1984.
Harvard Business School Press, Boston 02163

90 89 88 87 86   5 4 3 2 1

Library of Congress Cataloging-in-Publication Data

Donaldson, Gordon, 1922–
   Strategy for financial mobility.

   (Harvard Business School Classics ; 2)
   Includes index.
   1. Corporations—Finance—Addresses, essays,
lectures.   2. Resource allocation—Addresses, essays,
lectures.   I. Title.   II. Series.
HG4011.D575   1986   658.1′5   85–27207
ISBN 0-87584-127-9

PREFACE TO THE HARVARD BUSINESS SCHOOL CLASSICS EDITION

The occasion of a new edition of a book first published in 1969 inevitably raises questions of its relevance to the business world of today and to the current state of the art in management. In response, it is appropriate to begin by noting that the years since 1969 have been marked by exceptional turbulence in the economic and political environments of the western world, in fiscal and financial affairs, and in the competitive viability of major industries and firms. Thus the critical importance of *financial mobility*—the ability to adjust the magnitude and timing of corporate funds flows in response to unexpected events (opportunity or adversity) and thus to assure solvency and continuity—has been abundantly demonstrated.

By the time news of severe financial distress reaches the public, the parties involved, whether they be individuals, business corporations, farmers, or government, invariably are experiencing sustained operating deficits and an excessive burden of debt that is in danger of default. Even the U.S. federal government, while in no danger of defaulting on its outstanding debt, is defaulting on a wide range of "entitlements," once thought to be sacrosanct components of public policy.

These events, when they occur, represent the late stages of a chain reaction initially set in motion by a failure to anticipate and then to respond appropriately to unexpected change in funds flow. At this stage of the process, it is much too late to talk about a strategy of financial mobility. However, having once again learned from adversity of the need for defensive as well as offensive financial strategies, the leaders of the private and public sectors will be receptive to the subject's discussion. While this book is based on and addressed to the experience of profit-oriented business enterprise, the concepts apply to any organization engaged in the management of financial resources.

The economic and business climate of recent years suggests that the degree of uncertainty surrounding the solvency and continuity of individual business enterprise, and therefore the need for defensive planning, continues on a secular increase. Among the reasons for concern are the obvious vulnerability of the international banking system to Third World default, the growth of international competition, trade imbalance, the apparent inability of even conservative administrations in years of prosperity to bring federal spending in line with revenues, and the effects of deregulation. Many will conclude that the need for financial mobility on the part of the individual private enterprise will continue to increase.

This being the case, informed managers will respond by devoting more time and attention to defensive financial planning. Despite good intentions, however, the ability to respond may have decreased. For many industries the events of the last few years, in particular the combination of inflation and recession, have drained off most, if not all, of the financial fat that cushioned these organizations from sudden shock, and they have not had sufficient opportunity to recover.

At the same time, the wave of mergers and acquisitions with the accompanying threat to control has made managements highly sensitive to the conditions that attract the corporate raider, such as the appearance or reality of underemployed or unproductive resources and idle reserves. The more management focuses on maximum short-term performance in order to head off attack, the more it is prone to neglect long-term needs and contingencies. Thus, management often feels it has no choice but to take excessive risks with long-term survival.

There are positive as well as negative incentives to take

excessive risk, a notable example being the currently popular leveraged buyout. The opportunity for small groups (insiders or outsiders) to buy up the outstanding equity with the aid of heavy bank debt, take the company private, and repay the bank debt out of corporate funds flows has the potential for huge managerial and financial rewards. There is obvious danger to the corporation during the period of repayment of abnormal debt—when all of the available resources must be dedicated to this task—if the competitive and business climate is not exceptionally benign. The cycle is complete when the company, with a return to more normal debt-equity ratios, goes public again—in what is hoped will be a buoyant equity market, with substantial capital gains to those who have organized the buyout. Inevitably, all business is a balancing of risk and reward; exceptional opportunity for personal gain will continue to induce some to take exceptional corporate and personal risks, with little apparent regard for defense if things go wrong.

With respect to risk, in the past two decades the primary attention of the academic community has been focused on *portfolio theory*, the principles by which risk can be reduced through diversification. This concept has particular power with respect to large portfolios of financial assets, but also has some relevance to real assets in the business enterprise. In theory, diversification promises the elimination of *unsystematic risk,* those random, company-specific risks, leaving only the systematic risk arising from general economic phenomena common to all investment. Diversification is a powerful tool for portfolio managers, but of limited significance for business managers whose capacity for diversification has serious practical limitations and who, as custodians of the future of the individual enterprise, must necessarily be concerned with total risk in all forms.

Thus in practice, risk management in the individual business enterprise rests primarily on the operational defensive strategy outlined in this book. Such defensive strategy includes continuous scanning of the environment, translation of this information into specific financial consequences, and a plan of resource readiness that permits quick and effective response when adversity strikes. In recent years the term *scenario planning* has come to be used with reference to the careful exploration of the more likely future outcomes. Financial mobility requires an element of scenario planning but depends for its effectiveness on a sustained capacity for specific and appropriate response.

In implementing the concepts of this book, the most important change that has taken place in the past twenty years has been the development of new computer hardware and software. When the author was exploring the applicability of these ideas in the 1960s, the analysis had to be done on large main-frame computers using elaborate, time-consuming, tailor-made computer programs for the manipulation of data. Now, with the general availability of powerful desk-top computers and software packages providing comprehensive financial simulation and projection, there is no excuse for any company not to have the analytic tools and information on which to base an effective strategy of financial mobility.

In practice, the principal barrier to the development of a meaningful defensive financial strategy— one that is likely to persist—arises from the conventional mindset of corporate leadership. The typical chief executive sets aggressive goals and expects—and demands—full confidence in and commitment to these goals from the entire management team. The more aggressive the goals, the more likely it is that all resources—mental, emotional, and financial—will be committed to their achievement. It takes an unusually secure and independent chief financial officer to hold back some commitment of human and financial resources as protection against the possibility that, in the end, and despite the best efforts of everyone, the chosen strategy may fail. To do so may well be perceived as faintheartedness or even disloyalty. The role of conservator and custodian of corporate solvency is often times a lonely and unrewarding one, though vital to the ultimate corporate goal of long-term survival and continuity of the enterprise.

Boston, Massachusetts
January 1986   GORDON DONALDSON

Table of Contents

PART III. OBSERVATIONS OF PRACTICE:
THE COMMON ELEMENTS OF CORPORATE BEHAVIOR

PART IV. A STRATEGY OF FINANCIAL MOBILITY

Business Forecasting: Information or Control? . . . The Information Needs of Financial Mobility . . . A Computer
Model of Cash Flows . . . The Uses of Simulation Information . . . An Example of Simulation Results . . . Analysis
Without a Computer

Current Approaches to Measurement of Resources . . . A
New Kind of Financial Statement . . . Estimating Individual
Resources . . . The Managerial Uses of an Inventory of
Resources of Mobility . . . Reconciling Reporting of the
Past and the Future

Introductory Qualifications . . . The Problem Restated . . .
The Adequacy of Resources for Specific Contingent Needs
. . . The Adequacy of Resources at the Planning Horizon
. . . Priorities in the Commitment of Resources . . . Imple-
menting a Strategy of Mobility . . . Organizational Respon-
sibility for Financial Mobility . . . The State of Financial
Equilibrium . . . Debt Reserves and Debt Capacity . . . A
Last Word

List of Exhibits

Part I

The Concept of Financial Mobility

I
Introduction

This study of financial mobility grew out of the observations of a previous study reported in a book called *Corporate Debt Capacity*,[1] in which attention was centered on the practices of business corporations relating to the use of long-term debt. As the title of that book implies, the corporation was viewed as having the potential ability to use long-term debt as an integral part of its program of funding capital requirements. The book addressed itself to the problem of how best to determine the existence and magnitude of this borrowing capacity. In order to understand the management problem and relate to the circumstances and needs of the real world, a large part of the research effort was involved in field studies of individual business firms and in interviews with financial officers charged with the decisions under study. These observations were reported in Chapters 3 to 5 of *Corporate Debt Capacity*, pages 51 to 120.

Although I made every effort to approach these field studies without prejudice or preconception as to the findings, it is clear in retrospect that I had a distinctly normative bias derived from the way in which capital structure decisions have customarily been dealt with by students of corporate finance. This bias came from the conviction that the ultimate financial objective of the business firm is to increase or maximize the value of the owners' equity. This leads to a concern for the earnings on the equity investment and the price-earnings ratio through which changes in earnings are translated into higher or lower market values for the

---

[1] Gordon Donaldson, *Corporate Debt Capacity: A Study of Corporate Debt Policy and the Determination of Corporate Debt Capacity* (Boston: Division of Research, Harvard Business School, 1961).

common stock. Since the earnings per share, and possibly the price-earnings ratio also, are directly affected by the proportion of debt in the capital structure, it is obvious that an approach to maximum value of the equity must include a definition of the proper or optimum level of long-term borrowing.

Although there is considerable debate concerning the ultimate effect of corporate debt on the market value of the common stock, there is widespread acceptance by both practitioner and academic that some debt or "leverage" could be and commonly is beneficial in raising the per-share earnings and, therefore, the value of the common stock. In the company that has little or no debt but has the capacity to bear some debt-servicing burden, it would seem a highly attractive and relatively painless way of boosting earnings per share as compared with further increases in sales or internal economies of operation. In conducting this study of debt financing I had expected to find this attitude reflected by corporate financial officers, and any reluctance to use this source of funds was expected to be primarily due to the difficulty of determining how far to go, i.e., where to set the limits of corporate debt capacity.

It was therefore a considerable surprise to find widespread indifference among intelligent financial men in substantial corporations toward the prospect of refining the method of determining debt limits. Often they appeared quite content to continue to be guided by the vague rules of thumb of the financial community, rules quite unrelated to the specific circumstances of the individual business. Further, they appeared to have little or no inclination to fully utilize the debt capacity that these rules of thumb seemed to encourage. A debt level that clearly provided a substantial margin between corporate use and debt availability was not only tolerable but, in some cases at least, apparently desirable.

It was tempting to pass this behavior off as irrationality, ignorance, irresponsibility, or self-interest and thus to cling to the idea that the optimum policy is to take maximum advantage of debt leverage within rationally defined limits. With further reflection, however, it began to dawn on me that the frame of reference assumed by the optimum capital structure theory of corporate finance with its attendant logic was not necessarily the frame of reference of the managers being interviewed. Consequently, it was possible that another logic prevailed in their approach to decision making. The nature and significance of this distinction will be developed in succeeding chapters. It is sufficient to say here that whereas normative statements of policy focused almost exclusively on the magnitude of debt *in use,* managers appeared much more interested in the magnitude of the debt *not in use,* that is, on the reserve of unused debt capacity. Obviously, the value systems are quite different.

It does not take great insight to be aware that an important concern of the financial practitioner is for the needs of the future. It is also obvious that there would be a particular concern for needs that might emerge unexpectedly with insufficient time for response. It is therefore clear why a borrower might desire a reserve of unused borrowing capacity. But there remains the very sticky question of how this reserve shall be defined or measured so that it can be said to be adequate or "right." Having made some suggestions in *Corporate Debt Capacity* of how the measurement of total debt capacity of a company might be approached, I saw it as a natural next step to begin the exploration of an approach to a definition of debt reserves. Recognition of the possible conflict in viewpoint between theory and practice indicated that the first step in this exploration was to seek to better understand the viewpoint of the actual decision maker in this respect. This line of interest was the beginning of the ideas presented in this book.

It was not long, however, before the plan of the study broadened substantially in its scope. If the central problem lay in incomplete information about future funds requirements and the threat of an as yet undefined need, then the research question shifted from: How does/should a business determine the nature and magnitude of its debt reserve? to: How does/should a business respond to the knowledge that future funds flows are not precisely known and that from time to time major needs will arise that have not been fully anticipated? Although borrowing may be one of the primary means of defense against such needs, it is clear that it is not the only possible response and that there are likely to be several ways of closing the funds flow gap. This would seem to call for some sort of strategy for dealing with these events, a strategy of redirecting funds flows as new information changes the picture — what will be called in this book *a strategy of financial mobility.*

A point that should be emphasized early in this statement of the problem is that the challenge to management does not lie in change *per se* but rather in *unexpected* change. Substantial and irregular changes in funds inflows and outflows over time require careful planning of the company's investment program so that inflows match outflows at each point in time or liquid reserves are accumulated for those times when outflows will exceed inflows. In the absence of uncertainty as to the magnitude and timing of inflows and outflows this would be largely a mechanical process making little demand on the experience and judgment of senior management. However, the unexpected event is obviously an integral part of the real world experience.

DEFINITION OF TERMS

Two words have been long associated with dimensions of the problem discussed in this study. One of these is *liquidity* and the other is *flexibility*. Liquidity is commonly used to identify the degree to which the assets of a business are in the form of uncommitted purchasing power — cash or its equivalent (e.g., high-grade marketable securities). A high degree of liquidity is usually considered a positive sign since it indicates a capacity to meet obligations, an ability to move in new directions of investment, and a greater certainty in balance sheet values. On the other hand, liquidity also has its negative implications since the funds are at least for the moment out of work so far as profits are concerned and could imply excessive caution on management's part.

Liquidity is one of those values constantly being measured and reported. Normally, the item being measured is the reported cash balance, though a portfolio of marketable securities may be added in if the portfolio is being held as a liquid reserve and is available on short notice without danger of loss in value. It is recognized, however, by everyone who understands corporate finance that not all of the money shown on the balance sheet as "cash" is available for immediate investment in new specialized assets. Depending on the nature of the business, a major portion of the cash balance will be cash trapped in the transactions "pipeline." The magnitude of these transactions balances depends on the firm's system of collections and payments and on the volume of transactions being processed at any given time. The remaining portion of the cash balance will include funds accumulated for specific purposes in the near future, funds held as a "precautionary balance" against unexpected needs, and the involuntary accumulation resulting from a current excess of inflows over outflows. These differing elements comprised in the cash balance are not normally identified for the external analyst or even for management.

Liquidity may also be measured (and therefore defined) in a somewhat different way by adding other actual or potential sources of corporate purchasing power. A very familiar balance sheet ratio is the so-called "quick asset" or "acid test" ratio, which relates the magnitudes of cash plus marketable securities plus accounts receivable to current liabilities. This is presumably a test of the company's ability to pay off current liabilities out of full-value "liquid" assets. This liquidation value concept may have meaning to a short-term creditor but has little if any meaning for operating management since a continuing investment in credit to customers is an integral part of doing business with them. Funds tied up in accounts receivable related to a given level of sales are, therefore, unavailable for alternative uses and illiquid from a management viewpoint.

Less frequently, though more meaningfully, liquidity is measured by adding "free" cash and near-cash to the unused portion of a short-term line of credit with a commercial bank. The latter item does not, of course, appear anywhere on the company's balance sheet, and yet it represents a real resource for financial management in planning for future needs. Unused bank credit has the obvious disadvantage of an element of uncertainty about when it will be available and in what amounts, but management may have sufficient confidence in its banking relationships to ignore a small degree of uncertainty in this respect. It will be developed later that the basic intent of liquidity — free balances of purchasing power immediately available to implement management's decisions — is an important part of the concept of mobility.

Another term that has found a common usage in this general area is *flexibility*. The word is used in reference to capital structure decisions where a firm is choosing the particular mix of sources to be used in current financing. While the goal is usually considered to be finding the mix that minimizes cost and maximizes value at a point in time, some thought is given to undefined future needs and the ability to adjust the financing structure if events do not work out as expected. To be flexible in sources of funds is to have more than one alternative by which to deal with an uncertain future. This, also, is a part of what the author has elected to call *financial mobility*.

The subject of this book may be described as the management of funds flows over time in a world where the future is always in some degree unknown. Viewed in financial terms, business activity is seen as a continuous flow of funds into and out of specialized use, with the hope that it will generate a profit. It is the job of top management to choose where these uses or "investments" shall lie and to determine their evolution over time as the economic and competitive environment changes and as new management goals emerge in response to this change. Financial mobility is defined as the capacity to redirect the use of financial resources in a manner consistent with the evolving goals of management as it responds to new information about the company and its environment.

It will be apparent that this capacity to change the direction of corporate investment — at times abruptly and on a large scale — is in an important degree related to the company's "stock" of idle or uncommitted funds. Thus, there is a direct connection with *liquidity,* which is the stock of uncommitted funds in hand, and with *flexibility,* which relates to the stock of uncommitted funds available through negotiation with the capital markets. But this is only a part of the task of balancing the flows of funds over time. There is the equally important element of control over the flows themselves — the rate of release of funds from specialized use (inflows) and the rate and nature of commitment of funds to new uses (outflows). A deficiency in the flows at any given time may be provided for by any one or a combination of increases in inflows, decreases in outflows, and reductions in reserves. A fully developed strategy must recognize all three as an integrated and interacting set of alternatives. Thus, the issues raised by discussions of liquidity and flexibility are regarded as dealing with only

one part of the problem, and the abuse of imposing a new phrase
(financial mobility) is justified on these grounds.

THE APPROACH TO THE RESEARCH

The research and writing that have been done on the subject
of liquidity and flexibility in corporate financial management
might have been considered an appropriate point of departure
for a study of financial mobility. The general subject of cash
management and liquidity has been dealt with at two very different levels. There is the descriptive literature, which has been primarily concerned with the mechanics of cash flow and the minimization of idle or unproductive cash. In the post-World War II
period there has been a great deal of interest on the part of the
financial manager in such subjects as float, minimum bank balances, and the marketable securities portfolio. Here the writings
describe what is done — what might be called best current practice.

At another level are the academic writings, which have attempted to deal with the logic of how to determine the amount
of funds that should be carried as a liquid balance. This might
be called analytical and normative — not so much concerned with
what is done as with what should be done as a rational process of
decision making under optimum conditions. In this area the
problem has been identified as one that can be best handled by
viewing cash as an inventory and applying the statistical inventory model concepts developed for physical inventory decisions.
Thus, cash is seen as an item for which there are tangible gains
from carrying a stock and real costs for being out of stock; and
the analytical problem is how to assess in quantitative terms the
potential gains and losses at different inventory levels in order to
arrive at an optimum level. An assessment of the probabilities of
running out of stock at various cash balance levels will be a part
of those models that attempt to deal with uncertainty.

As previously indicated, the issue of flexibility has arisen in discussions of capital structure and new external sources of funds.
Invariably these writings deal with capital structure in the context of considering the set of financial policies that will maximize
the value of the company's common stock. The principal issues
are, therefore, the expected effects of various combinations of

contracts and sources on income and risk. The considerations of control and possible implications for further financing (flexibility) are generally brought in as qualitative aspects only and not as part of the explicit formulation. Indeed these aspects, which can be of great practical significance, are introduced largely as an afterthought in any theoretical writings. As a consequence, flexibility has not been seriously explored as an issue in itself, either descriptively or analytically.

A key characteristic of the analytical writings on both cash balances and capital structure is that they aim at an objective framework for evaluating changes in the structure of assets and liabilities. The measurement is in terms of anticipated change in the value of the business. Maximization of present value is the ultimate goal. The job of management is seen in terms of a single decision at one point in time, seeking the best obtainable outcome given the conditions at that time and whatever information is available at that time about the future.

The problem of financial mobility is inherently different. Instead of a concern for value at any point in time, it is a concern for continuity over time — continuity in funds flows so that the business can move forward to accomplish its goals. Instead of a primary interest in the single investment or financing decision, it is concerned with the linkage between decisions — the implications of present action for future alternatives and vice versa. From one viewpoint it is an operating problem in that it is vital to the continuity of the business as a competitive entity. From another viewpoint it may be regarded as a concern for the sustainability of value over time, which hinges on the ability to redirect funds flows so as to maintain earning power.

Given the desire and the opportunity to invest time in the study of financial mobility, different approaches might be taken. The more typical academic approach would be to deal with the problem normatively: How *should* a business make decisions that involve uncertainty about future funds requirements? What is the correct logical framework for dealing with the relevant considerations in a systematic and objective manner? This would be referred to as the development of a theory, conceptual scheme, or model for the problem so that it could be integrated with other dimensions of generalized models of finance.

Such model building inevitably means a retreat from the real world by simplification and abstraction in order to bring to bear the available tools of logic. Once the problem has been classified as to the relevant logical discipline into which it is assumed to fit — for example, Bayesian statistical decision theory — the primary capacities required of the researcher are the technical skills of the discipline and not an understanding of the real world. While such work is essential in getting the logic of the decision process straight, there is frequently a problem in bringing this logic to bear on real world decisions. The problem is partly semantic. The theoretician and the practitioner talk different languages, the one in quantitative symbols and the other in plain and sometimes imprecise English. The problem is also partly a matter of the oversimplifications of logic and the omission of important nonquantifiable elements.

There are significant difficulties in using the results of theory, but there is an even more basic potential problem. Almost invariably the theorist who undertakes to analyze a management problem brings to bear on it (1) a specific conceptual framework and set of analytical tools, which derive from the particular discipline in which he has been trained (e.g., econometrics, mathematics); (2) a motivation to make a contribution to better decision making through the application of his special talents ("better" in the sense of more systematic and logical and therefore closer to the right decision. By inference the theorist has little interest in how such decisions are, in fact, made by practitioners); (3) a preconceived set of standards by which he measures achievement toward optimum results (e.g., the maximization of economic value).

All of this appears to me to assume a more advanced state of the art of financial management than I believe to be the case. It would be a great advance to be able to say with conviction: Here are a set of (quantifiable) corporate goals; here is an analytical system for relating decisions to these goals; here is where a particular problem fits in the system; here are the relevant variables and the data upon which the decision should be based; here are the analysis and the results of that analysis. Unfortunately, all these dimensions are still in doubt. The evidence as to the doubt concerning goals, values, classification of problems, relevant discipline lies in the very wide gap still existing between academic theory and business practice.

For those who are concerned about bridging that gap in order to make reason a stronger partner of intuition and judgment, there is a need for another kind of research, of which it is hoped that this study is a sample. It involves a serious effort to learn from the businessman himself how he perceives the problem, what he sees as the relevant variables, and how he deals with them analytically in reaching sensible decisions. It means trying to understand his operational frame of reference instead of imposing one on him. It means taking what is for many academicians the giant step of assuming that the average businessman is both intelligent and rational in what he does.

This kind of research is often classified as "behavioral" as opposed to "analytical," involving an explanation of behavior as it is observed in real situations. It is also classified as "descriptive," an attempt to describe the world as it is, not as it should be. It would be unfortunate, however, if such work stopped short at the point of merely reporting on best business practice. The goal should be to look behind behavior to explain why things are as they are, to build a meaningful and understandable descriptive model of financial decision making, which can be compared with the logical or analytical model for purposes of bridging the gap between them. Both models are essential for recommendations of improvement in practice.

Thus, a vigorous attack at both ends of the research spectrum is needed, though unfortunately behavioral or descriptive research in finance is not in academic vogue at the present time. The well-being of the professional school of business administration depends not only on the existence of both kinds of research but also on a sense of responsibility in each approach to integrate with the other. The normative researcher should look to descriptive research for assistance in identifying and classifying the problems and in assessing the relevance of his results. The descriptive researcher should look to the results of normative research for help in identification of the relevant issues for exploration and for ideas as to how the present state of the art may be improved through logic and analysis.

The Research Question, Data, and Methodology

The general research philosophy behind this study having been stated, it is now appropriate to become specific about what was studied and how it was done. These facts were considered as given: that corporate funds inflows and outflows vary over time; that regardless of whether profits are realized or not, a deficiency of funds may develop from time to time; and that those charged with maintaining a balance between inflows and outflows have imperfect advance knowledge of the nature, magnitude, and timing of the need. The questions to which answers were sought in the descriptive phase of the study then may be summarized as follows.

(1) What is the process used for the identification of the nature, timing, and magnitude of future funds flows? What are the data used? How does the process reflect the fact that information is imperfect?

(2) What are the resources employed by financial management in meeting unexpected deficits in funds flows? How are these resources identified and measured? Is there evidence of a priority system persisting over time? What is the process by which resources are brought into play and what is the relationship among resources in this respect?

(3) What evidence exists to demonstrate a relationship between current action with respect to stocks and flows of funds and future requirements for funds, defined and undefined? Can this relationship be generalized by a series of observations of action over time?

(4) To the extent that action is required to maintain a balance of funds flows over time, is there an apparent strategy governing the action and if so what is its nature?

(5) Is there evidence to suggest the existence of a state of equilibrium in funds flows under certain conditions, and, if so, what are these conditions? (Equilibrium is defined as a state where a balance in the flows is achieved over several periods without overt action with respect to stocks or flows.)

(6) What is the relationship, if any, between a strategy of mobility and the set of financial policies that customarily circumscribe action with respect to dividends, debt usage, etc., and their effect on the value of the firm?

Since the focus of these questions was on expectations and their impact on current decisions, it was apparent that the research did not lend itself to an aggregate statistical approach. There are no public records of aggregate expectations, only of past performance. Even if they were available, however, I preferred to work by means of depth analysis of the individual business firm in seeking to understand individual behavior. The insights provided by the people actually involved represent a research resource which, if properly approached, is invaluable in reconstructing the managerial frame of reference. Although less rigorous than the manipulation of numbers and more relevant to the generation than to the testing of hypotheses, this method places primary emphasis on establishing the facts of the real world in complete form, even if there is some sacrifice in the elegance of the research method. It clearly makes those who read and use the results of this type of research more dependent on the maturity of the judgment of the researcher.

In view of the obvious problems inherent in attempting to reconstruct past decisions respecting financial action or even to make explicit the current thinking on any given topic (most of us find it difficult to explain our own reasons and motives to ourselves, let alone to others), it was necessary to adopt a research approach that did not place excessive reliance on any one source of evidence. Much has been made of the fallibility of interview data, and much depends on the integrity of both the researcher and the person being interviewed. Great demands are made on the capacity of the researcher to execute a subtle and unbiased interview and to judge when he is getting an honest and perceptive response.

However, the key to the use of such evidence — and the potential weaknesses are admittedly serious — lies in insisting on two or more independent bodies of data which, like a navigational fix on a target, come at the same point from different angles and provide intersections of information that corroborate each other. Many businesses possess a wealth of such information, which few researchers have taken advantage of but which is surprisingly available if a spirit of mutual respect and trust can be established. The use of multiple evidence in case analysis will be described below as it was applied to the study of financial mobility.

As previously explained, the research question related to the linkage between a sequence of financial decisions arising from uncertainty about future funds requirements. The objective of the study was to examine several series of sequential decisions and to try to identify an apparent strategy for dealing with the "unexpected" need where mobility was put to the test. The first challenge was how to identify an unexpected need, particularly after the fact. It was possible to ask questions about past expectations, but the data would be heavily filtered by subsequent experience and faulty memory.

It was determined, therefore, that the companies to be interviewed must be limited to those which had a formal forecasting procedure during the period in question and where the forecast records were still intact. In this way there would be, after the fact, a systematic record of expectations which could be used to verify the recollections of those who had lived through the experience. This requirement created some problems because the companies that had been using systematic forecasting procedures for five to ten years were not numerous. These forecasts customarily took the form of *pro forma* balance sheets and income statements with the forecast period varying from one month to five years, one year being the most common forecast horizon.

The second body of data required of each participating company was detailed financial statements to record the actual financial "events" to set alongside the forecasts. Because the study placed heavy emphasis on careful documentation of the precise sequence of events, it was necessary to insist that these statements be available for the period in question on a quarterly basis and preferably monthly. Such statements were usually those produced for internal use and often provided considerably more detail than published financial statements.

The analysis of such information in advance of interviews provided the basis for detailed questioning of the people involved, which was a third body of data. Here two techniques were employed to advantage in validating the record. One was to interview an individual not once but several times so that rapport could be established, issues could be probed in depth, and the same point could be approached from several angles. The other approach was to attempt to find two or more people who had lived through the same experience. Honest differences of viewpoint and perspective exist which, through contrast, tend to highlight the facts.

Finally, the records of the company often contained a rich body of data, which frequently were made available. These included minutes of meetings at the committee or board level, formal reports presented internally or to outside parties such as banks, memoranda kept by the people involved for their own use, books of record, published reports to stockholders, and reports to the government or regulatory agencies. Such information was often invaluable in determining the precise order of events, the mood and thinking of the time, the personalities involved, and the priorities that governed in particular decisions.

These were the elements of the research data used in this particular study. It must also be acknowledged that, being particularly attuned to the problem of financial mobility at this time, I was also seeking additional insights in my day-to-day contacts with businessmen. In some ways contacts with companies outside the formal research group provided more dependable data, since these relationships were often on a more intimate and enduring basis. Although it does not represent part of the formal evidence, such experience, which more nearly represents the "inside" point of view, was invaluable in giving insight into the problem.

In the choice of companies to form the sample of the business population to be researched, the primary requirement was access to the kinds of data above. Of necessity, this had two implications. It meant that the sample could not be described in any statistical sense as a "predictive" sample. That is, the data and findings so obtained could not be used to define with quantitative precision the characteristics of the population from which it was drawn. Research was done where research could be done. The other implication was that severe limits were placed on the number of companies that could be researched, since each company required a very large input of time to explore.

Thus, the findings became more for the purpose of generating than testing hypotheses. However, the research effort held to the objective of having something to say about how companies in general are likely to behave in this respect, and, in this sense, the research has a predictive character. The evidence on this point lies more in the appearance of consistent behavior among the companies under observation than in the methodology of selection of the sample.

It follows from the character of the data required that companies with this kind of data available are going to be relatively mature, both in the sense of having a number of years of performance behind them and also in the sense of having developed some sophistication in handling financial affairs. Although this does not necessarily mean that the companies also had to be large, the tendency was to rule out very small companies. It was considered desirable that the companies have access to the established capital markets, and this, too, led to the selection of medium-sized, mature companies. There was, in fact, a rather wide range of size within the research group.

One of the issues in the selection of companies was the type of need that gave rise to pressure on the balance of funds flows. In the preceding study, *Corporate Debt Capacity,* attention was focused exclusively on the business recession in this respect. The approach taken in that study was capable of analyzing other types of pressures, and it was considered a limitation that the study did not extend to other phenomena of uncertainty. Thus, in this study it was determined that a variety of causes of pressure would be included and industries and companies would be chosen with this in mind.

In order to give any hope of ability to detect patterns of behavior, it was necessary to establish situations in which the pressure on the balance of funds flows was substantial and sustained for some length of time. The causes of pressure had to be such that they affected the company in a major way. The more common types of pressure situations considered were as follows:

(1) Major cyclical fluctuations in volume of operations;
(2) Rapid and sustained growth in volume of operations;
(3) Secular decline in demand;
(4) Major changes in the technology of production;
(5) Serious erosion of competitive position because of product innovation or other factors.

The question will arise whether all these situations are likely to give rise to the type of need for funds properly described as "unexpected" — the need most likely to expose and test a strategy of mobility. One can conceive of events with major funds implications that could fall entirely without warning and with concentrated impact. They might be regarded as the ultimate hazard: events such as a natural disaster, or an arbitrary act of a competitor (e.g., a new product innovation), a government (e.g., a tariff change), or a court of law (an unexpected adverse judgment). More commonly, however, unexpectedness of events in business is partial rather than total—a matter of timing or degree of change. The events named above are known to happen and may even be anticipated by a given business as a part of its future experience. The problem arises because the event has not been foreseen soon enough to take the needed steps for funds acquisition or reallocation, or the full funds implications have not been correctly anticipated. In brief, the events with which this study will be primarily concerned are not so much unforeseeable as unforeseen.

In addition to the requirements that the sample of companies provide access to data in depth and that they represent a mix of causes of uncertainty, it was considered good research methodology to select companies so that all sectors of a simple grid of need for funds and the capacity to respond were represented. The intended meaning of this is as follows. On the basis of published information, it was possible to identify some of the kinds of funds flow pressures that the business had been facing in the recent past and to make a tentative classification of the company as to whether the imbalance or rate of change in funds flows was severe or mild. It was also possible to classify these same companies on a tentative basis as to whether they did or did not have the capacity to absorb a financial shock of this sort. This classification was primarily in terms of liquidity. The goal was to find companies representing all four combinations of these two characteristics. It was felt that this procedure would reduce the possible bias that would follow from a random selection disregarding the mix of pressures and capacity to respond.

The remaining consideration influencing the selection of the sample of companies was the desire to minimize the differences among companies that could be traced to the characteristics of the industry in which they were located. It is evident that cash flows are at times significantly influenced by industry characteristics and practices. A great diversity of industry would make comparison more difficult. The conclusion here was to aim for three or four companies from the same industry responding at about the same period of time to the same kind of financial problem. Ideally, the companies within a given industry would each represent one of the sectors of the grid of need and capacity mentioned previously. This was the model of company selection. In fact, it was only partially implemented for reasons to be described below.

The first step in the research sequence was a pilot study, which was a series of analyses and interviews with four companies regarded as "expendable" so far as the research sample was concerned. The purposes of the pilot study were as follows:

(1) To test the suitability of the concept of financial mobility as a meaningful concern of financial management.
(2) To test the validity of the research approach and the availability of data.
(3) To test the practicability of the research sampling process.

Certain modifications to the approach followed from these pilot studies. The first and perhaps most important was a recognition that to follow rigidly the full distribution of the need-capacity grid as the basis for sample selection would probably lead to an underproductive research effort. It was learned in the pilot study and in later case studies that those companies whose recent experience placed them in the segments of the grid involving low need or high capacity to respond—and particularly the two combined—had done very little thinking about and had undertaken very little implementation of a strategy of mobility. This observation tended, therefore, to shift the sample to a much heavier emphasis on companies that gave the most promise of serious thought and effort—the high need, low capacity segment.

A second significant modification related to the data available and to the approach to data analysis. As previously indicated, it was the intent to use formal funds flows forecasting as the basis of documenting expectations and then to compare the expectations with "actual" funds flows for the periods in question. This approach proved less satisfactory than was originally hoped for several reasons. One was that formal cash flow forecasting was still relatively new, and even among larger companies it was not easy to find one that had been forecasting formally and in detail on a consistent basis for ten years. A second reason was the discovery that forecast horizons were much shorter than expected, with heavy emphasis on the look one year ahead. Thirdly, and most significantly, it was found that formal forecasts were only a partial representation of the expectations of the financial manager, and often they were the least interesting part, showing only the most obvious, routine, and certain elements.

These points illustrate the importance of the pilot study in sharpening the research approach and method. They also explain why the final research effort did not come out as neat and tidy as the original specifications would appear to suggest. However, it is hoped that what was lost in the orderliness of the research approach was more than made up in greater significance of the findings.

THE PLAN OF THE BOOK

The results of the study will be reported in the following sequence. Part I, consisting of three chapters, provides in addition to this introduction a statement of the viewpoint that I bring to bear on the subject of corporate financial mobility. An understanding of this viewpoint is necessary to the reader in interpreting the report of field research and the analysis and conclusions based on these observations. This expression of viewpoint is most explicit in Chapter 2, where the traditional value-oriented viewpoint identified with most academic authors is challenged by what I regard as a managerial view related to the balancing of funds flows over time. Chapter 3 carries this viewpoint into a detailed statement of the concept of financial mobility. In this chapter financial mobility and the strategy related to it are defined in verbal and diagrammatic form. All of this is preliminary to any report on research findings.

Part II, also consisting of three chapters, begins the report of research observations in which the generalized abstraction of

financial mobility outlined in Chapter 3 becomes specific. It was
felt to be most revealing if the reader was taken first into the
dynamics of the problem as seen in the month-to-month unfolding of an individual case history. In these three chapters we
break in on the life cycles of three different businesses and for
a period observe how each company performed the difficult task
of keeping funds flows in balance under pressure. While there
is no basis for describing these cases as necessarily "representative" of the research population, they provide an intimacy of
information that aggregate statistics miss.

Part III moves from the specific to the general and reports
on research findings for the total sample of companies included
in the study. The material of this part is organized, not in terms
of comprehensive case histories, but rather in terms of a general
breakdown of the problem confronting management. Chapter 7
is taken up with the question of how these businesses looked at
the future and how they handled the dimension of time in financial planning. The concept of a planning horizon and the nature
of conventional planning are related to the need to respond to
unexpected demands for funds. Chapter 8 undertakes to define
the unexpected need for funds as observed in these companies
and proceeds to survey the various resources used to cover unexpected needs as they arose. Finally, Chapter 9 explores the evidence of a conscious strategy of financial mobility in the research
sample of businesses. The chapter presents a generalized model of
how companies were observed to cope with the problem of a persistent but uncertain deficit in funds flows and discusses the sequence in which available resources were placed in or withdrawn
from use.

The last section of the book, Part IV, presents my ideas for
improvements in corporate practice with respect to financial
mobility. Following the pattern of Part III, the first chapter of
this "normative" section, Chapter 10, presents ideas for a better
utilization of the resource of *time*. In particular, the discussion
centers on a new approach to the analysis underlying financial
planning. Chapter 11 deals with the need to take inventory of
the resources of mobility and to establish their nature and their
magnitude for some planning horizon. What emerges is a kind
of forward-looking balance sheet in contrast to the conventional

report of assets. The final chapter takes a tentative look at what a rational strategy for financial mobility should be and suggests a framework for organizing management thinking around the basic problems involved.

With this quick look at the organization of what lies ahead we now proceed to consider the first of two foundation chapters dealing with the question of viewpoint.

2

A Managerial View of Corporate Finance

Much of what I see as the differences between the findings of this study of corporate financial mobility and the teachings of modern financial theory with respect to normative financial policy can be traced to a difference in viewpoint. The typical academic theorist takes a clear position of identification with the economic interests of the common shareholder in matters of what *ought* to be done. This study asserts an identification with the viewpoint of professional management in attempting to explain what *is* done and further asserts that the interests of the shareholder on the one hand and of management and the corporate entity on the other are not necessarily identical.

Because the question of viewpoint is so fundamental to the observations and conclusions of the study, this chapter is devoted to an elaboration of the differences. The first three sections attempt to summarize in basic language some relevant portions of current academic theory. Since these sections are primarily for the benefit of the nonacademic reader, they may well appear over-generalized and oversimplified to the academic audience. Greater detail, however, would distract from the main theme. The fourth section (see page 34) begins the outline of my understanding of the managerial viewpoint, upon which later chapters build.

THE TRADITIONAL FOCUS ON OWNERSHIP VALUE

The overwhelming majority of those who have undertaken to generalize in print about the objectives of corporate financial policy have done so in a manner consistent with the legal traditions of private property rights in a capitalistic society. This familiar concept of the corporation owned by its stockholders and controlled by them through an elected board of directors is well embedded in legal precedent, regulatory practice, organizational behavior, financial reporting, and economic theory.

Statute and legal precedent clearly identify the link between corporate property, the title to which resides with the artificial personality of the corporation, and the real personality of the shareholder through the elective power of the certificate of ownership. Government regulation works to strengthen this link by supporting the information flow to the stockholder and his capacity to respond to information via appropriate voting procedures. Private regulation also reinforces stockholder control over corporate property by resisting dilution of the voting powers of common stockholders (e.g., the New York Stock Exchange policy manual). Business corporations adhere strictly to the rituals imposed by law concerning the relationship between corporate management and the board of directors on the one hand and between the board and the stockholders on the other. Recent events have created a high sense of awareness of accountability on the part of individual board members for acts affecting the material welfare of the stockholders. Financial reporting continues the "humble servant" image of management faithfully and continuously communicating with the ultimate authority of the stockholder group.

Economic theory sums this all up in depicting the ultimate purpose of corporate activity as the creation of transferable value for the stockholder. For those readers unfamiliar with the continuing thrust of modern theory of corporate finance some elaboration is in order.

It is the nature of economic and financial theory to seek rational description and explanation of financial phenomena in the economy and in the individual firm. Rationality implies objectivity, and objectivity demands a precise delineation of the characteristics of the problem being examined, the intention behind efforts to resolve the problem, and the criteria to measure achievement toward the stated goal. Theory has always involved abstraction from reality, a simplification of the problem to the point where objectivity is possible for the individual making the analysis. Unfortunately for the practitioner, theory has not made a practice of returning from the abstraction when the lessons of objective analysis have been learned.

To be specific, economic theory of the firm has consistently held to the concept that the economic objective of private enterprise in business is to maximize profit. The durability of this statement of objective is a tribute as much to its usefulness for abstraction and objective reasoning as to its validity in terms of real world behavior. It has the obvious advantage of being a single and unqualified goal: to make corporate profits as large as possible within whatever time dimension seems appropriate. Profit, being by definition quantitative, can be stated in precise terms and measured objectively. An established set of guidelines formulated by accounting practice makes the comparison of profit over time or between businesses reasonably meaningful. It is difficult to think of any other corporate goal that would offer anything like the same advantages for abstraction and descriptive or normative reasoning.

Further it is apparent that a focus on profit presents the very essence of an economic view of the business world since profit is an attempt to measure change in economic value over time. The principles of accrual accounting that underlie "net income" represent an effort to present a normalized picture of the change in the value of corporate assets between two points in time, dampening the temporary impact of irregularity in management's day-to-day decisions and actions (for example: purchasing, production, or equipment decisions). This year-to-year growth or deterioration in value as the accountant records it is transferred to the balance sheet, which is intended as an inventory of corporate values at an instant in time. Modern financial analysis has substantially discredited book value as a significant measure, but financial reporting doggedly persists in generating these numbers, presumably because no better alternative has been found.

In recent years the concept of profit maximization as the central theme of the theory of the firm has been blurred somewhat by the introduction of a substitute goal, that of profit optimization. Recognizing that an unqualified maximum profit goal is often too narrow a description of reality, when in fact the corporate business entity can be observed to be responding at various times to various objectives, some theorists have given explicit recognition to important constraints on how high profit will be pushed in practice. The optimum concept is therefore a modification of the maximum concept designed to indicate that maximization must be consistent with other nonprofit corporate business goals such as, for example, employee well-being. The target profit level becomes the "best" rather than the "most," taking all considerations into account. Whether this modification results in a loss in preciseness or objectivity depends entirely on how precisely the competing objectives can be described, since optimization is merely maximization within certain limits imposed by these objectives.

Translated into the terms of the ultimate property holder, maximum profits become maximum *earnings per share*. Since to the individual stockholder the value of the immortal corporate entity is something of an abstraction, the practical consideration becomes the exchangeable value represented by the market price of his stock. Thus the critical issue for him is the link between corporate *earnings per share* and *market price* of the corporation's shares and this, of course, is usually described in an *earnings yield* or *price-earnings ratio*. Put in these terms, there is no doubt that the stock market at least is very much concerned with profits and their growth over time.

In fact the identification of financial theory with the goals of the stockholder enables the theorist to get around the fuzziness of the optimizing concept and the observed limitations of profit maximization in a corporate sense. The separation of ownership and control has been a widely discussed phenomenon of modern capitalism. Deprived of the satisfactions of exercising real control over business resources — and largely incapable of the task anyway — the stockholder inevitably becomes an observer, preoccupied with the purely financial dimension of ownership and the game of watching value grow. Under such circumstances what other criterion of achievement can there be than the purely economic one of maximum growth in value? By shifting attention to the stock market instead of the business itself the theorist can restore his objective tools of analysis to rigorous employment.

It is little wonder that the focus of the theory of corporate finance in recent years has been on the determination of value in the market for equity securities. However, in this theoretical exploration it soon became apparent that a simple relationship between profits or earnings per share and market price was not going to suffice. It was obvious that maximizing earnings per share did not necessarily result in maximizing market value even though earnings per share are obviously a major determinant. The search for what makes value has extended to both the demand and the supply side of the equity market and has recognized emotional as well as rational considerations. The theory of corporate finance, however, has been primarily absorbed thus far with the relationships among a few key financial policies and market price. The primary considerations have been earnings, dividends, and the debt-equity relationship.

In the main, today's theorists are more interested in being normative than descriptive, more interested in what ought to be than what is. This is inevitable, for there is more freedom and more satisfaction in dealing with what is regarded as the ideal state. When financial theory prescribes an optimum set of corporate financial policies with respect to rate of investment, dividend payout, and debt financing it is usually with the objective of an impact external to the corporate entity — the maximum benefit to the holders of that corporation's common stock. (And it should be noted that this is regardless of whether the corporation has any intentions of additional equity offerings.) The benefits of the indicated financial policies are measured in terms of their anticipated effect on the present value of a future stream of financial benefits to the stockholder in the form of income (dividends) and capital gains resulting from liquidation of the ownership interest.

THE PORTFOLIO CONCEPT OF INVESTMENTS

The previous section considered financial goals in terms of the ownership value inherent in an individual business unit and from the viewpoint of the stockholders of that business unit as a unified group. Having followed the progression of financial theory to the point of its current focus on the factors influencing market value of common equities, the reader will not be surprised by the addition that theory recognizes the desirability and even the necessity of diversity in the investment programs of various categories of investors. Each investor, individual or institution, is assumed to have a variety of equities in his portfolio and to be continuously reappraising holdings of individual securities relative to the nature and performance of the others.

The basic objective of holding a number of different securities rather than one is obviously to reduce the dependence of the investor on any one company for the safety and growth of the investment fund. The future is unknown, data can be incomplete or misleading, and judgments can err. Diversification among various industries, companies, and types of securities operates, not to reduce the chance of loss per se, but to reduce the chance of a *large* loss from a single source. Such diversification can be and is carried on as an instinctive and more or less random process by many investors. It is increasingly recognized, however, that in large-scale diversification certain mathematical relationships can be utilized to serve the objectives of diversification in a systematic way.

The statistical approach to portfolio selection was given its original impetus by H. M. Markowitz,[1] who translated the concept of investment risk into statistical terms. He saw investment value to be related to an expected yield, and risk as the probability of variation from that expectation, defined by the statistical measure of *variance* from the mean. The operation of systematic portfolio selection can be used either to increase the return on the portfolio for a given variance or to reduce the variance (risk) for a given return.

The point of this reference to scientific portfolio management is to emphasize how far the investor in common equities has moved from the old idea of a loyal stockholder group, a sturdy band of risk-takers who invested in a company and then stuck by it through thick and thin. Investment by formulae applied to market values and expected return involves no identification whatever with individual businesses except to the extent that, and only so long as, the particular security serves the purely financial objectives of the portfolio. Professional investors do not invest at all unless there is a high degree of mobility in their investment position. They move in and out of companies as new

---

[1] Harry M. Markowitz, *Portfolio Selection: Efficient Diversification of Investments* (Cowles Foundation for Research in Economics at Yale University, Monograph 16; New York: John Wiley & Sons, Inc., 1959).

information reveals unexpected weaknesses or new opportunities. In fact, stockholder loyalty in the old-fashioned sense is now equated with naivety and lack of sophistication from the investment viewpoint — the viewpoint of financial theory — for it implies a willingness to concentrate investment and to hold to that investment for motives other than maximum financial self-interest.

OWNERSHIP VALUE AND FINANCIAL POLICY

In order to heighten the contrast between the current thrust of financial theory and the managerial viewpoint represented in this study it is necessary to indicate the direction of corporate financial policy that would be consistent with the theories of investor or ownership value. This will be taken up in terms of three major dimensions of financial policy: investment policy, debt policy, and equity policy. Conflicting viewpoints will be deliberately played down and the focus will be on the essential aspects of the most widely accepted theoretical positions.

(a) *Business investment* is generally regarded by financial theory as the allocation of scarce financial resources among abundant investment opportunities varying as to the magnitude and duration of financial benefits to be derived and as to the certainty of those benefits. Businesses are considered to have no boundaries on the range of their interest in investment opportunities except those imposed by a rate of return standard and the willingness to bear risk. Investment opportunities are seen as a continuing stream, from which management must select those expected to maximize the financial benefits for any given level of risk. Since the process is continuous, as soon as funds are generated by an investment the proceeds are immediately reemployed in new investment opportunities, consistent with the principles of compound interest.

When a new investment is being appraised, the single consideration on which it will be evaluated is the amount and timing of the change in corporate cash flows resulting from the particular decision to invest. When the new cash flow is generated, the funds are assumed to be channeled into new investment opportunities regardless of whether those funds are considered to be replacement of the original investment or incremental income.

The initial outflow of cash by which the company acquires the future financial benefits is compared with those future benefits by discounting their value at the time they are expected to be received to their equivalent value in the present, thus giving a precise mathematical advantage to those projects that promise a return nearest to the present moment. The power of discounting is such that one dollar to be received 10 years from now, when discounted at 10%, is worth only 38 cents today.

Thus the procedure for ranking prospective investments in order of desirability stresses the impact on cash flows and the time-value of money to the exclusion of all other management considerations. Investments are presumably classified by risk category where significant differences in the certainty of the return are apparent, so that investments with comparable expected returns but different ranges of possible variation can be distinguished. This refinement avoids the possible mistake of judgment of assigning to an investment promising a certain 10% return a lower priority than that assigned to another opportunity with an uncertain 12% return.

Given a reliable method of ranking investment proposals, the remaining step in the decision-making process is the choice of a criterion to separate acceptable from unacceptable proposals. Conventional business practice relies on a historical return on book value of assets, a cash flow payback period, or a target rate in excess of present performance. Financial theory, on the contrary, uniformly turns to some measure of the cost of capital as the appropriate hurdle or cutoff rate. The reasoning is that so long as new funds are available internally or externally, and the new investment promises a net return in excess of the cost of the funds required to finance it, the investment offers a financial advantage and should be undertaken. New investment possibilities would continue to be explored and additional investment projects undertaken up to the point where the declining returns on more marginal opportunities approach a rising cost of capital as the business pushes the limits of its available capital resources.

There is considerable debate as to how the cost of capital standard should be constructed and employed, but the most commonly used standard is a composite cost of debt and equity sources weighted according to the proportions found in an optimum capital structure. To the extent that this average cost of capital is derived from current market data it tends to reflect the average risk inherent in the current mix of corporate investment commitments (products, market areas, etc.). Unless this cost of capital is adjusted in the light of the unique risk level of new investment opportunities, the general application of such a standard would tend to favor high risk opportunities and discriminate against low risk opportunities.

Probably the most significant element in the whole cost of capital concept is the cost assigned to the dominant source of capital — owners' equity. There are two important aspects to this question. One is that in financial theory equity funds generated internally, whether for replacement of existing investments or as net profit, are assigned a cost just as new equity funds obtained from a stock issue are, though tax considerations may indicate use of different rates. The second aspect is that the cost assigned to equity money is not an out-of-pocket cost as in the case of debt but is an opportunity cost, which attempts to measure what the stockholder could earn if he had the funds available to him for investment outside the corporation. Thus the theoretical hurdle rate would prevent the corporation from reinvesting internally generated funds or investing new funds provided by stock issues unless the new investment opportunities available to this corporation under its present management were better than the next best external investment of comparable risk available to the stockholders. By implication this means that there could be a surplus of uninvested funds, in which case the surplus would presumably flow out to the stockholders in the form of increased dividends.

(b) The second set of considerations in relating financial theory to financial policy has to do with *the use of debt in the capital structure*. It has long been held that debt financing provides an opportunity for stockholders to magnify the beneficial effects of a given rate of return on assets by transferring the excess revenues derived from the investment of the fixed-cost debt capital to the credit of the equity holders. This is the well-known leverage effect. When the potential effects of new debt derived from conventional institutional sources on earnings per share are compared with the effects of comparable amounts of new equity

capital, the debt alternative invariably is shown to be much
"cheaper." Of course it is always recognized that a legal commitment to pay interest and repay principal involves risks not found
in equity contracts. Obviously the greater the proportion of debt
in the capital structure the larger the risk of difficulty if and
when there is a serious decline in the inflows to service this debt.
In general, however, the answer has been in terms of debt limits
prescribing "reasonable" levels of debt appropriate to the particular industry under consideration.

More recently a new approach[1] to the impact of debt on corporate finance has been advanced, leading to a reassessment of
the role of debt by many theorists. This approach adopts a strict
stockholder viewpoint and measures the supposed advantages of
debt leverage in terms of its total effect on the market value of
the common equity. Two key elements of the analysis are important here. One is the thesis that the leverage of corporate
income by the use of debt financing is no more than an extension
of the leverage that may exist in the investment position of the
individual investor. Thus the individual investor is in a position
to compensate for a lack of leverage in a portfolio of corporate
equities by borrowing on his own account for the acquisition of
those equities. The other important element of the theory is that
the negative effects of increasing risk associated with increasing
proportions of debt are felt directly by the equity market through
a deterioration of the price-earnings ratio. The result is considered to be a standoff between an improved earnings-per-share
effect on the one hand and an eroded price-earnings ratio on the
other, so that equity value is in effect unchanged by variations
in the debt-equity mix. The policy conclusion would appear to
be that management should no longer see any financial motivation toward higher debt levels.

(c) A third dimension of financial theory and its policy implications relates to *the use of equity capital*. I have already indi-

---

[1] Franco Modigliani and Merton H. Miller, "The Cost of Capital, Corporation Finance, and the Theory of Investment," *American Economic Review*,
Vol. 48, June 1958, pp. 261–297. Professors Modigliani and Miller have continued to develop and modify their theory, particularly in "Corporate Income Taxes and the Cost of Capital," *American Economic Review*, Vol. 53,
June 1963, pp. 433–443.

cated under the topic of cost of capital that financial theory encourages investment only when new opportunities promise a return in excess of capital costs, the principal component of which is equity cost. It was also noted that the essential element of equity cost is what the stockholders can do with the money in the next best alternative outside the business in question. The final criterion is the expected impact on the stockholder's personal investment position as measured by its current market value — not just his position in this business but in total. It should be noted that we are preoccupied with the viewpoint of the *existing* shareholders at the point in time just prior to any decision.

It is obvious that no business grows without some increments of equity capital. Let us assume then that a given business justifies some new equity financing under the opportunity cost guidelines. The next question is whether such equity funds will come from internal generation or new issues. Here the stockholder viewpoint becomes all-important because of the implications of the personal income tax on dividend payments. With the strong tax advantage accorded capital gains under the tax brackets of most stockholders there appears to be little reason ever to choose external over internal equity sources. However, a decision to reduce dividends as a means of increasing internal flow to new investment raises a hotly debated theoretical issue concerning the ultimate determinants of market value — whether the critical consideration is expected earnings or expected dividends. If it is the latter, then the hoped-for gains from the investment of retained earnings could be eroded by the effects of a dividend cut. Indeed, this could even be true in an earnings-oriented market if dividends were used as a prediction of management expectations.

Whatever the resolution of this problem, it is obvious that stockholder considerations permeate the discussion. The same viewpoint is clearly evident in discussions of the policy of repurchase of common equity. This use of funds is seen as an investment designed to restore greater leverage to the capital structure, with a significant potential advantage to the surviving stockholders.

DESCRIPTIVE THEORY AND PROFESSIONAL MANAGEMENT

The principal emphasis of current financial theory is on the question: How does/should the *stockholder* behave in order to realize *his* financial objectives? The principal emphasis of the research on which this book is based has been on the question: How does/should *professional management* behave financially in order to realize *corporate* objectives? This shift of emphasis has three dimensions:

> (1) from stockholder to management,
> (2) from external to internal,
> (3) from what should be to what is.

Most financial theory is strongly normative. It is concerned with the optimum state of affairs, and is often impatient with the descriptive base. Traditionally, financial theorists have been more interested in the logical superstructure than in the underlying assumptions and the evidence as to their descriptive validity.

I have no quarrel with the effort to develop normative financial theory. It is highly desirable that a substantial group of scholars devote their efforts to the development of a rigorous body of reasoning on matters of financial policy under the guidance of criteria that seek the optimum economic results. I consider it equally desirable, however, that there be a vigorous and concurrent effort to understand and describe real world behavior in financial management. If the ultimate purpose of theory is to influence practice for the better, there must be both a descriptive and a normative model, which are capable of being linked together. The development of more realistic explanations of what current practice is, and why, is the special responsibility of the professional school of business administration. The improvement of practice necessarily begins with business as it is and moves by steps that continually balance what is desirable against what is possible and practicable. Only by examining the real world with a minimum of normative preconceptions can we hope to relate the optimal to the operational.

The principal departure will lie in a serious effort to take a truly *internal* view of financial decisions. It is apparent that, although the business corporation in the legal sense is a fictional person that must be continuously linked to the real persons who make up the ownership group, such businesses do have a separate and distinct existence in an economic and organizational or human sense. It is also apparent that although in law the corporation has eternal life, the economic and human business entity making use of the corporate shell has no such assurance. There is therefore no question but that this business entity has objectives of its own relating to such matters as health, growth, and continuity. It is to be expected that the natural response of the men who run these businesses in the capacity of professional management will be to identify with the business entity and its self-centered objectives since their own personal goals in life are so closely tied to this activity. Thus it seems realistic to expect that financial and other management decisions will be considered first and foremost from the inside looking out rather than from the outside looking in as financial theory almost invariably does.

For purposes of exploring what this internal view may be and how it may bear on financial decisions it is necessary to break the umbilical cord to the stockholder. It is the identification with the stockholder that has forced an external view of finance on the financial literature. In order to make this break it is not necessary to argue that management *should* not identify with the stockholder interest; nor is it necessary to deny that there are means by which management may be compelled to adopt the stockholder view. The principal position is, rather, that there is a distinct internal viewpoint concerned with the business entity itself and that the self-interest of professional management tends to give this viewpoint priority unless coerced in some way to do otherwise. The central question is whether and in what ways financial policy might be modified if such internal viewpoint were held to the exclusion of the external stockholder viewpoint.

While the legal link to the stockholder persists in all its present vigor, the economic or financial link has for many companies, particularly many large and mature corporations, become extremely weak or nonexistent. The fact is that many businesses could get along very nicely without the stockholder. Indeed, in the stage of maturity it is the stockholder who depends on the corporation rather than vice versa, for the stockholder becomes a net drain on the economic resources of the business because of dividend payments and the absence of new equity issues. The stockholder is needed to give the business its initial equity base. Beyond this initial investment, however, retained earnings, debt capacity, and a reasonably stable growth rate permit many a business to be quite independent of the new equity market. Whether this is literally true or not, dependence on the stockholder group as a source of funds for growth tends to diminish over time. It becomes a matter of low probability, thereby decreasing the impact of the stockholder viewpoint on the self-interest of corporate management.

The break from the stockholder viewpoint will be regarded by some as an abandonment of the cornerstone of our free enterprise system and the institution of private property. There is no intention here of passing judgment on our traditional form of capitalism. It is always in the best interests of any institution to examine its evolution realistically and to anticipate the direction in which it seems to be headed. There is evidence that economic and managerial realities are diverging from the legal traditions, and the internal versus external view on financial problems is at the center of the divergence.

It would seem appropriate here to be somewhat more specific as to what has been called *professional management*. In general the term refers to the group of individuals who constitute the decision-making unit within a business entity and who hold that position by reason of career development in the employ of that business rather than by reason of authority conferred by an ownership interest. In considering financial decisions we may identify four subgroups of management that are involved in such decisions in one way or another: the board of directors, the chief executive officer, the chief financial officer, and the operating executives whose decisions and actions have major financial consequences. The concept of professional management includes the last three and may or may not include the first depending on its composition as an inside or outside board.

The key as to whether the external stockholder viewpoint has a natural priority in financial decisions lies in the composition and operation of the board of directors since all the others mentioned are career personnel. Although career personnel may be induced in various ways to adopt an external viewpoint, it does not come naturally or from self-interest and it cannot supplant the internal viewpoint but must exist side by side with it. The board, on the other hand, has responsibilities to the ownership group because of its organizational relationship to the voting power of the shareholders. These responsibilities are most visible in matters affecting preservation and growth of financial value. The fact that the board oversees and passes on key financial decisions, however, does not necessarily mean that the external viewpoint is dominant. In the absence of a dominant stockholder on the board, the board is unlikely to take an overriding external view of financial policy unless this view is also held by the chief executive and financial officer. Under such conditions it is to be expected that the initiative on financial policy will normally be taken by the members of professional management. The board (the external members) will normally respond to, and from time to time attempt to modify, this initiative.

An Internal View of Financial Goals

It will help this study if the way in which financial goals are modified by adoption of a strict internal viewpoint is made as specific as possible. The previous section stated that the corporate business entity "has objectives of its own relating to such matters as health, growth, and continuity." What is needed here is a statement of a goal that approaches in preciseness the "maximization of the present value of the stream of economic benefits expected to accrue to the stockholder." With current market value as a reasonable proxy for the present value of the stream of economic benefits and with dividends and future capital gains as proxies for the stream of benefits, this external concept of a financial goal is reasonably tangible and objective.

Question: what is the corporate equivalent? The financial objective of the shareholder is presumably to maximize his personal control over economic resources as measured by the exchange value of the ownership claims to which he has title. The exchange value of these ownership claims depends on the magnitude and certainty of the future flows to the stockholder. In the same way it may be said that the management of a business entity is interested in its control over economic resources. Management's power to do whatever it wishes to do depends in considerable measure on the ability to use economic resources. Management action regularly requires the allocation of resources to specialized use as a prerequisite to implementation of its decisions. It is reasonable to assume that the self-interest of management in pursuit of the power to implement action would desire to maximize the resources which, through corporate ownership or other means, it can direct to be used in the ways it sees fit.

These resources are not, as is commonly assumed, the specialized assets listed on the left-hand side of the balance sheet, for these are merely monuments marking the decisions of the past. What we are concerned with is corporate purchasing power for the future: *the anticipated flows of unspecialized funds feeding into a single business entity for its exclusive use and benefit.* Like the stockholder, management will be interested in the magnitude, timing, and certainty of the flows of funds which, as they materialize, may be committed or recommitted to risk on behalf of corporate objectives. Like the stockholder, management may be expected to prefer, all other things being equal, that corporate net funds flows be as large as possible, as soon as possible, and as certain as possible, because these spendable funds confer the power to plan and to execute action.

It is recognized that the corporate entity does not have the same perspective on future flows that the shareholder does. It does not have the option of consumption as well as reinvestment, though unwise investment may be regarded as a form of consumption and the payment of dividends or repurchase of common stock may also be so regarded. In contrast to the stockholder, the corporation is denied the ever-present opportunity of converting investments into cash. At best any such attempt at conversion by the corporate entity would not offer the same degree of promptness and certainty as to the outcome. Because of the relation of purchasing power to management action there will tend to be a stronger preoccupation with flows in the near term, the period over which explicit plans of action have been formulated, than may be true of the equity investor. There is no apparent equivalent to the capital gains associated by the security investor with ultimate liquidation, since management would not under ordinary circumstances deliberately terminate the economic base of its future activities.

The grid in Exhibit 2A has been constructed to assist summarizing the potential differences between the internal and the external views of financial policy. It is based on the following broad definition of an investment objective, applicable to both the ownership group and the corporate business entity itself:

> Given a limited amount of capital to invest and given a judgment about the risks the investor is willing to assume, the investor will try to select from the total group of available investment opportunities that set of investments which will yield a future inflow of funds having the greatest present worth.

It is in the definition of "present worth" — to whom and for what purposes (and thus how it is to be measured) — that the basic differences lie. The following paragraphs are designed to fill in the "boxes" on the grid as an explanation of the contrasts in viewpoint.

EXHIBIT 2A

GRID FOR SUMMARIZING DIFFERENCES BETWEEN INTERNAL AND EXTERNAL VIEWS OF FINANCIAL POLICY

Issues Viewpoint → ↓	Ownership Group	Corporate Entity
Range of Investment Opportunities	(1)	(2)
Constraints on Investment	(3)	(4)
Nature of Funds Flow Stream	(5)	(6)
Capital Inputs and Their Cost	(7)	(8)
Target Risk Level	(9)	(10)

(1) Range of Investment Opportunities — Ownership

The investor in common equities is free to invest for any desired time period in any business entity that offers its shares to the public in sufficient quantity to establish an orderly market. The key considerations of eligibility are risk, return, and mobility of capital. The nature of the enterprise is important only as it bears on these investment considerations.

(2) *Range of Investment Opportunities — Corporate Entity*

The group of investment opportunities for a specific business entity is essentially a subset of the opportunities available to the ownership group. Theoretically, an operating company could invest in any of the equities available to its shareholders. Practically speaking, however, operating companies do not consider a purely investment position in the common equity of other operating companies as an appropriate use of corporate funds. Thus investments are limited to the opportunities open to direct managerial control by the investing company. In the case of acquisitions the assets of the acquired company will likely be taken over outright or by an investment in excess of 50% to assure a dominant voice in operating and policy decisions. In practice management tends to limit its investment horizon to activities that are a direct enlargement of the existing product, market, and geographic base or a logical extrapolation of these activities to gain added leverage from the corporation's unique resources.

(3) *Constraints on Investment — Ownership*

Diversification of investment activities offers the opportunity to reduce the risk associated with a given level of expected return or, alternatively, to increase the expected return for any given level of investment risk. Theorists have recently been indicating the opportunity to apply statistical concepts in the management of security portfolios with the goal of developing the potential advantages of diversification to a higher level of productivity. Professional investors are showing increasing interest and it is apparent that security investment offers the greatest opportunity for more scientific diversification policies. The ownership groups would appear to be the most likely beneficiaries of these ideas. This follows from the opportunity of spreading moderate sums of capital widely, easily, quickly, and cheaply. Investment mobility has been developed to a high degree.

(4) *Constraints on Investment — Corporate Entity*

In a business organization the concept of financial risk cannot be handled in purely financial terms, because financial considerations are a means to an end, serving basic organizational objectives. This is so even though financial risk may be regarded as a convenient summation of various operational risks (of competition, product, market, production technology, and so on). The problems are not a simple trade-off between risk minimization and financial return. Other and competing goals are involved, too, such as competitive rank, share of the market, size, and technological leadership. It should also be noted that management's *perception* of risk is strongly influenced by familiarity. Accustomed risks are minimized and unaccustomed risks, even though they afford diversification of risk, tend to be inflated.[1] Many managements reject diversification for this reason.

It is also apparent that real investment takes place much more slowly than financial investment in securities. Major time lags are involved in both investment and disinvestment, particularly the latter. The obvious effect is a great reduction in the mobility of investment as well as increased uncertainties in the decision-making stage. The process of developing a product and market position or of shifting into new positions may extend over the entire career of any one chief executive officer.

The factors above tend to combine to restrict in a major way the range of alternatives open to management at a point of time and therefore substantially reduce the opportunity to apply objective diversification concepts to practical advantage.

(5) *Nature of Funds Flow Stream — Ownership*

For the owners the expected benefits from an investment consist of a stream of dividend payments and a capital gain when the investment is terminated. These sums must be adjusted for the tax treatment of dividends and capital gains, which varies substantially depending on the nature and circumstances of the recipient. It is generally agreed that current investment value must be related to the magnitude and certainty of these receipts,

---

[1] Should this appear irrational, the reader is reminded that this volume is primarily concerned with explaining behavior, not saying what it ought to be.

though the form of the relationship is under debate. All other things being equal, the larger the dividend or capital gain, the greater the value.

(6) Nature of Funds Flow Stream — Corporate Entity

For business and its management the comparable flows are the expendable funds generated by an investment. These can be readily identified for the business as a whole, but there may be considerable difficulty in breaking them down by investment centers in a degree comparable with that possible in the security portfolio. For the corporation these flows are largely if not entirely defined as income for tax purposes, and they are taxed at a single rate for all corporations within broad categories of business activity. In a very real sense the matters of concern to ownership flows are of no direct consequence to the corporate flows from which they are derived except with respect to dividend payments. Here what increases one decreases the other, for it is the residual flows after dividends that are the basis of future management action.

(7) Capital Inputs and Their Cost — Ownership

For any given ownership group new capital inputs are primarily derived from the earnings of the existing portfolio, unused debt capacity based on the value of the portfolio and its related earnings stream, and the liquidation of existing investments. The potential costs of these inputs are the forgone revenues of alternative investments, actual out-of-pocket costs involved in the transfer of funds from one investment to another, and possibly a change in risk characteristics reflected in a lower price-earnings ratio. Total costs are summed up in their negative effect on the value of the portfolio. The investor, of course, hopes that the new investment will have a net positive effect on the portfolio value.

(8) Capital Inputs and Their Cost — Corporate Entity

For the corporation the new capital inputs are primarily derived from net inflow from operations, unused debt capacity related to these flows, and occasionally the liquidation of particular investments. Since market value is external to the corporation, the shareholders' measure of cost — the effect on the value of the portfolio — cannot be used for internal operational purposes. Building on the concept that future flows are the source of economic power for management, we would measure the costs of capital inputs in terms of the negative effect on future inflows. Such costs would be either explicit out-of-pocket costs, such as interest, or implicit opportunity costs, the lost revenues of the next best alternative. Again, the hope would be that the positive returns from the inputs would more than offset the costs. In any case it is the change in *corporate* flows, not investor flows, that matters to management.

(9) *Target Risk Level — Ownership*

The attitudes of any individual investor toward risk-bearing and the rewards necessary to compensate for risk-bearing have a strong influence on his investment decisions. Whether the investments are personal or institutional, the decisions concerning them tie back ultimately to personal, subjective attitudes which must be taken as given. For the given investor or ownership group the description of a common risk posture is extremely difficult because of the heterogeneity of most such groups in terms of age, economic circumstances, investment objectives, and other characteristics. Nevertheless it is theoretically possible for such a group to have a composite target risk level.

(10) *Target Risk Level — Corporate Entity*

Since risk is considered a subjective phenomenon it might be assumed that a corporate entity cannot have a target risk level independent of its owners. The corporation does have a management, however, and these people have a strong personal stake in its future. Indeed, they are likely to regard themselves as having more of a stake than individual shareholders since they are much less mobile. They certainly do have concerns about all the risks of the business, including financial risk, and inevitably these risk attitudes bear on decisions. As the officers find themselves in the position of having to make such judgments on behalf of ownership, inevitably these judgments will reflect their personal evaluation of corporate risks and will be influenced by the desire to preserve and expand the corporate entity on which their personal fortunes and reputations rest.

3

The Concept of Financial Mobility

Continuing the point of view expressed in the preceding chapter, which identifies a goal for the corporation and its professional managers distinct from that of the owners, we now begin to examine the operational implications. The corporate goals, whatever their tangible forms, are regarded as having a common denominator in the need for the preservation and growth of the business entity. Consider a company engaged in the production and sale of a product line such as, say, builders' hardware. At any point in time this company has one or more plants with a related labor force capable of a certain output. It has a supervisory and management group, a set of established and prospective customers, a distribution network, a defined market area. As an ongoing business it has a continuous sequence of work routines centering around solicitation of orders, production schedules, purchase orders, employment procedures, shipments, collection of accounts, and so forth.

All of this frenzy of activity requires careful planning, organizing, and decision making if it is to have any chance of keeping on going and keeping on growing. If we assume intelligent and experienced management, it can be expected that these various activities will settle into a pattern which may be regarded as successful, judged by the common business yardsticks of success. In the process the business will have adapted to its own industry environment, developed a competitive position that it can hold and perhaps improve on, and found a means by which the internal threat of inefficiency and misjudgment will be contained within tolerable limits.

Given a pattern of performance that has proved successful —
more and better products, larger and more efficient plants, more
employees, more customers, larger trading area, expanded management team — management's principal task is to keep it that
way. In a dynamic economy, active or latent threats to an established market position derive from change: change in the industry environment of consumer behavior or technology, change in
the action of competitors, and change within the business itself.
Again assuming an intelligent and experienced management, it
seems reasonable to conclude that where change can be anticipated the threat can be avoided. For example, a pronounced
seasonal swing in sales and operations usually presents no great
problem.

The challenge to management is therefore to be found in *unexpected* change of substantial proportions affecting an important aspect of operations. "Unexpected" implies that a significant
time constraint is imposed on efforts designed to respond to the
new set of circumstances by the revision of existing policy and
action. Implicit in this time limitation is some uncertainty about
the ability of management to make an appropriate adjustment to
the new situation, either by minimizing or neutralizing adverse
change or by taking full advantage of beneficial change.

It may be argued that it is the role of management to assure
that all change is expected change, from which it follows that
there is always enough time to take appropriate action, and therefore that there is no uncertainty about a favorable outcome.
Modern management expends a good deal of effort in attempting
to forecast change in economic, technological, financial, and other
dimensions of the business. However, it is unrealistic to assume
that a given management can consistently turn in a perfect score
in this respect. There are bound to be some significant respects in
which the future was not fully anticipated. Further, for the purposes of this study it is not of major consequence whether a particular event *could* have been anticipated. The important thing
is that it was not foreseen and therefore response under time
pressure was called for.

The response of management to evidence that change is taking
place rests on three key elements:

(1) an understanding of what is happening and how to adapt,
(2) time to act, and
(3) the capacity to act.

In this study the first of these elements will be assumed to exist.
Actually the understanding of the problem may be a matter of
degree and there is likely to be some trade-off between number
one and the other two. This is to say, the process of getting on
top of a problem once one becomes aware of it usually takes
time; the faster this can be done the more time there is for response. Similarly, the better the understanding of the problem
the greater is the capacity to deal with it. However, the focus of
this study will be on the key component of management's capacity to act over some finite time period.

The capacity of management to act in response to unexpected
change in the external or internal environment depends on its
control over the resources of the business. By exercising judgment
in the use of these resources management can hope to influence
the stream of events that make up business experience. The resources of the business may be classified as human, technological,
economic, and financial. Economic resources are defined here as
the various tangible assets of the business which represent a past
commitment of financial resources to specialized use in the interests of future income potential. The financial resources are the
various claims by means of which a business may have access to
additional human, technological, and economic resources. *This
study focuses on economic and financial resources (particularly
the latter), which are regarded as the key to management's capacity to act in the face of change.* At any given time the financial
resources are deployed in some pattern of use that presumably
will bring optimum results. Change necessitates some redeploy-
ment of these resources, and management must have the power
to redeploy as well as the intelligence to direct such power effectively.

FUNDS FLOW FORECAST

The starting point of management strategy with respect to
change is an attempt to anticipate it far enough in advance to
provide a reasonable period for response. The change with which

we are concerned is that which has a substantial impact on corporate funds flows — the purchasing power by which management exercises control over economic and other resources. The word "funds" is meant to designate cash or its equivalent in other forms of purchasing power.

Business does not usually report financial performance in the form of funds flows or purchasing power as defined above but, rather, reports what is considered to be the primary concern of ownership — the value of the ownership claims and changes in value over time. The balance sheet shows this value at a point in time and the income statement reports changes in value, that is, profit, over a period of time preceding the balance sheet date. As a consequence of this form of reporting, it has become common practice in many businesses to forecast financial change in the form of pro forma income statements and balance sheets. In the process of their construction the business obtains a crude measure of funds flows and reserve positions, which under certain circumstances may be sufficient to alert management to the need for action.

There is now a growing interest in dealing directly with pro forma funds flows and in being more precise about magnitudes and timing. This is particularly true in companies that by reason of having fully committed their resources to specialized use need to be very careful about modest changes in flows. Such companies find it useful to reconstruct the conventional financial statements into a funds flow statement projecting key sources and uses of funds. Ultimately such companies develop rather detailed cash forecasts for periods up to a year or more. Here they are looking directly at the components of cash inflow and outflow rather than a crude measure of aggregate flows from the income statements.

For such cash or funds flow forecasts the time period may range from one week up to ten years. In most cases the deterioration in ability to anticipate events does not follow a continuous path as the time horizon grows more remote. Rather, there are distinct breaking points in the ability to see the future, centering around such intervals as the current production season, the customer buying cycle, the budget year, the limits of the current capital expansion program, a long-term industry cycle. Thus, for example, in the automotive industry forecasts are heavily dependent on the input of information provided by early trends in new model purchases. The companies begin then to firm up forecasts of the current production year. With some lag these data are transmitted to the machine tool industry, which then firms up sales expectations to the automobile manufacturers up to but not beyond the next model change. For most businesses that reach out in forecasts beyond the two- or three-year implications of a surge in capital expenditures to, say, a five- or ten-year forecast, the forecast becomes largely a linear extrapolation of current trends and has rather limited usefulness for financial strategy.

In any case, the clear intent of the forecast is to reach forward in time to identify the events likely to require reallocation of financial and economic resources and thus to provide ample time for this process to take place at minimum cost or to maximum advantage. One of the key issues in the area of financial mobility is the trade-off between mobility of resources and time. We shall be returning to this issue frequently.

FUNDS FLOW EQUILIBRIUM

Much of the discussion of corporate financial management in the literature of finance is in terms of goals, policies designed to achieve those goals, and criteria for measuring achievement. As such the literature is concerned more with the guidelines of action in financial management than with the action itself. The action itself — the day-to-day, month-to-month job of managing company finances — may be summed up in basic terms as the maintenance of balance in funds inflows and outflows over time. This is the essence of solvency, which is an obvious prerequisite of corporate continuity and growth. It is, however, more than just paying bills on time and keeping a positive bank balance.

Funds outflows may be defined as the commitment of corporate purchasing power (usually cash) to specialized use in behalf of corporate objectives. Specialized use will of course mean a variety of things, such as the purchase of machinery, payment of a payroll incurred in creating inventory values, an expenditure for advertising designed to generate future demand for the product. The purpose generally is to produce, directly or indirectly, funds inflows or new purchasing power greater than that originally expended. Inevitably there are time lags of varying duration between commitment of purchasing power and accomplishment of purpose.

Obviously, in a going enterprise funds are released from specialized use at the time funds are being committed, or recommitted, and these are called funds inflows. The primary source of new purchasing power is the collection of accounts receivable following sale of the company's products, but other sources, usually much more discontinuous, also contribute to the flow. Common usage sets the reference point for flows "in" and "out" as possession by or control over the funds by the corporate entity and its officials duly authorized to make expenditure decisions. Because of the random element in business activity it is unlikely that the current inflow of funds resulting from past decisions and actions will be exactly equal to the current outflows on behalf of the future. Left to their own behavior we can expect flows to be frequently if not continuously out of balance, with an excess or a deficiency depending on the vigor of present actions compared with the past.

Consequently there is a need for planning and constant supervision so that the available purchasing power will be equal to the needs set by events and by management decisions. The word equilibrium is used here to refer to this condition. It implies not only a balance or equality of funds flows at a point in time but also a tendency to remain in balance. Further explanation of this concept is required.

In conventional terms funds flows refer to both change in form and growth in the value of assets. The funds flow statement is a composite of changes among the uses and sources of funds as reflected in a comparison of two successive balance sheets coupled with the growth in asset values as reflected in the income statement for the period. In a naive accounting sense funds flows are always in balance thanks to the precise application of double entry bookkeeping. But this accounting convention conceals the necessity for conscious management action to assure that the funds required for essential corporate purposes are matched by equivalent corporate purchasing power at the time of need. This does not happen by accident or by grace of accounting principles. Accounting merely records the fact of the match in flows that has been achieved in the past.

Equality of flows may be achieved by cutting back on planned expenditures as well as by increasing the inflow of expendable funds. While the variability of expenditure patterns is always an alternative open to financial management and one of considerable practical significance, it must be assumed for purposes of sound financial planning that action which compromises essential corporate purposes will not be a part of the appropriate strategy. Admittedly this is a vaguely defined constraint but it is one of real importance nevertheless. Financial management must operate in such a manner as to bring about the equality by careful planning of and control over the inflows of purchasing power.

Equilibrium in connection with funds flows implies more than equality or balance, however. It indicates also a tendency to remain in balance over time. The rate of flow will not always be the same, but if changes in flow occur there will be a movement to a new level of equality. On first thought it would seem that there is nothing inherent in corporate funds flows that would tend to preserve a balance of inflows and outflows over time. Business affairs are too subject to nonperiodic events and to the vagaries of human effort to result in an inflow from the past equal to outflows into the future. However, if equality is not taken literally it is conceivable that circumstances could exist where funds flow equilibrium would be a practical fact of financial affairs in a company over an extended period of time. Such would be the case of a company holding to its traditional position in an industry with stable demand and little change in market share. Here the inflows resulting from past actions and events would tend to equal outflows for future benefit; and any temporary dislocation, for example, plant modernization, would in all probability be followed by a return to equality.

Similarly one can conceive of conditions where funds flow disequilibrium would fairly describe the state of affairs. A company in a stage of rapid growth or, alternatively, of decline and unprofitability would tend to have a persistent excess of outflows over inflows. Obviously such conditions would have a profound significance for financial policy. Nevertheless, it may be concluded that states of equilibrium or disequilibrium are not necessarily inherent in corporate financial affairs. Random events and random responses produce irregularities of flows over time. If equilibrium is to be attained, it must be the result of conscious effort on the part of management.

Hence the concept of equilibrium as used here as a goal of financial planning is an extension of the initial step of balancing inflows and outflows; it is seeing that they remain in balance. This condition will not be considered to exist unless the equality of flows that is achieved is consistent with established financial policies and the action taken is within the boundaries defined by these policies. The desirability of equilibrium lies in the obvious advantage of a pattern of financing that promises continuity of the capacity to service corporate objectives without the constant strain and stop-gap actions associated with a situation persistently out of balance.

A simplified illustration of funds flow equilibrium as a goal of financial planning follows. Exhibit 3A shows the cash position of an actual company as of January 1, 1962. It also shows the additions to and deductions from cash for the first quarter of 1962 as they actually occurred. These changes are represented in the company's customary accounting terms and as such do not tell precisely the story of actual cash flows. However, in the end they do reveal the principal sources and uses of cash and they balance out to the actual cash balance at the end of the period. It can be seen that during the first quarter the main drains on cash were payment of federal taxes, a substantial increase in inventory, and an unusual expenditure for fixed assets — equipment in this case. It is also clear that inflows from normal internal sources would have been quite inadequate to balance the outflows of this quarter, and the action taken was a substantial increase in the company's notes payable at the bank in the amount of $2.1 million. In spite of this the company's bank balance declined by $1.5 million.

The exhibit then shows the forecast of flows quarter by quarter to the end of 1962 and the total estimated flows for the year. These projections represent, obviously, an expectation of balance or equality in flows quarter by quarter. Whether they also represent a true equilibrium position is another question, the answer to which is not apparent from the figures. The forecast of equality of flows (actually, some excess of inflows) for the rest of 1962 may be more than a passive report of events considered likely to

EXHIBIT 3A

ANALYSIS OF PROJECTED CHANGES IN CASH POSITION: YEAR 1962
(In thousands of dollars)

	Actual Year to Date (1st quarter)	Est. 2nd Quarter 1962	Est. 3rd Quarter 1962	Est. 4th Quarter 1962	Estimate Year 1962
Cash Balance — Beginning of Period	$ 3,989	$ 2,467	$ 2,585	$ 2,591	$ 3,989
Additions to Cash					
After-tax earnings	$ (359)	$ 300	$ (37)	$ 35	$ (61)
Provision for depreciation	192	193	192	193	770
Increase in notes payable	2,100	—	—	—	2,100
Increase in advances from customers	45	161	150	(70)	286
Increase in accrued payroll and expenses	39	(49)	(115)	53	(72)
Provision for current year federal taxes	139	273	175	266	853
Total Additions to Cash	$ 2,156	$ 878	$ 365	$ 477	$ 3,876
Deductions from Cash					
Additions to property, plant, and equipment — net	$ 770	$ 256	$ 253	$ 253	$ 1,532
Increase in notes and accounts receivable	89	809	21	269	1,188
Increase in refundable federal taxes	664	(490)	165	—	339
Increase in inventory	1,883	(909)	(88)	(435)	451
Increase in prepaid expenses	55	25	(41)	(62)	(23)
Decrease in accounts payable	650	172	(83)	(177)	562
Payment of federal income taxes	724	692	91	222	1,729
Dividends	126	—	—	—	126
Increase in investments and other assets	55	170	6	1	232
Total Deductions from Cash	$ 5,016	$ 725	$ 324	$ 71	$ 6,136
Net Increase or (Decrease)	$(2,860)	$ 153	$ 41	$ 406	$(2,260)
Special Adjustment Deferred income on acquisition	$ 1,338	$ (35)	$ (35)	$ (35)	$ 1,233
Cash Balance — End of Period	$ 2,467	$ 2,585	$ 2,591	$ 2,962	$ 2,962

happen. It may in fact represent a *forcing* of that balance by management action. The company is in some difficulty, showing a small loss for the year as a whole, though in a cash flow sense operations still are expected to provide $700,000. Under the circumstances the holding of capital expenditures to $250,000 a quarter, the steady decline in inventories, and the termination of the cash dividend all suggest a deliberate plan to match inflows and outflows without any further increase in bank borrowings.

Thus a forecast is at the same time an anticipation of events and a plan of action, the combination of which is expected to keep cash or funds flows in approximate balance. Beyond this is the question of whether this represents a *stable* balance or equilibrium, which can be maintained without serious strain on the company or its management. The evidence of the forecast, together with knowledge of the company beyond this exhibit, suggests that it is not an equilibrium position. The requirements of an equilibrium position are that the outflows are adequate to fulfill the corporate objectives; that these objectives are not seriously compromised to bring the flows into balance; and that the balance is achieved within the framework or bounds set by accepted financial policy, including consistency with the risk posture of the management.

The facts of the case were that the company was experiencing a period of depressed sales volume, excess capacity, and low profits. Debt had been used in an effort to lift the company out of the doldrums by acquisitions and internal rejuvenation, and the addition of $2 million of bank debt in the first quarter of 1962 raised total debt to or above the bounds considered prudent by management. Under the circumstances financial management was endeavoring to keep a tight lid on capital expenditures and to bear down on what was regarded as an excessive inventory position, and it planned to eliminate the cash dividend to stockholders. By these means it hoped to bring about a gradual improvement in the cash position of the company during the rest of 1962, ending the year with $500,000 more in the bank than at March 31.

It is unlikely that this modest improvement, if achieved, would indicate that an equilibrium position had then been reached. It is conceivable that outflows of around $500,000 a quarter could be continued without further erosion of the cash position or increase in debt. However, with substantial expenditures for revitalization pending, with high debt and a suspended dividend payment, the balance in flows would not be consistent with either corporate objectives or financial policy. Continued disequilibrium and financial strain were in prospect for the indefinite future.

THE CHALLENGE OF THE UNEXPECTED EVENT

Departing from the previous example, let us assume that we have a company with its flows in balance and in a state of equilibrium as previously defined. Note that equilibrium does not mean an absence of change but only that change is generally foreseen and that the response is within the guidelines set by financial policy. As previously stated, we are concerned with the impact of the unexpected event having major financial implications. It will be helpful to be more specific about what these events are, what their financial impact may be, and what reallocation of resources is required to restore the desired equilibrium of funds flows.

The events in which we are interested result in a major increase in outflows of funds or decrease in inflows, or both, and consequently demand action if the revised outflows are to be met. It is recognized that a decrease in outflows or increase in inflows also represents a disturbance of equilibrium and indicates that action is necessary to restore equilibrium. However, the excessive accumulation of liquid funds does not represent the same kind of pressure as an anticipated deficiency and the latter is a better subject for research on management behavior. An earlier statement indicated that the word "unexpected" signifies a significant time problem in response — insufficient time to think, to plan, and to act. This is admittedly a relative concept; at some point it depends on the caliber of management as to whether it is a problem at all. The most useful definition is to say that the event *is now expected to occur within the customary planning horizon of the business and was not anticipated at the time the original plan or forecast was made.*

In such events, leading to an identified deficiency of liquid funds at some point or period in time, certain distinctive characteristics may be recognized. In the first place, the need for funds may be either aggressive or defensive. If the event calls for an increased outflow, the outflow may be required to take advantage of an opportunity that has suddenly presented itself (this may be called an *aggressive* need) or it may be required to protect the company from some form of adversity (a *defensive* need). This study has tended to direct field work to an examination of the problems of response to a defensive need simply because they tend to deny the alternative of postponing action and to have a more apparent sequence of response by management. The aggressive need, however, is equally appropriate to the problem of funds flow equilibrium.

Another characteristic of significance is whether the need is a single sum required at a point in time, for example, the payment of a tax judgment or of damages under a legal action, or whether it represents increased outflows over an extended period of time. This is the contrast between a payment that although perhaps large is nevertheless precise in amount and timing and a series of payments that may be and may continue to be indefinite as to both amount and timing. The latter would be illustrated by an unexpected change in production technology. It is undoubtedly the more difficult problem to handle.

Finally, there is some significance in the question of whether the unexpected event that promises to disturb funds flows is external to the business unit itself or internal. An illustration of an external event would be some action taken by a prominent competitor, and an illustration of the latter would be some action taken by its own management. One might assume that events initiated from within are therefore known and consequently cannot be called unexpected. In practice, however, those responsible for funds flow equilibrium sometimes find the behavior of their own management the most difficult element to predict. This may be illustrated by a president who has embarked on a series of personally negotiated acquisitions. The point to be made here is simply that the challenge of the unexpected is not confined to events in the external environment.

In the field studies reported in later chapters a number of specific events giving rise to imbalance in funds flows are brought under observation for the manner of management response. These events will be found to fall under one of the following general categories of unexpected change having a major impact on funds flow equilibrium:

(1) A change in the general economic environment — the occurrence of a major industry- or economy-wide recession in business activity.
(2) Product innovation — the introduction of a competing product with potential to cause substantial loss of volume in traditional product lines.
(3) Change in production technology — the introduction of new ways to produce the product in larger quantity, with better quality, or at lower cost.
(4) Change in consumer behavior — resulting in shifts in demand, distribution systems, marketing approaches.
(5) Competitive action — a strategic move on the part of important competitors which has not been anticipated and which demands a response if market share is to be preserved.
(6) Management behavior — a move on the part of the company's own management affecting the patterns of funds flows.

None of these changes is inherently unpredictable. The fact that they were not predicted or were only imperfectly predicted in the companies studied gave rise to the need for rebalancing funds flows and reallocation of resources.

FINANCIAL MOBILITY DEFINED

The continuing operational problem for financial management is to maintain balance in funds inflows and outflows, to maintain or work toward equilibrium in these flows, and to be prepared to respond to unexpected events that cause a distortion of the expected funds flow pattern. Let us be clear on what we mean by funds flows. Funds have been defined previously as corporate purchasing power — usually, though by no means always, cash — and flows represent a rate of conversion of this purchasing power into specialized use (so-called *outflows*) or alternatively a release of purchasing power from specialized use (*inflows*). *Specialized use* generally means the acquisition of a tangible or intangible asset with income-generating potential.

At any point in time corporate resources will be subdivided into those committed to specialized use, and hence restricted as to alternative application, and those in relatively unspecialized form and hence available for alternative use. Earlier in this chapter the former resources were called economic resources and the latter financial resources. Over any given period of time there will be a flow or transformation of resources, the net effect of which may be expected to alter the balance between specialized and unspecialized resources, though it may leave the total unchanged.

The task of maintaining equilibrium in funds flows when these changes take place centers on the control exercised either through the reduction of outflows representing applications of funds to specialized use or through increase of inflows representing a release of funds from specialized use. *The capacity to influence the rate of change of economic resources from one form into another and hence to determine the mix of resources at a point in time will be referred to in this study as financial mobility. The ultimate aim of financial mobility is to achieve a state of equilibrium in funds flows consistent with essential corporate objectives.*

It is uncertainty that gives rise to the need for a reserve of unspecialized or uncommitted resources and as a consequence causes withholding of funds from income-generating use. It is uncertainty that requires financial mobility of a high order and a strategy for applying this mobility. Thus the observation of the impact of and response to the unexpected event provides not only the best opportunity for identifying what the strategy of mobility may be but also the chance to observe financial policy in the form of a constraint on that strategy. It may be said that the economic function served by a strategy of financial mobility is the opportunity to reduce unproductive resources to a minimum without violating the company's financial policies or risk posture.

Before leaving this definitional section a practical consideration must be recognized. So far we have been talking of *corporate* mobility. We shall continue to emphasize the company viewpoint. It is a practical fact, however, that financial officers at times choose or are forced to adopt a personal or functional concept of mobility as opposed to a corporate concept. This phenomenon will be developed in more detail later in descriptive chapters dealing with field studies. The corporate concept of mobility implies a control over or ability to influence total corporate funds flows. If in practice this influence is only partial on the part of the financial officer, then his behavior with respect to his financial responsibilities may be expected to diverge from what might appear to be optimum corporate strategy. Thus, for example, if the only resources he has direct and full control over are cash balances and the marketable securities portfolio, then his strategy of mobility may give undue emphasis to these dimensions of the total picture. These are matters of considerable practical significance.

THE STRATEGY OF FINANCIAL MOBILITY

In considering management action for maintaining financial equilibrium under conditions of uncertainty it is helpful to attempt to identify in advance the basic elements of a fully developed strategy of mobility. Even though practice may not reveal conscious attention to these elements, they will be a useful framework for observation. Practice may indicate modification or refinement before normative conclusions are reached. The following aspects are considered to be a logical breakdown of this critical dimension of financial management.

(a) A plan for the preservation or achievement of funds flow equilibrium under known existing and expected conditions.

A business unit has explicit corporate goals leading to a plan of management action requiring the expenditure of corporate purchasing power. These planned outflows must be matched by expected inflows supplemented as necessary by management action modifying the flows or adjusting the balance between committed and uncommitted resources. If these planned flows represent an equilibrium position sustainable within the bounds set by financial policy, then the achievement of balanced flows will be sufficient. If they do not represent an equilibrium position, then further modification will be necessary in order to move toward such a position. This, however, is not necessarily to be accomplished within the current planning period.

(b) Identification of key financial policies with respect to such matters as use of debt and payment of dividends. These policies act as constraints on the action respecting balancing of funds flows.

The development of an explicit policy on key aspects of sources and uses of capital is usually regarded as a statement of a single optimal course of action. In actual practice policy is more commonly a consensus of key management personnel on a *band* or *range* of acceptable behavior — for example, with respect to the form, amount, and timing of dividends. So long as action does not violate the limits set by this range, which may be broad, no penalty will be assumed. The identification of these limits of acceptable behavior is essential to a rational strategy of mobility. Such a strategy may contemplate the possibility of violating policies under certain conditions but presumably would take account of whatever penalty was involved.

(c) A program of search, which continuously scans the future within the planning period and is designed to identify hitherto unexpected events at the earliest possible moment.

The obvious intent of financial forecasting is to reduce uncertainty about future events affecting funds flows. As the time available for action increases, there is a decline in the importance of mobility in corporate resources permitting rapid or instantaneous management response. The more efficient the early warning system on approaching disturbances, the more fully can resources be committed to income-generating use. The strategy of mobility will be geared to what experience has to say about the accuracy of company forecasts.

(d) Identification of the resources that may be called into play in the event of an unexpected need.

Such an inventory requires an estimate of the amount of funds that will be available for conversion to alternative use, the timing of release, and the probability of release from existing uses where for one reason or another there is uncertainty about availability. The resources of mobility are very different from the list of assets shown on a conventional balance sheet. They are the resources that are to be committed or may be committed in the future — a very special kind of balance sheet.

(e) Development of a tentative strategy or set of strategies for responding to the unexpected need. Such strategies consist of the circumstances and order in which the resources identified under (d) will be drawn into use.

This priority list would represent a joint judgment on the several considerations affecting the action to be taken, including speed of response, certainty of response, cost broadly defined, and so on. In practice there will be a sequence of responses over time as the nature of the need becomes more apparent, circumstances change, resources change.

(f) As a matter of practical significance there will be consideration given to the extent to which the required outflows or "need" may be modified as an alternative to the conversion of resources from existing uses.

This has two dimensions: the corporate dimension, which relates to the ability to influence the external environment; and the functional (financial) dimension, which relates to the internal environment and the financial officer's influence thereon. This aspect of strategy implies tampering with corporate goals, which at least for normative purposes were to be taken as "given" in this study. In practice companies and managements do modify their goals in the light of new information or changed circumstances. They may also revise their risk posture, which was also assumed as "given" for normative discussion.

The Resources of Mobility

As previously indicated, the customary image of corporate financial or economic resources is the left-hand side of the balance sheet. The point that has already been made is that the balance sheet shows how certain resources have been invested in the past for purposes of generating income. The viewpoint of mobility requires that attention be shifted to the resources available to support management action in the future. Some important points of difference in these two concepts of financial resources will now be considered.

One of the steps to be taken in developing this concept of resources related to future decisions and future funds flows is to discard the restriction of *ownership* which is inherent in the balance sheet. Ownership has been associated with the concept of control and hence might seem very relevant to financial mobility as previously defined. In a practical sense, however, in the large business organization of today the fact that the corporation owns an asset does not mean that top management, and particularly the financial arm of top management, can convert it to alternative use at will. To illustrate: a major segment of what is shown as cash on the balance sheet is permanently clogging the transactions pipeline and is unavailable for alternative use as long as the volume of transactions remains at or near existing levels. It makes for a reassuring statistic on the balance sheet but is operationally useless in balancing funds flows. Similarly, other assets appearing on the balance sheet may for a variety of reasons be temporarily or permanently beyond the reach of management for the purpose we have in mind even though clearly owned by the corporation.

At the same time there are resources not owned by the corporation that can and often do play a key role in funds flow management. An obvious example is the unused line of credit at the bank. These are resources that either formally or informally have been committed for use by a particular business as and when needed, and the business will make plans on the assumption that it can reach out for them if funds flows get out of balance. So it must be emphasized that when we talk of the resources by means of which equilibrium in funds flows is maintained, we are speaking of resources both inside and outside the company.

Referring again to the conventional balance sheet concept of resources, it is also important to recognize that although assets are given a monetary value for accounting purposes they do not necessarily have a monetary or purchasing power equivalent. The important questions are whether an asset or a resource can be converted into alternative use in a given interval of time, and if so what is the magnitude of the potential purchasing power or funds flow. In a sense this question appears related to the degree of specialization of an asset, that is, the range of alternative use inside or outside the business. In general, the less specialized the asset or resource, the more useful it is in the management of funds flows. (On the other hand, it might also be generalized that the more specialized the asset, the more productive it is likely to be in generating earnings, since the purpose of committing assets to specialized use is the generation of income.)

Thus at one extreme we would have bank balances and at the other special-purpose machinery. However, some cash is in fact extremely immobile and at certain times some machines may have a very ready market. It will be apparent that both the timing and the time interval involved in conversion to alternative use are important in identifying the mobility of particular resources. It will also be apparent that we are dealing with the separability of an asset. Can it be "spun off" into alternative use inside or outside the company without adversely affecting the basic corporate objectives (such as a sales or an earnings target or some other goal)?

These illustrations thus far have been drawn from resources that exist and are in some sense at the disposal of management: cash, salable assets, assured borrowing power. Since the whole discussion relates to financial planning for some future time interval, it is appropriate to include the resources expected to accrue during the planning period or even beyond. These expectations are contained in the funds flow or cash flow forecast.

It might appear that these resources (or income) are completely mobile since they cannot be actually committed to use until they are received. However, the forecast usually draws its management sanction from a budget and that budget represents an agreement among members of management as to how future funds inflows are to be allocated. Consequently, a reallocation of these anticipated inflows to uses other than those described in the budget may involve some degree of internal negotiation. The expected incremental inflows cannot be automatically assumed to be completely mobile.

This raises the important point that the management of future resources frequently involves negotiation both internally and externally. Some resources, such as cash, may be under exclusive corporate or financial control; but many, perhaps most, of the potential resources of mobility involve agreement on the part of other parties that their use be changed since they are already "employed" in some sense.

Another major difference between past and future resources is the obvious one that assessment of resources to be available is more complex, involving three dimensions of amount, timing, and probability. The assessment of probability is an attempt to reduce uncertainty to a measured adjustment of resource values. This is a very difficult judgment, but as a practical matter the judgment will have to be made or it will be implicit in the action taken. Thus, for example, a decision to treat a certain resource as totally unavailable for unexpected needs amounts to a judgment that its availability on short notice has a probability at or near zero. Whether and to what extent explicit probabilities can be brought into practical decision making will be discussed later in this book. In any case it is clear that these considerations are absent from the usual balance sheet concepts of asset value related primarily to historical cost at a point in time now passed.

Finally, there is a dimension of mobility which is of very real importance but which the balance sheet and accounting conventions ignore. This may be summarized by the terms "competitive lead" and "competitive lag," referring to the extent to which past expenditures have given a company time to maneuver before competitive pressures cut into current earning power. Accounting conventions are necessarily arbitrary in the extent to which they recognize, through the procedure of capitalization, that past expenditures have a future rather than a current benefit. Customarily expenditures on tangible assets having extended physical life are capitalized, whereas intangibles such as advertising, market development, and research are not capitalized but are normally written off against income in the year incurred. Nevertheless, intensive market cultivation and product research over a period of many years may be the key to a genuine competitive lead that sustains future earning power; and this is the only thing that gives past investment any real present value.

This staying power of current earnings, though difficult to measure, is of very real consequence when funds flows have to be modified to take account of unexpected pressures or opportunities. It is a key resource relating to the effectiveness of past expenditures although much of it is unrecognized on the balance sheet. By contrast, if it is absent it largely denies the values claimed on a balance sheet.

DIAGRAMMATIC REPRESENTATIONS

As a supplement to the preceding pages, which have attempted to present the concept of financial mobility in words, this section adds further clarification in the form of a series of diagrams. These visual summaries may assist the reader in relating his own notions of the meaning of "financial mobility" to those which I have in mind.

Exhibit 3B

The total economic and financial resources of a business unit, the combination of resources to which it has legal title and re-

EXHIBIT 3B

SUMMARY OF CORPORATE RESOURCES: ONE POINT IN TIME

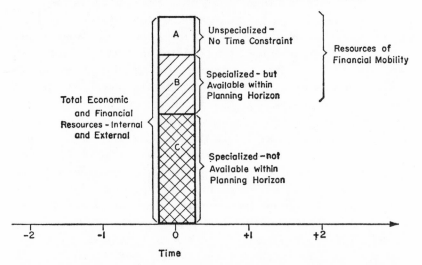

sources to which it has access outside the firm, are regarded as a finite amount at a point in time. These are represented by the height of the bar at point zero. Similar representations could be made at any other point in time either as a fact with respect to the past or as a prediction of future position. Such resources are here classified on two bases:

(1) Unspecialized and hence available as purchasing power for alternative uses without time constraint (A); or specialized, i.e.,

committed to income-generating purposes and hence not immediately available for alternative use (B and C).

(2) Mobile, i.e., actually or potentially available for alternative use within the company's planning horizon (A and B); or immobile, i.e., committed on such a long-term basis that the funds are not available for alternative use during the planning period (C).

The resources with which this study will be concerned are those in categories A and B. It is implicit in this concept that the various resources can be not only identified as to nature but also measured.

Exhibit 3C

Exhibit 3C extends the concept of Exhibit 3B to indicate that the plans and expectations for the business generate foreseeable

EXHIBIT 3C

THE CHANGING MOBILITY OF RESOURCES OVER TIME

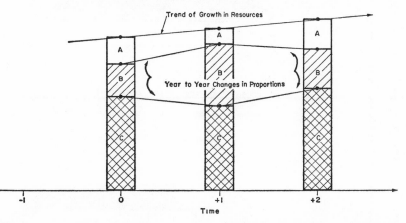

changes in the company's resource position both as to total resources and as to the distribution of these resources in their potential for mobility. The diagram suggests that there will be an expected trend in total resources and periodic shifts in the boundaries between proportions of resources in categories A, B, and C. These resource positions are the result of a corporate plan developed at point zero, based on best estimates of conditions through the end of the planning period and a program of management action geared to corporate goals and consistent with existing fi-

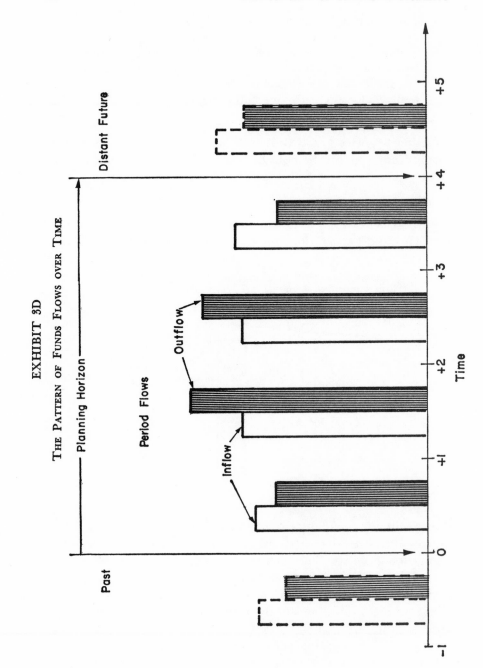

EXHIBIT 3D

THE PATTERN OF FUNDS FLOWS OVER TIME

nancial policies and corporate risk posture. The positions reveal a changing financial mobility or capacity to respond to the unexpected, and presumably harmonize with an established strategy of mobility. The decreasing or increasing proportion of unspecialized assets is assumed to be consistent with or to reflect a movement toward an ultimate equilibrium situation.

Exhibit 3D

Exhibit 3D suggests a shift in attention from the static inventory of financial and economic resources illustrated in Exhibits 3B and 3C to the dynamic flow of funds over time — the planned changes in the allocation of resources. These flows are represented by bars for Inflow and Outflow (release and commitment) of cash or funds, period by period. The flows are unlikely to be equal from period to period and Inflows are unlikely to equal Outflows for any period if one excludes changes in the cash balance as a "flow." The company involved will have a finite planning horizon, in this case assumed to be four periods hence, over which it has specific expectations and plans for the balancing of flows and the distribution of its resources. Beyond that horizon there may be some vaguely defined expectations suggested by the broken bars of period five.

Exhibit 3E

The problem addressed by this study is what happens when the planned flows prove to be in error and in one or more of the periods within the planning horizon a substantial unplanned deficit in the flows appears. When such a need arises there may be and often is a choice as to whether the need will be accepted within the planning period. Thus, the first set of alternatives with respect to the unexpected need may be expressed as follows:

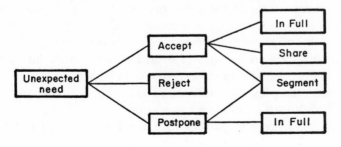

If outright rejection of the need is either impossible or inadvisable, then there may be an opportunity to postpone to a later planning period. If postponement is inadvisable, then it may still be possible to reduce the financial impact of the event or action by either sharing the burden with another business or finding a way to segment the payments over a longer period, which is a form of postponement of the need.

If the company follows the path of accepting the need for funds in full or in part within the planning period, then the resources of mobility must come into play. Here the two basic choices lie between the commitment of reserves and the modification of previously planned flows during the period in question. The reserve alternative may be depicted as follows:

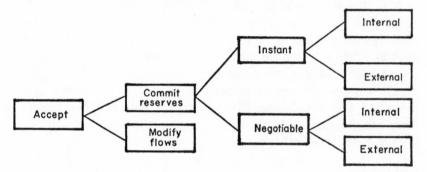

Here corporate reserves are classified as to (1) whether they are instantly available or negotiable, that is, subject to a time and uncertainty constraint, and (2) whether they are available within the assets to which the business has title or are reserves that are currently the property of persons or institutions external to the corporation.

If the company accepts the need and either has no reserves or chooses not to commit them to this use, then the remaining alternative is to modify planned outflows so that the new need is absorbed by displacing another need of lower priority, thus preserving the previous balance of total inflows and outflows. Since the choice under the modification of flows alternative is somewhat more complex and difficult to visualize than the use of reserves, Exhibit 3E is presented as an effort to summarize the basic alternatives. Here one pair of bars for Inflows and Outflows is

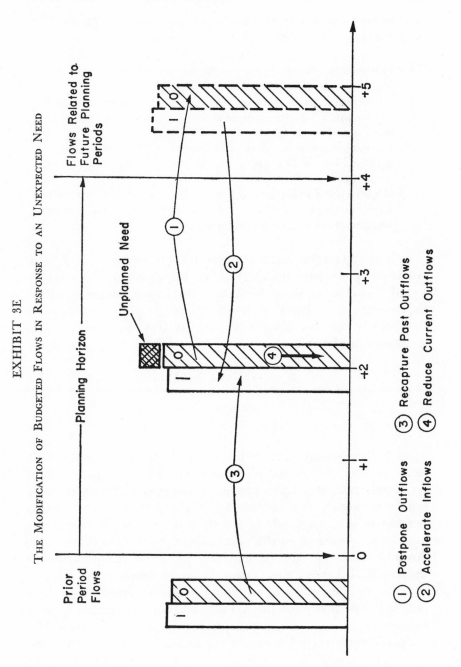

EXHIBIT 3E

THE MODIFICATION OF BUDGETED FLOWS IN RESPONSE TO AN UNEXPECTED NEED

used to summarize the entire plan of funds flows over the planning horizon. The alternative choices are seen as:

(1) Postponing outflows related to future period income to a later planning period, e.g. market development.
(2) Accelerating inflows previously expected in future periods— not common, but an example would be a series of price reductions on durable goods.
(3) Recapturing past outflows—in effect reversing past investment decisions by the liquidation of the asset acquired, as in a sale and leaseback.
(4) Negotiating a reduction in the outflows related to current inflows, as might happen in an unexpected business recession when wages or salaries might be reduced.

As a further refinement of these choices attention will focus particularly on the modification of planned outflows. It was found useful to break outflows down into four categories which, depending on circumstances and management attitudes, are likely to be treated differently in a strategy of mobility. This classification of outflows is:

(a) volume-related
(b) scale-related
(c) strategic
(d) value-related

(a) Volume-related expenditures are expenditures for such items as direct labor, raw materials, and purchased parts. These are closely related to units produced and sold and normally cannot be reduced unless volume declines and then largely in proportion to the magnitude of the decline. Of course, inventories may be accumulated to the point where, for a period, a scaling down of these expenditures may take place without a decline in units sold. Likewise, the decline in units produced may for a time exceed the decline in units sold. However, a decline in these outflows is normally conditional on and follows a decline in sales volume.

(b) Scale-related expenditures are basically related to the general scale of operations and only imprecisely related to the number of units produced and sold. They are roughly defined by the size of the corporate entity and the position it holds in the competitive structure of the industry in which it operates. They cover a wide range of expense categories in both current and capital budgets, including indirect labor, office staff and management payroll, and advertising. As the company grows in size these expenditures inevitably increase, but at any given time the budgeted sales for the immediate planning period would be largely if not entirely unaffected by sizable changes in these outlays.

(c) Strategic expenditures, a more vaguely defined category of expenditure, include those assigned a high priority rating by top management because of a unique role they currently play in the corporation's long-run strategy. In management's judgment they are vital to the future of the organization. Examples of this class would be certain capital expenditures related to new product development, certain research and development outlays, market development outlays, and acquisitions. These expenditures are a matter of judgment at a point in time and can only be identified by the people involved in the decisions. By definition they would not be open to manipulation for purposes of normal strategy of financial mobility.

(d) Financial, or value-related, expenditures are a number of expenditures not directly related to the tangible economic function of the business entity — the nature or scale of operations or the number of units produced or sold — but are related to the value of the business as an investment and the rate of growth of value over time ("income"). Whether a business owns or rents property, performs a certain production process with a labor or a machine input, refunds a bond issue to gain a better interest rate, or pays an increased cash dividend — these choices do not have any direct effect on the number of units produced and sold in a given time span or on the company's productive or marketing capacity. They do affect the cash outflows, however, and they do directly affect the size and distribution of the earnings stream and therefore the equity value of the business. Thus they have been labeled "financial" or "value-related" expenditures to distinguish them from the first three categories.

As a classification similar to these four broad categories, there are some comparable distinctions to be made among capital expenditures. The classification suggested below can be fitted into the categories above, but because of the size and importance of capital expenditures in strategies of mobility these groups need separate description. Distinctions among capital expenditures may be made as follows:

(i) Maintenance of capacity. Replacing a roof, a boiler, or an electric generator that either has broken down or threatens to do so is obviously essential to the continuity of production and sales. In most mature facilities there are a number of "must" expenditures each year.

(ii) Expansion of capacity. Preparation for growth in established product lines may come after capacity has been strained for some time or may come comfortably in advance of the need. In either case it represents movement toward a new scale of operations. Here there may be more leeway as to timing and magnitude than in category (i).

(iii) Cost reduction. Many proposals come forward each year that are defended on the grounds that they will do basically the same job as existing investment but more cheaply. A machine that has run three years of a 15-year economic life may be replaced by a technological innovation because the latter offers substantial savings over the former. The ultimate impact is on the net profit line of the income statement rather than on the product or the customer.

(iv) Strategic advances. A number of capital expenditures for such items as machinery or warehouse space represent the capital required to implement a strategic decision to move into a new product or a new market. They are viewed quite differently from the first three.

(v) Noneconomic expenditures. Finally, there are certain capital expenditures that do not have any *direct* or measurable relationship to production, sales, or value-creation but are judged desirable, such as the classic examples of landscaping or the employee recreation room.

These five categories of capital expenditures fit reasonably well into the first four broad categories as follows: (a) — (i), (b) — (ii), (c) — (iv), (d) — (iii). The fifth category would presumably underlie and relate to both (a) and (b).

Exhibit 3F

As a device for putting together the concepts of financial mobility, as to both resources and strategy, a decision tree is presented in Exhibit 3F. This diagram summarizes the basic choices open to management when an unexpected need arises. It defines both range and sequence of choice. It will be used as one of the means of summarizing the action in the descriptive chapters of Part II. The various branchings are intended to represent both circumstances and choices. For example, the first alternative respecting the deficit is a question of fact, whether the change in expectations leading to a prospective deficit is regarded as discretionary or nondiscretionary by management. If it is discretionary, then management has a choice: to accept, to reject, or to postpone the need for funds. In the diagram choices are represented by diverging arrows.

Among the alternatives presented is the option to reject or defer a need — valid alternatives under many circumstances. However, this raises the prospect of compromising corporate goals and requires an evaluation of costs and risks. It also requires a judgment of how much time, in addition to the time gained by the forecasting procedures used to spot the need, is necessary to achieve the desired reallocation of resources. In the main this study will look only at the Accept decisions and the manner of fulfillment. The implication is that these are the situations where the cost of a Reject or Defer action was judged to exceed the cost of reallocation.

MOBILITY AND THE MANAGEMENT VIEWPOINT

The descriptive chapters in Part II will attempt to examine the manner in which managements practice the art of maintaining mobility over time. From this examination is expected to come some characterization or "model," to use the current word, of strategy as it is in the real world today. Since the sample of companies investigated is small and not scientifically chosen, the evidence will not be held out as conclusively representative of business practice but rather as a serious hypothesis as to intelligent business practice.

Before making the study I had a prior hypothesis about the

EXHIBIT 3F

THE STRUCTURE OF CHOICE FOR A STRATEGY OF FINANCIAL MOBILITY

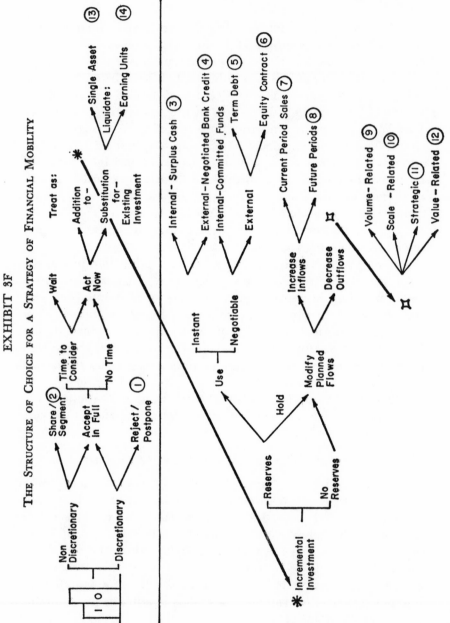

managerial view of finance, which is spelled out in detail in Chapter 2. In this view the preservation of the corporate entity and the achievement of its operating objectives are regarded as paramount and financial policies are considered to serve the purpose of facilitating these objectives. Although this is not necessarily in conflict with the traditional financial goal of maximizing stockholder value, there are times when a choice must be made as to priority and the management view would then place stockholder value in a secondary position.

The strategy of financial mobility is a critical element in keeping the corporate entity not only solvent but capable of supporting management action in pursuit of its goals with the necessary corporate purchasing power, regardless of whether the necessary action can be accurately determined in advance. Chapter 3 has developed the concept that a rational strategy of mobility includes the identification of the resources of mobility, measurement of their magnitude, assessment of their availability, and development of a ranking of resources whereby the order in which they will be called into use will be tentatively planned in advance. The focal point of the managerial viewpoint becomes the one or more key resources of mobility that lead the priority list and are the principal defense against the unexpected need. The hypothesis presented here is that management in general, and financial management in particular, will attach the utmost importance to the preservation of its key resources of mobility, and that mobility will tend to dominate financial policy even to the violation of the financial policies generally considered to serve stockholder value best.

Observation of the validity of this hypothesis is regarded as a significant test of the existence of a management viewpoint as distinct from a stockholder viewpoint in financial affairs. The hypothesis would argue that if the financial officer follows the assumptions of financial theory and is highly sensitive to the stockholder interest, it will be because he derives his financial mobility from the stockholder through manipulation of the dividend or new issues of stock. On the other hand, if he is denied mobility by this source because of a fixed dividend policy and resistance to new issues, he will tend to become insensitive to the stockholder interest. Similarly, if the financial officer draws his primary mobility from negotiated debt, he will tend to bring the viewpoint of the creditor to bear on corporate financial policy.

It follows from this line of reasoning that the greatest identification with a corporate viewpoint, as distinct from the viewpoint of ownership or capital supply, will be achieved under circumstances where mobility is an internal matter. This suggests that primary mobility would be derived either from a substantial reserve of liquid funds or from a capacity to negotiate reallocation of flows and stocks when the unexpected occurs.

Part II

Observations of Practice:
The Dynamics of Individual Experience

Introduction

The time-worn taunt of the business practitioner to the theorist that he has never had to meet a payroll has a grain of truth in it. There is nothing like the pressure of responsibility and the threat to one's income and prestige to sharpen the mind and separate the relevant from the irrelevant. The obvious fact that many business leaders today are highly intelligent men must mean that their behavior under these conditions of pressure is bound to be informative as to the relevant considerations and how they may be evaluated. The information I particularly sought in this study was evidence of the resources regarded by management as important in preserving mobility over time, the manner in which these resources were used, and the policy that integrated their use into some pattern of operation over time. It is a basic assumption of the study of practice that a careful recording of *the sequence of action over time* for several companies under a variety of circumstances will be informative in these respects.

Part III of this book presents generalized conclusions on company behavior, based on the total sample of businesses observed. The weakness of any generalization is that it squeezes out the unique elements of each situation, both economic and human. Thus, much of the dynamic continuity is lost. It is essential to an understanding of financial mobility that the flow of interrelated events over time be understood, and it is for this reason that the three case histories of Part II are included. The reader does not necessarily have to read all three before proceeding to Part III, though each case is quite different from the others and significant contrasts can be observed.

The company described in Chapter 4 is a basically sound and

profitable company, which has to deal with the recurring phenomenon of a short but severe sales decline that it is unable to predict. It is a good example of the healthy company responding to an adverse event of a type it has experienced before.

The second detailed case history, described in Chapter 5, is that of a company in a weakened competitive position facing severe and prolonged industry recession at a time when other events are compounding the funds flow problem. This company is an example of the multiple adversity situation — the coincidence at one period of time of events not inherently correlated.

The third case history presents a quite different set of funds flow problems straining the company's capacity for financial mobility. This company faced secular erosion of competitive position, due primarily to faulty product mix and a failure to keep up with technological advances, coupled with an underlying problem of scale. The somewhat random impact of efforts to overcome these problems, along with the usual ups and downs of sales volume in a weak profit situation, placed great strains on the balance of funds flows. Chapter 6 outlines the way in which the company responded, and attempts to construct the strategy for mobility.

4

Company A: Mobility and the
Business Cycle

The Emerging Impact of Recession

Company A is a manufacturer of capital goods, much of which are produced to customer order. The highly cyclical industry has conditioned management and employees alike to the event of a serious decline in orders. In spite of this general awareness there is a notable absence of confidence in ability to predict when a turning point in business will occur and how prolonged the decline will be. In conversations the company's chief financial officer stressed repeatedly that the company did not have an involved planning approach. Forecasting even one year ahead was regarded as difficult, and substantial errors were made in one-year forecasts. From time to time, but without any real success, the company had undertaken studies to relate orders to various economic indicators. Substantial and erratic changes from month to month in orders booked made the timing of a change difficult to identify quickly.

Thus we begin this recorded experience by noting the severe limits on preparation for response that the management accepted for itself. A recession could be in process for two or three months before it was recognized as such. The resource of time to act was essentially nonexistent. The key indicator used was the company's own record of Orders Booked and all management eyes were focused on this index as a guide to action. A decline in orders for two or three successive months was the clue to an adverse trend. If this was consistent with the best information on other companies and with anticipated industry trends, it was accepted as a signal for action to head off an anticipated imbalance in funds flows.

The monthly record of orders booked from January 1954 to December 1961 is shown in Exhibit 4A. This period was chosen because it spanned the impact of two successive downturns in business, the first in March 1957 and the second in February 1960. The graph of orders covers the period leading up to the first recession and through the end of the second. The pattern of demand is anything but smooth; though with hindsight the trend lines become apparent, they were not so in advance. Interpretation of this graph must allow for the impact of periodic price increases, which traditionally are announced far enough ahead to lead customers about to place orders to accelerate these orders by a month or so. During the period covered by the graph there were three such increases, the effects of which are seen as sharp but temporary improvement in orders in September 1956, October 1960, and October 1961.

In order to give some perspective on the first of the two recessions (March 1957) and to indicate the lack of ability to forecast coming events in the business, some comment on the preceding experience is necessary. The graph shows a long period of up-trend in orders from January 1954. By 1956 the company had decided on a major addition to its capacity and had made arrangements to finance the addition by a new issue of common stock. Management was unwilling — and perhaps unable — to raise this sum ($3.8 million) by a commitment of its debt capacity and in any case reasoned that "bricks and mortar" should be ownership money. Further, the common stock price at that time was regarded as favorable, that is to say, above book value. The issue momentarily increased the company's cash position from the low level of $3 million in June 1956, but the plant expenditures and inventory accumulation reduced cash plus marketable securities back to $3.7 million in February 1957. The company therefore entered the recession period with a low reserve of liquid funds.

For many years the company had adhered to a dividend policy of a stable quarterly amount that the directors felt confident the company could maintain, plus year-end extras when earnings proved to be good. A second sign of management's expectations in 1956 was the declaration at the November board meeting of an extra dividend larger than those of the two preceding years. Perhaps more significant was the fact that at the same time the board increased the regular quarterly dividend from 27½ cents to 35 cents.

Against the background of a strong 1956 and a promising level of orders in January and February 1957, orders booked in March dropped noticeably. The downturn was masked, however, by a rise in April orders over March, so that it was only when May and June proved to be down again below the March level that the alarm bells began to ring. With this evidence in hand of a potential decline in funds inflows, management made its first move to assure future balance by cutting outflows — at first very tentatively. This first step, an internal rather than an external one, was to begin laying off productive labor, also shown in Exhibit 4A. When the orders of July and succeeding months continued the decline, the layoffs became more drastic. In the early months of the recession some glimmer of hope for a turnabout persisted, as evidenced by the fact that a slight rise in September orders over August bookings produced a slight rise in direct productive labor in October. However, the layoff was quickly resumed in November.

Thus, with a planning horizon near zero and the prospect of a sharp decline in demand of unknown duration, the only assurance of balance in funds flows was to insist on operational mobility and tie employment as closely as possible to orders booked. In all, over 25% of the direct labor force was laid off during the first six months of this recession period.

The company's cash position (see Exhibit 4A) should be in mind before the other steps taken by management are considered. In general the recession years of 1957 and 1958 were years of improvement in liquidity. The cash position improved from a low point in February 1957 to a high point in November and then declined to a level just under $6 million, which was maintained throughout 1958 and most of 1959.

The quick response of control of outflows, particularly those directly related to new inventory, was obviously a key factor in determining the cash position. Also of importance were the company's borrowing practices. Short-term bank loans (Exhibit 4A) were used strictly as a reserve against short-term deficiencies of cash *after* these deficiencies had become apparent. The company

EXHIBIT 4A

COMPANY A: GRAPHS OF SELECTED FINANCIAL DATA
JANUARY 1954–DECEMBER 1961

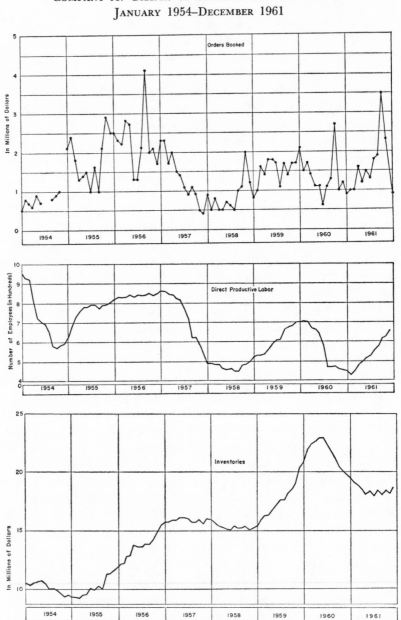

EXHIBIT 4A (continued)

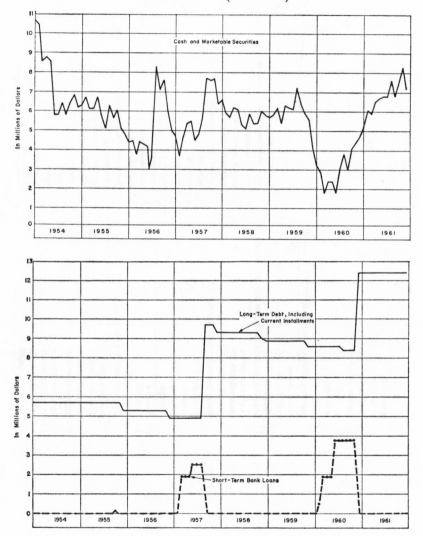

EXHIBIT 4A (concluded)

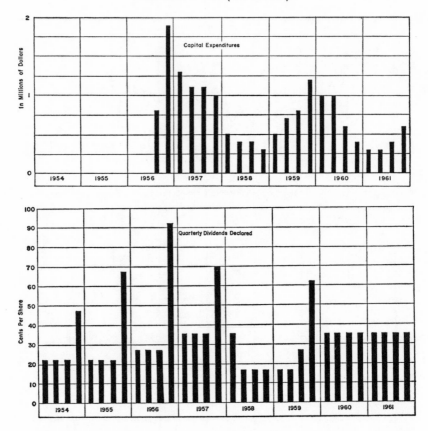

borrowed $1.9 million in March 1957 and another $600,000 in June. The first borrowing had no direct relation to the forth-coming recession. The second loan was not used to anticipate a need but did relieve a typical "bind," which occurred as a result of the inevitable one-quarter lag in the response to a decline in orders.

The real act of anticipation in borrowing came in September when the company negotiated a term loan for $4.8 million (Ex-hibit 4A). Since it was now apparent that the money borrowed on short term could not be repaid in the near future without reducing cash to a level considered dangerous, management acted to hold these funds by converting the borrowing to a term loan. Further strengthening was provided by borrowing an additional $2.3 million. This use of external negotiated reserves represented the second step in the response to balance funds flows and came roughly six months after the downturn in orders began. The replacement of short-term notes by the term loan was re-garded by management as restoring its reserve of short-term borrowing power, which it valued highly as a means of respond-ing to a need "after the fact" with speed and confidence.

During this recession the primary internal control on funds flows was the contraction of direct expenditures related to cur-rent inventory building, to current orders, and therefore to current income generation. In the main, expenditures relating to the income of future periods were not immediately affected. This is best illustrated by capital expenditures, also shown in Exhibit 4A. The high level of capital expenditures initiated in 1956 continued through 1957 at a rate of approximately $1.1 million per quarter. However, in the last quarter of 1957 the annual capital budget came up for its customary examination. The net effect of this internal negotiation was to cut the 1958 budget substantially below that of 1957 to a rate not in excess of $0.5 million per quarter.

This third explicit act by management came approximately nine months after the downturn in March. The fact that it was not accelerated indicates a certain confidence in the measures already taken. Indeed, management has asserted that the cut in capital expenditures was due to uncertainty in sales and profits rather than immediate funds flow requirements. It is clear, however, that although the action taken had no direct relation to near-term sales, it certainly did have a significant and beneficial effect on the near-term cash position, conserving about $0.7 million per quarter.

By these means the company survived a year of substantial adjustment to a new and lower level of funds flows. Before 1957 was over another act of significance occurred. The board had continued to vote the quarterly dividend set in January. In November the issue was presented as to whether an extra dividend should be declared for 1957. The evidence was that, in spite of the obvious recession in progress, recorded sales and earnings for 1957 would approximately equal those of 1956. In the face of this evidence the company did declare an extra dividend, though it was approximately half the amount declared the previous year. Thus through the end of 1957 and into the first quarter of 1958 the company continued to protect the stockholder from the pressures of financial mobility. Dividend declarations are plotted in Exhibit 4A.

At this point some vagueness in the evidence appears. The facts of action taken are clear; the reasons are not. The facts are that in April 1958 the quarterly dividend was cut in half, to remain at that level for five consecutive quarters, and the year-end extra for 1958 was omitted. This amounted to a "saving" of nearly $1 million in 1958. The total 1957 dollar payment was not equaled again until 1963. By April the evidence of a substantial decline in sales and earnings for 1958 was there for all to see. Thus management clearly had the basis for curbing shareholders' expectations. By April also the company's cash position had eroded by 20% and appeared on a downward trend. Among other things the lag in meeting tax commitments was now catching up with Company A. The action taken appeared drastic and inconsistent with previous dividend policy. On the other hand, it cannot be proved that cash pressures were the cause of the action. The short-term cash gains were of course substantially smaller than those realized by actions previously discussed.

Somewhere during the period of these two recessions dividend policy began to shift under the pressure of events and the changing views of management. The concept at the outset of the period was a low and stable quarterly rate plus a variable extra, which could be relatively large in good years. The pressures of prosperity brought about nearly a doubling of the quarterly rate in three years without abandonment of the extra. Events proved that the stockholders could not expect such dividends to be sustained during years like 1958. Although the year-end extra reappeared briefly in 1959, this device for achieving mobility in outflows to stockholders was then abandoned. It was concluded that the market price did not respond to the extra as it did to increase in the quarterly rate.

This research study began with the general hypothesis that financial policy, including dividend policy, is one of the key constraints on the management's task of gaining equilibrium in funds flows over time. That is, dividend policy would be a long-term given, and funds flows would be balanced so as to preserve the policy intact. The question is whether there is a substantial interaction of the short-term needs of mobility and long-term financial policy. The answer to that question — to be raised again and again — is very significant. It certainly is not answered here by Company A.

Through 1958 funds flows appeared to level off at the new lower level of operations and to be at least temporarily in equilibrium. No further borrowings were necessary. Cash moved in small variations up to and down from the $6 million level. Direct labor employment was more or less stable, with only a slight drift downward through September. Profits were much lower but still showing. In spite of reduced capital expenditures the plant was considered in excellent shape.

RECESSION NUMBER TWO

We now turn our attention to the second recession which began in February 1960. Again we need to set the stage by some comments on the preceding period. In September 1958 orders began an upward trend from the preceding recession. During the period that followed, the industry and particularly this company's management gained the impression that the early 1960s would be a period of boom conditions. The phrase "the roaring Sixties" was repeated as the mood of expectation at the time. In the month following the pickup in orders (October 1958) recall of the work force laid off in the preceding recession began, and the payroll climbed steadily from that point forward. In spite of the fact that inventories (Exhibit 4A) had not declined substantially in the preceding recession (down from $16.1 million to $15.0 million) the company began to build inventory in anticipation of future demand. From October 1958 to June 1960 inventories rose from $15.3 million to $22.9 million.

At the same time plant expenditures were rising again to previous quarterly levels ($1 million) in anticipation of these needs. This change was most noticeable in fiscal 1959. As another measure of management's mood and timing, in July 1959 the quarterly dividend was increased and in November an extra was declared (the last time this was done). In January 1960 the quarterly dividend was restored to the level of January 1958. At the beginning of 1960 a steel strike temporarily unsettled expectations but management fully expected that settlement would bring about a surge of orders.

When the surge did not come, management was quick to sense a possible error in expectations. Its record inventory levels and sharply weakened cash position were strong reasons to be highly sensitive. Cash balances had begun a decline in September 1959 and by January 1960 were at a record low point of $3.3 million. Even with a return to short-term borrowing ($0.5 million) in February, cash balances declined to $2.9 million. With the first turndown of orders in February some action was taken, though at first tentative. This was the decision in March to cut out all overtime work. March required additional short-term borrowings ($1.4 million) and again cash declined — to the unheard of level of $1.8 million. As in the previous recession there was a misleading pickup in orders for one month (March) and then the decline took over. Exhibit 4A shows that layoffs began in April and for April, May, and June decreases were continuous but moderate.

June again recorded severe cash pressures. Even additional short-term loans of $1.9 million did not prevent cash balances from declining again to the $1.8 million mark. Layoffs increased sharply in July and August. Orders booked took a sharp drop in July. It would appear that the recession response to balance funds flows was identical with that of the preceding recession. The major burden of response was again internal and fell on expenditures directly related to inventory building. Short-term borrowings were used in a supplemental role to cover cash shortages as they developed and to carry the company through the first few months of recognition and growing response to the event of recession.

There were important differences, however, which can be attributed to the distinctly more acute problem of management of short-run funds flows in 1960. In this recession cash balances were half what they had been in 1957, and whereas previously bank loans had resulted in an improved cash position, this time cash declined further in spite of substantially larger short-term borrowings. The differences in responses were as follows:

(1) Layoffs extended this time to indirect as well as direct labor and to office as well as plant personnel. The accounting staff was cut substantially and, in fact, had not been fully restored four years later. Ironically, one of the jobs to suffer was forward financial planning. Even management salaries were reduced by 10% to 20%. The sequence was: overtime elimination, layoffs in plant and reduced work week, cut in office staff (lagged by one month), salary cuts.

(2) Capital expenditure revisions did not await the normal round of negotiations at the end of the year. This time the third quarter 1960 expenditures were cut in half and the last quarter expenditures were down to $400,000.

(3) Quarterly dividend payments were unaffected, either at the time of the decline or later. This evidence appears to support the assertion of management that dividends were geared to earnings, not cash position. Total sales for 1960 turned out to be about equal to those of 1959. Although profits were down, they were still quite adequate to support the regular dividend.

As events worked out, this decline was shorter and less severe than the preceding one. The magnitude of the response was clearly related to the "shock" of a gross error in expectations and the exposed liquid position of the company. In fact, orders began to recover in August and rose very sharply — though temporarily — in October following announcement of a price increase, thus indicating the intentions to buy beyond that date. By reason of the drastic curbs on expenditures the cash position began to recover strongly. By October cash was above $4 million. In

December, with cash up to $4.7 million, the company "restored" its short-term borrowing power by converting the outstanding short-term debt into a $4 million term loan, as it had done in the preceding recession.

It is interesting to note further that by the first quarter of 1961 the recovery was well established. In spite of this, however, the recall of the plant labor force did not commence until March. By this time inventories had worked down to $18.8 million from the peak level of $22.9 million. The company appeared to be still in a state of shock in all areas of operations. After the fact management indicated a keen awareness of its misjudgment of events and felt that the response had been more drastic than it would have preferred, calling on a degree of mobility within the organization that was in some sense harmful. The implication was clear that this degree of internal mobility was not a part of planned strategy and would be avoided in the future if possible. A similar comment was not made about the adjustment of 1957.

A Strategy of Mobility: Constraints on Action

From these two recession experiences it is possible to infer a strategy of mobility to deal with sudden and unexpected declines in the rate of cash inflow from sales. The details just outlined can be put in a more general context by reference to the elements of a strategy discussed in Chapter 3 and the diagrams of the decision alternatives. Company A's plan for balancing funds flows in the immediate future was very short range, centering around the record of orders booked currently and in the preceding months. For Company A, in the bar chart in Chapter 3 showing a hypothetical projection of inflows and outflows (Exhibit 3D, page 66), the four periods more appropriately would be months rather than quarters or years. During the period in question there were no abnormal concentrations of expenditure, such as a major plant addition or an acquisition, so that the flows were primarily those associated with the sales volume of the immediate future.

It is apparent that the task of balancing funds flows over time was being performed within boundaries set by certain key long-range operating and financial goals and policies, which were designed to promote maximum corporate well-being including, presumably, the needed growth in economic resources. Most important among these goals was the desire to be a leader in the industry: to have a margin of advantage over the competition with respect to technical excellence of the product, price, and production facilities. Information gained not only from the company but also from some of its competitors indicated that it had in fact achieved a substantial advantage in this respect. This competitive leadership was of critical importance to financial mobility and yet was essentially a nonfinancial phenomenon. It was the key to the ability to shorten the expenditure horizon from time to time without immediate adverse effects on inflows. It also implied a pattern of long-run expenditure enabling the company to maintain technological excellence.

Also of importance in the set of constraints on funds flow management were certain financial policies respecting sources from which new infusions of funds might come. Specifically these were dividend policy and debt policy. Dividend policy prior to the first recession was one of regular cash dividends to stockholders, at a level that the company hoped to be able to sustain under these kinds of variations in earnings levels, plus year-end extras varying with the earnings performance of the immediate past. Thus funds flows were protected by omission of the extra dividend but only after it was demonstrated that earnings were significantly below normal. Debt policy was such as to permit without serious question both medium-term and short-term debt, with a general maximum long-term debt guideline of 25% of capitalization. A high premium was placed on strong bank relations. In addition to these policies there were the usual conventions of one-year operating and capital budgets, which functioned in such a way as to stabilize expenditure patterns until the next budget negotiation was opened. This appeared to have greatest relevance for expenditures not directly related to units of output.

Within these broad guidelines funds flows were managed largely on a month-to-month basis. Planning might almost be called retrospective rather than prospective if one puts literal interpretation on the "orders booked" guideline. However, this is not accurate. Despite its protests that forecasting was extremely

unreliable, the management was obviously on the alert for any
signals about the future; for instance, from competitors, from
industry data. It was against this fragmentary evidence that the
developing trend of orders booked was assessed and a response
determined. Whether the response was fast or slow depended
in part on the consistency of the evidence and in part on the
current ability to withstand funds flow deficits. In view of the
short horizon, the financial management had to be very sensitive
to significant changes in funds flow patterns.

A Strategy of Mobility — Resources and Sequence of Use

The range of choices that formed a part of Company A's
strategy of mobility can best be described by reference to the
decision diagrams of Chapter 3. The relevant choices are summarized in Exhibit 4B, which shows the "branching" observed
to be in use during these two recession periods. Certain significant choices were denied the company under these circumstances.
One set of these related to the urgency of the need. The unexpected need or deficit was not such that it could be avoided,
deferred, or shared. The event of a sudden decline in customer
orders was clearly beyond management's influence at that point
in time. Second, the resource of time was absent or at a very
minimum — time that could have been used to modify the need,
negotiate sources, adjust other flows. Its absence obviously restricted the options open to management when the event occurred.

The primary resources of mobility in the first recession period
were:

> (1) cash balance,
> (2) short-term bank loans,
> (3) contraction of planned outflows.

An important but secondary line of defense was:

> (4) term loan.

These resources are listed roughly in the sequence in which they
were used as the recession unfolded. With very little warning of

EXHIBIT 4B

DECISION TREE REPRESENTING COMPANY A's STRATEGY OF MOBILITY

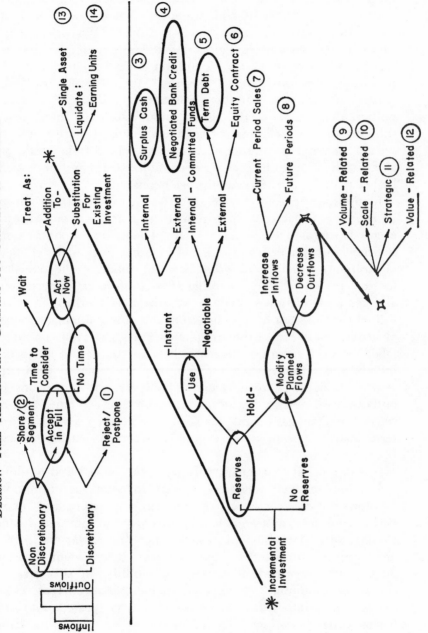

the impending decline in inflows and with some initial uncertainty as to how serious and prolonged that decline would be, the natural response was to absorb the initial cash deficit through reduced cash balances. At the outset of the first recession, balances of about $5 million were below a mid-1956 peak of $8.3 million but still "average" for the company. Later experience indicates that there was then a cushion of $2 to $3 million. A point that the reader should have in mind when thinking of cash balances is that many financial officers are uncertain of what minimum transactions balances they can get along with. As a result they may respond as if the minimum was higher than experience would prove necessary.

In the case of Company A a decline in cash balances almost immediately triggered a short-term bank loan. The sequence of events is summarized in Exhibit 4C. These two responses were sufficient to cover deficits for 3 to 4 months. They had the effect of cushioning the organization from the shock of the recession for this period of time, enabling it to confirm its expectations and get itself mentally ready for the next step, which in effect shifted the problem of mobility from the purely financial sphere of activity to the operational sphere. Through layoffs of direct labor the work force now began to bear the burden of balancing inflows and outflows, and the company was able to gradually restore its depleted cash reserves. However, the reductions in outflows were not so drastic as to enable the company also to repay the short-term bank loans. These were converted into a term loan to permit a more gradual return to earlier reserve positions.

It is significant that during this first recession reduced outflows were almost entirely related to current inventory accumulation. Outflows not directly associated with units of output and "extra period" outflows (postponable outflows) were not affected during the first year. A revision of capital expenditures was made only at the normal time and for the next year. It is evident that the management regarded its strategy of mobility in this first recession as optimum. The company had the financial reserves to protect operations until the recession was confirmed, allowing for an orderly scaling down of inventory outflows, protecting committed outflows until the normal review period, providing

EXHIBIT 4C

SEQUENCE OF COMPANY A'S RESPONSES IN RECESSION

Events →

Reaction to the Need	Source of Mobility	1957 Decline in orders begins / Decline ends				1958 Orders level off / Orders pick up				1959 Peak of orders				1960 Decline begins / Orders level off				1961 Orders pick up			
		1	2	3	4	1	2	3	4	1	2	3	4	1	2	3	4	1	2	3	4
I. Modify Amount or Timing	Reject/Postpone Share/Segment																					
II. Accept as Incremental:	Instant:																					
(A) Commit Reserves	Internal	U	R	R	U	U							U	U	U	U	R	R	R	R	R
	External—Bank Line	U	U	R	R																R
	Negotiable: Term Debt			U	R				R				R				U]				
	Equity																				
(B) Modify Flows	Increase Inflows: Current																				
	From Future Periods																				
	Decrease Outflows: Volume-Related	U	U			U						R	R	U	U	U	U				
	Scale-Related													U	U	U					
	Strategic						R		U	R								R			
	Value-Related										R	R									
III. Accept, but as Substitution for Existing Investment	Liquidate: Single Assets																				
	Earning Units																				

Symbols: C—Consider U—Use]—Limit R—Restore

for a quick restoration of cash and short-term debt reserves and a gradual restoration of long-term debt reserves.

The second recession can properly be described as having caught management off guard. Thus it put the strategy of mobility to the test. Because the company was caught with depleted cash reserves, it shifted a greater burden of mobility to a contraction of outflows and therefore onto the shoulders of the operating organization. This is evident in an accelerated and more drastic cut in direct labor, reduced pay to indirect labor and management, violation of budget conventions regarding revision of extra-period expenditures such as capital expenditures, and new highs in long-term debt. These differences can be seen in the changed timing of responses in Exhibit 4C. At the same time the sequence of use and restoration of liquid reserves — cash and short-term debt capacity — followed the previous pattern. This indicated very high priority on the continuity of these reserves, a priority found to be not unusual among the field sample of companies.

The responses in the second recession period were regretted by management because they cut more deeply into the stability of organizational funds flows than management thought "right." Although management was determined to try to avoid such deep cuts in the future, it believed that the ability to adjust expenditure patterns quickly was an essential element of mobility in its industry.

Management believed that the capacity to absorb the impact of a severe recession in the industry internally and to balance flows by a rapid contraction of expenditures was based on an organizational flexibility deriving largely from a position of leadership in the industry. This had more than one facet. For instance, it meant the ability to price the company's products so that there would still be a positive cash flow from operations at the bottom of the recession, if not an actual profit. To rephrase for emphasis, current operations would not be a drain on the cash position at that time. Some evidence of the company's confidence in its competitive leadership is seen in the timing of the price increases previously cited, at points when demand was still at depressed levels.

Organizational flexibility was also considered to depend on

product leadership. Being ahead of the competition in product innovation made it possible for the company to slacken the pace for a period without an immediate adverse effect on sales. The same head start was also apparent in productive capacity and efficiency. The average age of the company's equipment was below that for the industry, permitting cutbacks in capital expenditures without an immediate cost in efficiency.

Another main ingredient of internal means of financial mobility was considered to be a management willing to run the risks of quick and bold response to partial evidence. The reaction to an apparent downturn is always tricky, since too sharp a response to a short-lived drop in orders can lead to lost orders and even lost customers. If errors of judgment lead to the interpretation of excessive caution or financial weakness, then loss of confidence internally and externally may result. On the other hand, failure to act quickly can lock up substantial funds in inventory for extended periods of time.

An important aid to management in following a policy of quick response is an organization accustomed to sharp swings in corporate activity and willing to bear some individual share of the job of absorbing the shock. This would clearly imply some substantial degree of immobility on the part of corporate personnel, who presumably would prefer greater personal stability.

Long-Run Policy vs. Short-Run Mobility

One of the interesting questions raised by this study is the relationship between a set of policies presumably aimed at maximizing the long-run growth in economic value of the firm and the strategy of mobility designed to assure operational continuity. Nothing is inherent in this relationship to make it necessarily harmonious, and it would seem almost inevitable that on occasion at least the policies would be in conflict. On such occasions the outcome of the conflict provides an insight into how management perceives this relationship.

The experience of Company A through two recession periods provided a test of both dividend and debt policy under the short-run pressures of financial mobility. To take dividend policy first, it has previously been explained that dividend policy was in transition during the period. Before the first reces-

sion, dividend policy appeared more closely tied to and dependent on the current balance of funds flows through the use
of the extra dividend. The amount of the extra was determined
entirely by circumstances at the time and had no long-run implications. On the other hand, the option to reduce or eliminate
the extra could be made only at year-end and was conditional
on the coincidence of sharply reduced earnings. Thus it was unlikely to be part of the strategy of early response to falling inflows.

The abandonment of the extra after 1959 precisely because it
lacked any long-run implications for the investor meant that
the dividend policy and the strategy of mobility were now, potentially at least, completely independent. Only when the funds
flow deficit happened to coincide with a visible and sustained
drop in earnings was there hope of using a dividend cut as part
of the balancing mechanism. The second recession was a test of
this new dividend policy, which came through unscathed. Regular dividends were not reduced even though earnings were substantially lower in 1960. This does not deny that under some
circumstances regular dividends might be cut in order to cover
a cash deficit, but the precedents were strongly against a cut not
"justified" by a record of declining earnings. Also, the company's
avowed strategy of substantial instant reserves to stand the first
shock of an unexpected cash deficit tended to insulate dividend
policy as well as other internal flows.

On the surface at least, debt policy also appeared to stand up
under the substantial internal strains of recession funds imbalance. The company used its short-term borrowing power as
a liquid reserve for short-term emergencies and managed to live
within the self-imposed 25% long-term debt limit. On the other
hand, in December 1960 it moved to a long-term debt level of
approximately 25%. While this was presumably an acceptable
level within the risk preferences of management, the question
is raised as to whether the company's strategy of mobility was
still intact, since unused long-term debt capacity was the key to
a quick restoration of short-term borrowing power.

At this point in time the short-term borrowing power had
been restored by a $4 million term loan but cash levels were
only at the normal level of around $4 to $5 million. The validity

of the strategy of mobility was at this point contingent on receiving only one shock at a time — on the orderly internal adjustment to a cash flow deficit before other demands were placed on the system. The possibility that the management may have felt somewhat overexposed under these circumstances may be evidenced by the fact that cash balances were subsequently permitted to climb to the unusual level of $8 million in November 1961. It is worth noting, however, that at the 25% level the management felt it could still raise "substantial amounts" of long-term debt, though interest rate and other covenants would be under pressure. One conclusion could be that the company's strategy of mobility recognized the possibility of brief periods of overexposure to risk, which did not in themselves trigger action respecting other resources of mobility.

These observations respecting dividend and debt policy as well as those relating to company norms on cash balances suggest that financial policies are evolutionary phenomena which are periodically tested against the realities of funds flow fluctuations and progressively redefined. In the event that they prove in conflict with the demands of financial mobility they may be modified. The experience of Company A in these two recessions seemed to suggest that minimum cash balances were lower than originally assumed and debt limits possibly higher. Until new experiences proved these conclusions difficult or dangerous, the interaction of policy with the results of a strategy of mobility could be described as having produced a new policy for the future. The new norms would then survive until experience proved their validity (i.e., they did not get the company into trouble) or new pressures once again caused revision.

5

Company C: The Response to a
Severe Recession

The account of Company A in the preceding chapter shows a
company in good health experiencing the normal pressures of
cyclicality in its industry. The account to be presented in this
chapter shows a company subjected to demands for financial
mobility far beyond those experienced by Company A as to
both severity and duration of the pressure. This was so for four
basic reasons. One is the difference in the duration of deep
recession. The recession period for Company C began in 1957
and even by 1963 the company was only beginning to emerge
from the low level reached at the end of 1958. A second reason
is that Company C was weak competitively even though it held
a respected position in its industry (capital goods). It did not
have the same share of the market, did not have the same degree
of product innovation, and did not have the product diversification of Company A. A third and important reason was that by
unfortunate coincidence it entered the recession period with certain key resources of mobility already fully committed. In this
respect its experience was somewhat similar to the second recession experience of Company A. Finally, again by apparent
coincidence, the problem of recession was combined with other
problems which made the adjustment more difficult.

Pre-Recession Commitments

Exhibit 5A, showing the monthly pattern of sales and income
from January 1952 through December 1963, indicates that for
several years preceding 1957 the company had enjoyed a relatively strong market except for a decline in 1955. This experi-

EXHIBIT 5A

COMPANY C: NET SALES AND NET INCOME, MONTHLY
JANUARY 1952–DECEMBER 1963

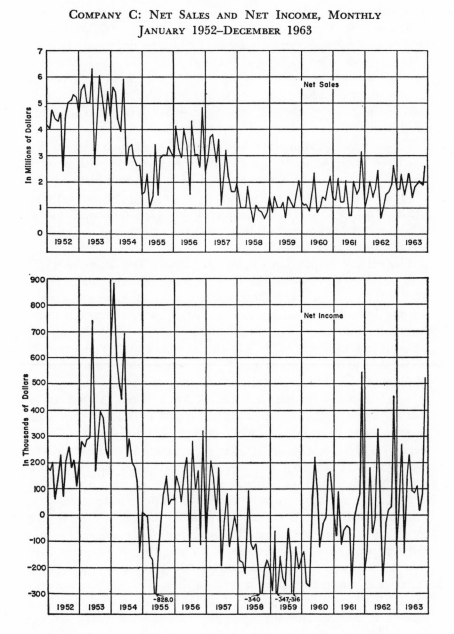

ence had created a mood of confidence and optimism in the company, which was reflected in a high level of funds flows. This can best be exemplified in an action that preceded the recession of 1957 and contributed materially to the difficulties. In 1954 it was decided to expand plant capacity to include the production of an important component traditionally purchased from a supplier. The stated purpose was to obtain cost reduction, part of which was to derive from "greater flexibility in scheduling production."

To do this the company required $5.7 million, which it did not have in its possession at the time. Negotiation with a term lender indicated that although this sum was well beyond the company's debt capacity, the lender was willing to put up half the amount, provided it was matched by a common stock issue. This arrangement was completed and the common stock sold on a rights offering in mid-1954.

The plant had just been completed by the beginning of 1957, one year late and costing $1 million more of debt money than expected. Thus in 1957 the company faced the future with a substantially diluted equity position (20% more shares outstanding than in 1953) and long-term debt capacity fully committed, or even over-committed, to "bricks and mortar." The pressure of needs had led to substantial short-term bank loans as well. Needless to say, the cash position was also low.

This condition of financial immobility was not lost on financial management, which in mid-1956 urged that action be taken to free up short-term borrowing power "against possible future needs." The recommended course of action was a return to the equity market for $3.8 million, which would equal the short-term debt at that time. It was clear, however, that the equity market was not particularly receptive. The management was unhappy with what its current investment banker had been able to do and wanted a change. The opinion was expressed within the company that "today there is no one in the financial field that is interested in us." Nevertheless, an effort was made to get someone to undertake to raise $3.8 million on "the best possible basis." By November 1956, however, the stock market was in a moderate decline and the company forecast for 1957 did not match 1956. Therefore, the decision was made that the sale of additional securities would be "too costly" and must be dropped "at this time."

It was then decided that the restoration of funds flows to an equilibrium position should be undertaken by the slower and more managerially painful internal route of contracting outflows. There was a renewed emphasis on cost reduction across the board. When the dividend came up for discussion in February 1957, continuation of the 25-cent rate, which had been raised from 17½ cents in mid-1956, was approved only after considerable debate. The company had a policy of responding to changes in net income by changes in the dividend with only a short lag. For instance, the dividend had been cut to zero following the sharp but short dip in early 1955. Cash conservation appeared to be an important reason for the rapidity and magnitude of response.

The gathering concern at the beginning of 1957 was in contrast to the mood only a half year earlier when it was reported that "the present rate of activity is now expected to continue well into the first half of 1957, in contrast to a previous expectation of a substantial drop by the end of 1956." Obviously the ability to see even six months ahead was very restricted. The management had periodically shown concern about the cyclicality of its industry, and called consultants in for recommendations early in 1957. The consulting report rather predictably recommended diversification through acquisition and suggested that the financial executive be given the search for acquisitions as one of his growing number of responsibilities.

THE PERIOD OF SHARP DECLINE

1957

Against the background of concern and sensitivity to change came the collapse of orders in May and June 1957 to the lowest point since 1954.[1] There was an immediate cut in production to avoid building inventory, but the cutbacks were not fast enough or sharp enough to avoid some increased dependence on short-term bank loans. Bank debt, which had declined from the $3.8

---

[1] Exhibit 5B depicts the changes in several series of financial data from January 1956 to December 1963.

EXHIBIT 5B

COMPANY C: GRAPHS OF SELECTED FINANCIAL DATA
JANUARY 1956–DECEMBER 1963

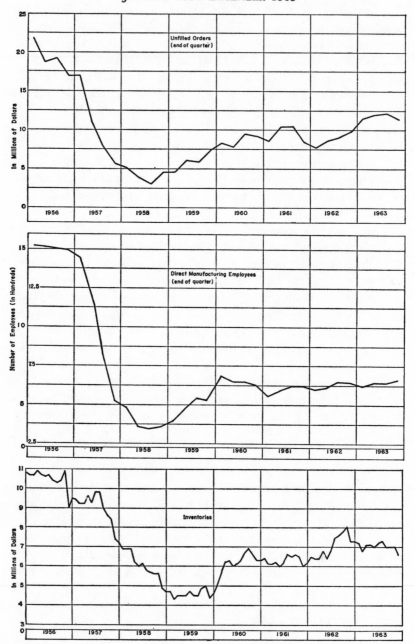

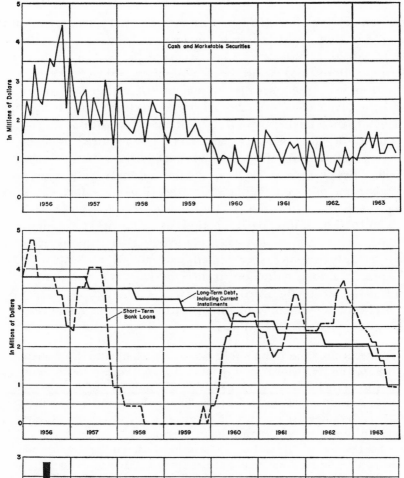

Cash and Marketable Securities

In Millions of Dollars

5
4
3
2
1
0

1956 1957 1958 1959 1960 1961 1962 1963

Long-Term Debt,
Including Current
Installments

Short-Term
Bank Loans

In Millions of Dollars

5
4
3
2
1
0

1956 1957 1958 1959 1960 1961 1962 1963

Annual Additions to Property
Plant and Equipment

In Millions of Dollars

3
2
1
0

1956 1957 1958 1959 1960 1961 1962 1963

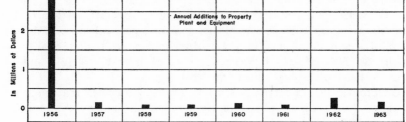

Quarterly Dividends Declared

Cents per Share

30
20
10
0

1956 1957 1958 1959 1960 1961 1962 1963

million level in late 1956 to $2.4 million in February, was up
to $3.5 million in March and rose again in June to $4.0 million.
It remained at this level until it dropped to $3.3 million in
October, 1957, to $1.9 million in November, and to $0.95 million
in December. It was soon clear that drastic action was in order,
and the layoff of direct labor as orders declined had to be supplemented by a general pulling in of the expenditure horizon, a
reduction in all expenditures not absolutely required to generate
current inflows. By June capital expenditures were down to
$500. They were zero in July, and by the end of the year pro-
posals were not even being submitted. Further effort got into
high gear in August. To set the tone of internal austerity, the
officers took a voluntary reduction in salary of 10% effective
August 18, "to be restored when net profits after taxes exceed 5%
of quarterly shipments or an annual rate of $1,200,000." On
August 27 a 50% reduction in directors' fees was voted and the
cash dividend for the third quarter was eliminated.

A chronology of some of the operating decisions taken during
the second half of 1957 follows:

> AUGUST 16. The second shift was to be eliminated by Septem-
> ber 20, and by October 26 the ratio of hours worked to inventory
> was to be reduced 30% from the first five months of 1957. Several
> tasks were to be eliminated by the financial section by September
> 21, for example, the report of time spent on salvage and the re-
> port of hours worked by purchasing personnel.
>
> SEPTEMBER 26. A cutback was ordered in janitor service (no
> more dusting of desks and cleaning of ash trays).
>
> OCTOBER 15. Executives held a meeting to consider further re-
> ductions in indirect personnel and expense, e.g., release of sales
> trainees and employees in purchasing, tool control, and quality
> control. This last group was reduced to 31 from 67 in July and
> the foremen picked up some of the work.
>
> OCTOBER 18. The targets set for further personnel reductions
> were 285 in indirect labor and 190 in direct labor by the end of
> November.
>
> NOVEMBER 12. The Management Committee voted to close all
> open authorizations for capital expenditures, effective immedi-
> ately.

From an earnings viewpoint these actions were designed to

reduce the imminent threat of an operating loss and cut the accumulation of inventory to bring it down to a better relation to sales. From a funds flow or cash flow viewpoint the action was obviously to restore some sort of balance between sharply reduced inflows and outflows. This was by no means easy or certain. There was in fact substantial resistance to cuts in personnel where there was not a direct and obvious relationship to units produced. For example, the following quotations are from reports by the executive in charge of a major staff function:

> SEPTEMBER 11. "In evaluating the stringency of this objective it should be noted . . . after having cut back employees from those originally authorized, we have been asked to make further reductions of 30% since July 27. By comparison, although clerical requirements are seldom lessened in even the same proportion as manufacturing work loads, the number of direct labor workers in the shop is scheduled to be cut by only 19% between the same dates."
>
> SEPTEMBER 18. "I have prepared a formula which would result in the same relationship of personnel to level of production as for the rest of the company based on ratios as of June 16."

These comments indicate both an appeal to bargains previously made ("those originally authorized") and to the principle of parity in bargains now being made among members of the management team concerning their own areas. With his own perception of what was vital to the future of the company each executive tended to protect his own department. The fact that there was considerable "heel dragging," which materially impeded the balancing of cash flows, is seen in the following report on November 8: "The planned layoff of 475 people during the six-week period ending November 30 is not moving rapidly. As of November 8 only 75 have been laid off. A speed-up is urged." On November 14 the advertising manager submitted a budget for 1958 unchanged from 1957. He was asked to resubmit giving effect to an overall cut of 25%.

Now let us take stock of where the company stood at the end of 1957. Sales were continuing their sharp decline, net profit had turned into a net loss, and cash flow from operations (depreciation added back) had reached zero. Operations were at the point of becoming a net drain on the company's cash position. However, the action taken to curb cash outflows had so reversed the inflow-outflow relationship of June that by December the bank loan had been paid down to $0.95 million. This, at least, was encouraging to the management charged with the essential task of maintaining solvency and forward motion. With the prospect of operating deficits in 1958, however, and no apparent end to the recession, there was little reason to feel relaxed about the state of financial mobility. Long-term debt was still high and new equity was out of the question, reducing external mobility to the mercy of the company's commercial bank so far as defensive needs were concerned.

1958

When the first quarter of 1958 produced further declines in orders and deepening losses, a new and more vigorous attack on outflows was called for. A memorandum on March 28 referred to a situation "so critical that drastic steps must be taken immediately." Action was called for in the areas of executive salaries, sales expense, hours of employment, and supervisory expense. Discussions followed at which specific action was hammered out. The final decisions reached in mid-April included:

(1) A second salary cut of 10%. (This was followed shortly by a third 10% cut for executives. Other salaried personnel had two 10% cuts.)
(2) Study of sales expense, with target reduction of $28,500 a month called for.
(3) Abandonment of the production schedules for inventory; with some exceptions, all units to be built only to customer order.
(4) Four-day workweek.
(5) Reconfirmation of need for diversification, but consultant on diversification dropped.
(6) Drastic cuts in prices of some finished goods inventory to move it out.

In addition, throughout this period there were a number of early retirements, demotions, expansion of duties, and other ways of getting more work out of fewer people. Certain areas were protected: "Long-range welfare requires continuation of engineering and sales at as high a level as possible and these have not been reduced in proportion to the drop in volume" (Memorandum of April 16, 1958). At the same time, however, there were some cuts: fewer salesmen, resort to commission dealers, and a 50% cut in the advertising budget.

In cash flow terms these efforts in the first two quarters of 1958 produced an approximate balance in cash flows and held the cash account to about the $2 million level, $475,000 of which was used to pay the bank loan down to $475,000. Pressure and resistance to pressure continued. For example, in late June the chief executive expressed the view that supervisory personnel had not been sufficiently reduced. The executive in charge countered that supervisors "were working a fifth day without overtime, were working very hard, and were doing work subordinates formerly did in addition to their own duties."

It is not surprising that, as the recession deepened, thoughts turned to more wide-ranging means by which the company could obtain relief from the pressures and sacrifices necessitated by internal balancing of current outflows with current inflows. As early as August 1957 some consideration had been given to sale and leaseback of the new facilities, which had been completed only a year before at such a considerable sacrifice of financial mobility. How vigorously this proposal was pursued is not clear, but no action resulted. By mid-1958 active consideration was being given to another potential means of sudden change — merger. An investment banker assisted in exploration of merger with a substantially stronger company in the same industry, but in the end the negotiations were dropped because the price to Company C was too high — an exchange of stock at a value 25% below market and transfer of full management control. The management of Company C preferred to struggle on alone. The door was left open, however, to other such opportunities.

By September 1958 orders began to level off at a very low volume though this was not clearly apparent at the time. Total employment within the company also bottomed out, and the numbers on the payroll at the end of the second, third, and fourth quarters were approximately equal. Management was still requesting further reductions while recognizing that "greater reduction may not be permitted by the work level." Here and there overhead was edging down. In spite of "sharp disappointment" the time-honored Christmas gift to employees was cut out at a saving of $160,000. Even the children's Christmas party narrowly missed being dropped to save $1,000. With "indirect areas as tight as they can be" there was word of some grumbling in the shop, but fairness of treatment seemed to be the test of acceptance of sacrifices.

In August the last of the bank loan was paid off and for the rest of the year the cash account held at the $2 million level. The company remained free of short-term debt from that point until November 1959. Capital expenditures for 1958 totaled $70,600. A decline in sales to 40% of the previous year's total made it difficult to present an optimistic annual report for 1958. However, management reported that it had "held together a solid core of skilled employees, continued product research and development, maintained intensive sales activities, and kept both plant and machinery in good operating condition." Hopes expressed for 1959 were very guarded.

STAGNATION AND SLOW RECOVERY

1959

The year 1959 proved to be another year of struggle to spend as little as possible. By year-end the record showed sales slightly above 1958 but not enough to demonstrate any real evidence of an upward trend. Losses continued heavy. Orders fluctuated substantially from month to month and only with hindsight can 1959 be seen as the very uncertain beginning of a long, slow climb back to normal. By the end of 1958 usable inventory had been largely consumed as a substitute for current expenditure and a modest pickup in orders meant some rehiring. Over the year employment gradually began to rise until at the end of the third quarter totals were back at fourth quarter 1957 levels, still less than one half of the level in March 1956.

The first step was the restoration of the 5-day week in the first quarter of 1959. Although forced into more hours to meet current sales, the management had no intention of relaxing its austerity program under below-breakeven conditions. All salary cuts remained in effect throughout 1959. Capital expenditures exceeded those of 1958 by a mere $7,000. All other indirect expenditures remained at a low level until toward the end of the year, when selling expense and new product development showed very modest gains. In summary, with some slight improvement in orders, but well below the breakeven level, direct production expenditures began inching up while the lid remained tight on expenditure for the future.

It is significant that during this whole period the position of the financial officer had been gradually rising in the executive structure. He became a vice president in 1958 and executive vice president in charge of sales, finance, and diversification efforts early in 1959.

In cash flow terms the month of June 1959 may be regarded as a key turning point. The company had now been "out of the bank" since August 1958. Beginning in May 1959 cash was invested in short-term securities. This portfolio was short-lived, however. It reached a peak of $1 million at the end of June, dropped to $0.5 million in July, and disappeared in August. Cash outflows were beginning to creep up again, and yet the end of the recession was nowhere in sight. To get through November a one-month loan of $475,000 was required.

1960–1961

The gradual improvement in orders and gradual increase in direct labor hours crept along into 1960. In March the financial officer presented a highly significant report to the board. After reviewing the prospects for the industry and calling attention to an earlier prediction of a long, slow recovery over the next couple of years the report said in part:

> The forecast of Cash Flow shows that the Company has lost its financial independence, even at this rather low volume for 1960. For any volume at or above the breakeven area, the Company must have bank loans to finance its daily operations with no foreseeable plan or prospect of sufficient cash inflow to provide our own financing of a reasonably normal level of operations. Thus, short-term bank loans are now being used to provide semi-per-

manent financing — a condition not acceptable to banks for a very long period. . . . Bank loan requirements will total $1,800,-000 in the second and third quarters, with a balance of $1,200,000 at the year end.

In short, the Company has exhausted its cash resources — there is insufficient cash now available to finance even a breakeven operation. With no marked improvement in the near future, the Company will be hard put to justify the future extension of credit in the present amounts.

The balance sheet positions for 1960 are shown. These graphically show the financing of the increase in Inventory by bank loans.

So much for the brighter side of the picture. What is going to happen if the economy and/or the industry turns down in the second half of 1960? Where does the Company get financial resources to continue in the event we have a loss of say $1,000,000 this year? This could rather easily happen if sales slid off modestly.

That briefly highlights the Company's present situation. To summarize, the Company is in a precarious position and if we do not do something about it in the next few months, it will be done by someone else. We are already getting repercussions from our present financial position.

What are the alternatives?

1. Sell out to someone like Textron, on *their* terms.

2. Continue as we are and hope for the "gold ring" to materialize — if it doesn't
    (a) Get taken over in a proxy contest
    (b) limp along and wither away
    (c) go into bankruptcy

3. Try to effect a program of acquisitions and consolidations in the next four months.

For the first time since early 1957 we have a quarter coming up — the second quarter of this year — in which we expect to show a profit.

   (a) This is a wonderful opportunity for obvious reasons to try to consummate a stock deal.

The only program we have been able to develop at this time is the following. There is nothing definite in any part of it but at least it is something that has merit, there is indicated interest on the part of other companies, and we can work at it now. I would like to give the outline of it, as I see it; others will endeavor to fill in some of the details. It should be remembered that our knowledge of these other companies is very preliminary and sketchy and will have to be checked out, of course, before any final action is taken. Most of this program has been discussed and approved in principle by the Executive Committee.

There then followed a description of two acquisitions that appeared particularly worthy of exploration. The criteria being used were the opportunity to put excess capacity to work, the immediate addition of the earning power of the acquired company, and diversification of product line. Company C appeared ready to face the dilution of equity involved but still expected to retain control. The hope was that one or two favorable acquisitions would considerably improve Company C's bargaining power for other acquisitions later. There was the expectation of cooperation from the bank and the term lender in any additional cash required.

In spite of these ominous views on the loss of financial independence and the unprotected needs for the future, together with exploration of a means of escape, the succeeding months and years saw no dramatic change. Sales improved from 1960 on but the usual month-to-month gyrations confused the trend and the upward movement was excruciatingly slow. The period 1960–1962 may be summed up as the challenge of survival at the break-even level. Profits fluctuated around zero — in some quarters above and in some quarters below. With hindsight the gradual upward movement is apparent, but it was certainly less apparent to those directly involved at the time.

As presented in the previously quoted memorandum, Company C was vulnerable in both directions. Further declines meant immediate losses and the prospect of dissipating funds in the process of generating current sales. On the other hand, any improvement, however modest, called for an immediate infusion of more capital. It was the latter event that occurred. This is apparent in the figures for employment and in the accumulation of inventory, which had to grow to complete orders as they were received. Those costs not directly required to generate current inflows were held down tightly: investment in plant and equipment, in managerial and supervisory personnel, in new products, in new markets. Gradually, however, even these so-called postponable expenditures began to inch up as the time purchased by past expenditures began to run out. The dramatic cutbacks of 1958 and 1959 were no longer possible. Annual reports continued to refer to "further gains in reducing overhead," but the figures show an unavoidable drift to higher levels as volume gradually began to pick up.

During this period the commercial bank played a vital role in the essential task of balancing month-to-month funds flows — a matter of sheer survival at this point, the luxury of financial equilibrium being far out of reach. The question of cash solvency obviously underlay the hope of preserving the corporate entity and its existing management. Having reached the point in 1958 and 1959 of being completely paid off, the bank permitted itself to become substantially recommitted to Company C in 1960. In January 1960 the bank loan stood at $475,000; by July it was up to $2.85 million, where it remained until the first half of 1961. A temporary decline to a low of $1.7 million in May 1961 was followed by a rise to $3.3 million in October. The classic pattern of the use of short-term funds for long-term purposes was becoming apparent.

1962

The early part of 1962 did not appear to aggravate the problem, however, because of what was reported as a "sideways movement" in orders. The bank loan dropped to $2.4 million in January, moved to $2.6 million in May, and then suddenly rose to $3.3 million in September, $3.5 million in October, and $3.7 million in November. At this point the alarm began to ring in the bank, which called for a meeting with the company on November 7 "to discuss present and possible future financial plans and prospects for 1963."

The following memorandum covers the meeting from Company C's viewpoint.

> Specifically, the bank is concerned about the following:
> (1) The forecasted increase in bank debt at the end of 1962 as compared with that at the end of 1961, and the reasons for such increase.
> (2) The continuing lack of profitability at present level of business with no apparent upturn in 1963.

(3) The continuing use of short-term bank credit at prime rates of interest as a substitute for capital and long-term debt.
(4) Apparent need for increased borrowings in the event of an appreciable increase in volume of business.
(5) No apparent means in the immediate future, at least, for reducing amount of short-term borrowings.
(6) The small amount invested in recent years in new machine tools and equipment, and possible effect of this on present and future operations (ability to turn out competitive products, capacity, costs).

The officer representing the bank stated that the bank valued its long association and business dealings with the company and wanted to do everything that it could to be of help. The bank was mindful of the fact, he said, that the company had demonstrated its ability to liquidate its loans in a down cycle through inventory liquidation. The bank was much concerned, however, about the present financial situation and felt that somehow a definite plan should be worked out to provide for the elimination of short-term bank loans as a source of capital at the present level of business. He added that the bank officers wondered whether the company was doing everything possible to improve its profitability, improve its position in the industry, acquire or merge with a profitable company, and diversify its activities.

The company discussed the following factors with the bank representative:

(1) Our full awareness of the financing situation.
(2) The major steps taken since 1957 to preserve the company and its capital, and to balance out cash needs with cash resources.
(3) Forecast for remainder of 1962, possibilities for 1963, and the possible acceleration that could occur in demand.
(4) Probable improvement in profitability if orders increased 25%.
(5) Activities since 1957 to conclude a suitable acquisition or merger that would diversify activities, add more load to current operations, or use up the accumulated tax credit; and the effect of the financial situation on consummating any suitable acquisition.
(6) The current lack of bargaining position to acquire a suitable source of profits and to refinance the short-term bank loans.

(7) The expectation that a substantial upturn in demand would have occurred by 1963 and that the resulting improvement in profitability would open up one or more possibilities for acquiring a source of needed capital.

This meeting was followed by a second meeting two weeks later at which more company and bank representatives were present. At this meeting the bank stated that "the company must somehow evolve a plan or plans to pay off the nonseasonal portion of the loan (about $2,400,000) in the not too distant future, and that progress must be accomplished before the Credit Committee took drastic action." The alternatives raised by the bank were:

(1) improved volume through new product developments
(2) acquisitions to use capacity
(3) sale of portion of existing plant
(4) merger upstream to get capital and/or volume
(5) improved quality and quantity of engineering staff
(6) increased profitability on existing volume

All of these alternatives had been considered previously and some had been acted upon. The more drastic from management's viewpoint, 3 and 4, which recommended a partial or total "sell out" by existing management, had been toyed with but real opportunities had been passed by as too "costly" to ownership and management. Yet, of all the points listed, these were the only real prospects for the quick relief sought by the bank. At the conclusion of these discussions the bank officers appeared satisfied that the company was doing all it could, and they were aware of more optimistic expectations for 1963.

1963

This review of the history of Company C ends with 1963; for in that year the company began to experience a substantial increase in demand, which saved it from the unnamed threats of the bank. Volume had increased some 20% by the end of 1963 and, justifying the previous opinions of management, a significant profit was recorded. By reason of continued very tight controls on expenditures and the accumulation of inventory the company was able to reduce the bank loan substantially to a level of $950,000 at year-end. The experience had left the company in a very weakened condition competitively and still extremely vulnerable. However, the hope was that a sustained period of improving demand would enable the company to regain its competitive and financial strength. Indication of the renewal of optimism was the directors' vote of a special year-end dividend to the stockholders, and the waiver obtained from the lenders to do so.

MANAGEMENT'S CONCLUSIONS FROM THIS EXPERIENCE

How did financial management view this experience through which it had passed? What lessons had it learned? First, there was a keen sense of regret that the company had permitted itself to become so fully depleted of cash and debt reserves in order to construct the plant addition in the year preceding the collapse of sales. It was clear that this was not a financially oriented decision but a necessity resulting from a policy decision at top levels—a decision made largely in terms of production needs and long-term corporate development and apparently without regard to near-term financial risks. Present financial management did not participate in this decision but, as a result of having to live with the effects, had resolved never to commit debt capacity in the future to "bricks and mortar."

A second topic keenly recollected by financial management was the frustration of attempting to forecast requirements when the only hard data on which to build such a forecast were orders on hand. It is interesting that financial management had forecast with considerable accuracy the timing of the ultimate recovery period — years ahead — but was virtually blind beyond six months during the period of decline. Related to this is the strongly expressed assertion of financial management that it could not develop a long-term strategy but rather took one step at a time, hoping that each one was the most sensible that could be made.

A third major conclusion from this experience was that the primary cost of inadequate financial mobility was the erosion of the company's resources of first-class personnel and management talent. This occurred because of layoffs, failure to replace on retirement, doubling up of jobs, and in general a less attractive working environment. Though the problem was not exclusively or even primarily financial, there was clearly a direct connection with the inability to financially sustain key areas of activity and development. The management position was summed up in the comment, "I'll trade money for people any day."

A somewhat related observation concerns the problem of scaling down inventory levels. This was regarded as the most difficult assignment; indeed, it was asserted that finance does not exert much control over inventory levels. The problem lay in the fact that personnel would have had to be cut back very sharply in order to bring inventories down quickly: too sharply for sustained operations at the new lower levels and more quickly than line management was willing to concede. There was also the inevitable problem of an unbalanced inventory in relation to current demand. Payroll was the key to rebalancing cash flows.

It was noted by management that the financial effects of the period of severe pressure were not all negative. In some areas genuine savings were effected, which perhaps could not have been brought about without such pressures. These areas were listed as reduced interest costs as debt was paid down, reduced local taxation on inventories and plant value, reduced selling expenditures such as advertising, which were "of doubtful value anyway," reduced margins to distributors, elimination of dividends, reduced pay to employees, more work from a smaller staff, reduced pension payments. On the other side of the account there were explicit costs in addition to the loss of personnel, primarily deferred maintenance, aging plant and equipment, and heavy retraining costs when the staff was once again on the rise.

In the management of funds flows through this period no use was made of either liquidation of tangible assets or the addition of new equity funds through the issue of common stock. The primary restraint on liquidation of assets was the fact of general industry recession and the concentration of plant on one geographic site. Management did consider the sale of the new facility constructed just prior to the slump but the sale was never consummated. New equity played a potential role as the vehicle by which acquisitions would have come about. Discussions on this subject did not make clear the extent to which the depressed market value of the stock inhibited serious consideration of acquisition or merger. It is my opinion that it did seriously inhibit any deal where the balance of control was in question.

A dominant issue for management in evaluating the resources of mobility, second only to that of internal controls on outflows, was the handling of borrowing power. The record previously cited indicates the vital role played by the commercial bank in the survival of the management team and the corporate entity. The commercial bank stated that the personal behavior of the company's financial officer had played a large part in maintaining bank support. In particular, his ability to project requirements and repayment schedules, his ability to "deliver" on these projections and to demonstrate that he was in command of the financial situation, his integrity, his willingness to take the initiative on full disclosure, to advise before rather than after the event: these were the ingredients holding the situation together.

It is not an overstatement to say that during this period the financial officer was conscious of being as much a representative of the bank in the corporation as he was an officer of the corporation. This was reflected in his ability and willingness to reflect the bank viewpoint and argue it in management councils. The financial officer was portrayed as being in a delicate negotiating role, which he found possible only by avoiding complete dependence on either party.

Toward the end of this experience the financial officer began to count resources in terms of months of survival time left. At one point he gave the company 18 months, which was his measurement of the remaining reserves for support of necessary outflows unless a strong recovery of orders manifested itself. The bank negotiations reported previously indicated that the bank officers shared these gloomy predictions.

CONSTRAINTS ON MOBILITY: PRECEDING POLICY AND ACTION

In reviewing a period in the history of a company such as that just outlined, it is essential to keep in mind that the particular sequence of events observed may be conditioned by the accident of its starting point. Certainly one must be fully aware of the general conditions preceding the period and their probable influence on the set of responses being observed. In the case of Company C this is particularly significant.

By undertaking the plant expansion just prior to the long period of recession the company denied itself certain key resources in the following period. The plant financing committed the company's entire long-term debt capacity to this purpose. In addition, the related issue of common stock diluted the equity base to the point of inhibiting an issue of common stock for other purposes in the near future. Nor did the use of this money do much to defend the company against the pressures of recession. The purpose had been to provide the capacity and obtain the cost savings of owned rather than purchased sources. At a much lower volume of operation these hoped-for advantages largely disappeared without adding anything to the extent or salability of the company's product mix.

Hindsight shows that the timing of this action was about the worst possible so far as corporate mobility was concerned. Recognition of the danger was indicated by the suggestion of issuing more common stock, a suggestion that might have been more palatable to the stockholders except for the fact of the recent common issue. In the end, the decision was reached to try to restore more mobility by internal means. As a practical matter it must be recognized, of course, that the commitment of one resource may be the necessary prerequisite to the opening of another resource. Many of the resources of corporate mobility require negotiation and there is considerable strengthening of the bargaining position if it can be demonstrated that there is no other alternative. Thus the ability to transfer the problem of mobility from external sources to internal sources may depend on proof that external sources no longer exist. This can hardly be accepted as a desirable element of strategy but it appears to be a common fact of life.

Another potential constraint on financial mobility is the set of policies designed to protect and enhance the value of the stockholder interest. These may result in certain self-imposed rigidities with respect to the extent, timing, and use of sources of funds, which can limit a strategy of mobility under certain circumstances. In the case of Company C the use of long-term debt as a defensive measure in recession was not given an opportunity for testing because of its prior commitment to plant expansion. However, it was clear that the company was not inhibited from its use by a concern for the risks involved. On the contrary, it was clear that the company would go to the limit of availability from regular institutional sources.

With regard to the use of a common stock issue, there were several pieces of evidence that the management felt restrained because of the potential dilution of market value. The subject came up just before the recession period, when it was proposed that common stock be issued to provide greater financial mobility. It also came up later when the prospect of a merger or acquisition as a way out of the financial difficulties again raised the question of the possible effect of more shares on the current market value of the company. It is not clear now what, if any, were the specific criteria by which the potential effects on market value were evaluated. It is clear that the management was, at the least, willing to seriously consider this alternative as a source of funds under these circumstances.

With respect to dividend policy there was considerable precedent for adjustments down and up in the cash dividend per share. In fact there had been recent precedent for suspension. During 1954 earnings had declined significantly and in the first quarter of 1955 the cash dividend was cut in half. In the third quarter, against the background of a loss recorded for the second quarter of 1955, the cash dividend was suspended and it was not resumed until the first quarter of 1956. Thus the general policy was one of close correlation with fluctuations in earnings with just enough lag so that the public record on earnings was established before action was taken.

Beside the constraints of precedent action and value-oriented financial policy, there is the consideration of past experience, which is of special significance to the relationship between financial and operational mobility. The fact that the phenomenon that imposed the discipline of shrinking outflows — an industry recession — was not an unfamiliar experience in the industry and the company made it easier to get quick acceptance of the internal controls necessary to balance flows internally. Management and workers knew that surplus financial resources were not adequate to protect the organization from the shock of adjustment to new low levels of sales and earnings. Workers, management, and suppliers all had to absorb some of the responsibility for the adjustment. Generalizing for a moment, it can be argued with conviction that the cash flow problem of mild fluctuations in sales may be greater than for sharp fluctuations since in the former case the organization is more likely to resist the liquidation process that can be a key element in a strategy of mobility.

A STRATEGY OF MOBILITY: RESOURCES AND SEQUENCE OF USE

In considering Company C's strategy of mobility we should first consider the nature of the need and the resource of time to respond. A serious business recession is a completely nondiscretionary cause of imbalance in funds flows. Having elected to operate in a given industry and to do so without the protection of diversified activities with offsetting funds flow characteristics, the business cannot escape the inherent fluctuations that stem from product, technology, and market.

Thus in the decision tree sequence of Exhibit 5C there is no choice but to "accept" the prospective deficit, no alternative of either rejecting or postponing the impending need for funds caused by a shrinkage in inflows below previously anticipated levels.

The only question then is whether there is a resource of time in which either to await confirming evidence or counterbalancing change or to act to anticipate the need. Of course, the situation in the real world is not as clean cut as the diagram suggests — time vs. no time. The question of time is a matter of magnitude, whether there is a lot or a little. In Company C's case the judgment has to be toward the "little" end of the scale. Management was well aware that it could and would experience serious recessions sometime. Consequently the general phenomenon had to be a part of its forward thinking. Beyond that there was an expectation in 1956, by financial management at least, that a recession could be in the making and that if it occurred it could be a long one. The proposal to sell common stock in the latter part of 1956 attests to that belief.

On the other hand, no one knew the precise timing of either the downturn or the upturn until the record of orders booked showed an unmistakable downward or upward trend. Thus the compelling evidence was such as to produce a lagged response rather than anticipation. Somewhat akin to the need of a record

EXHIBIT 5C

DECISION TREE REPRESENTING COMPANY C's STRATEGY OF MOBILITY

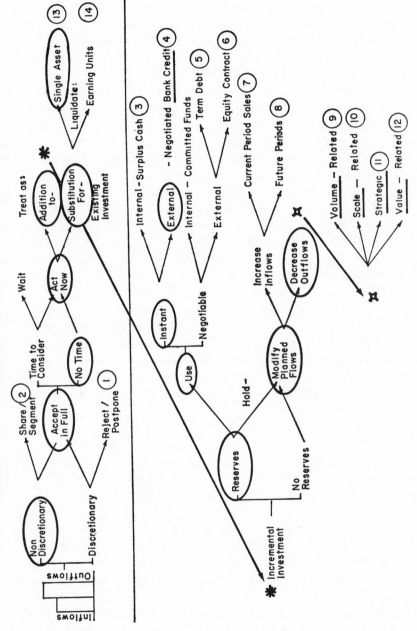

of declining earnings in order to justify a cut in the cash dividend, this record of declining orders is often the evidence necessary to convince operating management that counter measures are necessary. Thus it is essentially accurate to describe the situation of Company C in the early months of 1957 as a "No Time" circumstance demanding immediate Action.

The next question is whether Reserves existed at that time which could be used to cushion the impact of the recession on the organization. External negotiated reserves of either long-term debt or equity were already fully committed to the plant expansion. The remaining reserves would be of the "instant" variety — surplus cash or negotiated bank credit. Cash reserves, which had been high in 1952–1954, were regarded as nonexistent in 1957. The only real reserve at the beginning of 1957 was therefore whatever remained of an unused line of credit at the bank. Bank loans had been reduced during 1956 from $4.75 million to $2.5 million. Thus unless the bank radically revised its willingness to lend — which it had not done — it was apparent that there was at least $2 million of short-term credit available. However, knowing that this amount could easily disappear into working capital in a couple of months, financial management was understandably sensitive to a change that would suggest a deficit in cash flows.

In summary of the strategy of response during the recession period, the following resources of mobility were either used or contemplated for use:

      (1) control (reduction) of outflows
      (2) instant reserves (bank credit)
      (3) recapture of past outflows
      (4) reduction of need by sharing

The actual sequence of use of these resources is summarized in Exhibit 5D. The major burden of mobility fell on the control of outflows and on short-term bank borrowing.

The degree of vulnerability and sensitivity in Company C in early 1957 can be seen in the timing and sequence of action with respect to the different categories of outflows. Even before the recession was properly under way the company cut back sharply

EXHIBIT 5D

SEQUENCE OF COMPANY C's RESPONSES IN RECESSION

Reaction to the Need	Source of Mobility	Events →																											
		1957				**1958**				**1959**				**1960**				**1961**				**1962**				**1963**			
	Yr / Qr	1	2	3	4	1	2	3	4	1	2	3	4	1	2	3	4	1	2	3	4	1	2	3	4	1	2	3	4
	Events	Sharp decline in orders		Inventory starts down	Losses appear	Operating cash deficit	Balance in cash flows	Low point in orders		Inventory levels off	Orders slowly rising		End of sustained deficits	Inventory rising				Alternating profits and losses: '60–'62				Capital expenditures edge up				Sales rising / Profit			
I. Modify Amount or Timing	Reject/Postpone Share/Segment							C						C												C			
II. Accept as Incremental:	Instant: Internal																												
	External—Bank Line		U		R			R	R	R	U	U	U	U	U	U		R	U	U		R	U	U	U	R	R	R	R
(A) Commit Reserves	Negotiable: Term Debt																												
	Equity																												
	Increase Inflows: Current	U	U	U	U	U	U	U																					
(B) Modify Flows	From Future Periods		U	U	U	U	U	U																					
	Decrease Outflows: Volume-Related	C	U	U	U	U	U	U																					
	Scale-Related									R			R					R				R				R			
	Strategic									R			R					R				R				R			
	Value-Related												R																R
III. Accept, but as Substitution for Existing Investment	Liquidate: Single Assets, Earning Units			C →				U																					

Symbols: C—Consider U—Use]—Limit R—Restore

on capital expenditures. This move was in contrast to that of Company A, described in Chapter 4, which tended to give the capital expenditure area more protection and to defer reduction until a later date. The response of Company C seemed to suggest the expectation of a serious and prolonged recession, which called for cash conservation in discretionary areas at the earliest possible date.

As soon as the actual decline in orders began (second quarter, 1957) the volume-related outflows, direct labor and materials, were cut back quickly and sharply. Cuts in scale-related outflows (overhead categories) followed in the third quarter. Value-related outflows, dividends and cost-reducing capital expenditures, were being reduced at the same time. This vigorous "across the board" attack on outflows in the first recession year spared only certain key strategic expenditure categories in such areas as engineering, product development, and sales. Of course there was considerable resistance internally to these pressures and they were not as immediately or uniformly successful as top management hoped.

Nevertheless, the management was remarkably successful in balancing funds flows under the sharply declining sales curve. The second line of defense, short-term bank debt, was called into action only during the second quarter of the year and then only to a midyear maximum level of $4 million. After that point the control over outflows was so effective as to produce a surplus of cash inflow, which was used to reduce the bank loan during the rest of 1957. The action was, of course, at considerable cost to those who were out of a job or on reduced pay, those who had to assume heavier duties, and those who had to experience the massive readjustments in scale and methods of operation. On the other hand, it saved interest costs and — of much greater importance — impressed the bank that management was in control of funds flows and doing its best to get its house in order. This had much to do with the lender's willingness to re-enter the situation later when its support was vital to survival.

By the fourth quarter of 1957 there was evidence that the tight control over outflows had extended to what have been called strategic areas — related to long-run issues of product superiority, technology, competitive position, market share. The company was properly sensitive to reduced outflows in these areas; yet modest reductions were in fact taking place. The most obvious elimination was in the capital expenditure area, where in 1958 only $70,600 was spent on capital expenditures of all kinds, compared with an annual average of $1.6 million in the period 1952–1956. Given better circumstances, expenditures in these areas would probably have increased in 1958. The company did not have the competitive lead that would justify a "safe" interruption of these outflows.

This first phase of mobility strategy was coming to an end about the end of 1958. Sales volume had leveled off at a very reduced order rate and the company appeared to be reaching the limit of its ability to balance flows by reducing outflows. By the third quarter of 1958 the company was out of the bank and cash balances reached a peak in the second quarter of 1959. From that point on, since deficits still continued to plague the company, the second and critical reserve took over: short-term bank debt. For the next three and a half years the commercial bank kept flows in balance and kept the company alive. The bank was a reluctant partner and its patience began to wear thin toward the end. On the other hand, it is highly significant that the loan had been completely cleared up for five quarters before this last phase began.

Exhibit 5D shows that other means of balancing flows were given active consideration at various times but without significant result. Quite early in the experience an effort was made to reverse the decision to expand plant, which had tied up long-term sources in 1956. An attempt was made to sell this new plant to provide substantial relief, but it was unsuccessful. There was also some sale of inventory at distress prices. In addition to these efforts at liquidation of asset values there was evidence on three separate occasions of serious attempts to find relief by joining forces with other and presumably more affluent companies. These attempts also were unsuccessful. Potentially they promised quick relief from serious financial pressure but either the price was too high or the prospective partner unavailable. The longer the situation continued the more costly this alternative became. The question was whether management preferred the certainty of loss of the company's identity by merger or continuation of the risk of losing it by bankruptcy.

It is probably incorrect to suggest that recapture of past outflows by liquidation of assets and modification or elimination of the need by merger were elements of a strategy. They were more in the nature of alternatives of desperation and not consciously selected strategic possibilities. Indeed, the earnest critic may question how much of all that occurred is properly described as a "strategy" of mobility. It is difficult to document the evidence of a conscious strategy. In part, what has been described as the sequence of response may be better referred to as the *implicit* strategy of a set of acts.

The evidence indicates that the conscious strategy of mobility was reflected in the decision in late 1956 to rely on internal control over the nature and timing of outflows supplemented by a modest instant reserve in the form of short-term debt capacity. The decision, of course, was taken without knowledge of the severity of the impending recession. This choice and the following events forced on the company the consideration of other means of balancing funds flows, which undoubtedly were not anticipated when the decision was made. The possible use of these alternatives was implicit in the choice, however, given an event of the severity that occurred. Undoubtedly some of the measures taken to curb outflows and also the degree of dependence on the bank were acts that management, with hindsight, would not have selected. The same conclusion applies to sale of the new plant and certain proposed mergers. Assertions by management suggested that such "mistakes" in strategy would not be repeated in the future. In effect the company gambled on the severity of the recession and lost—almost for good.

Financial Policy vs. a Strategy of Mobility

The concept of value maximization attempts to lay down certain guidelines about such matters as (a) the relationship between expected return on investment and the cost of capital, (b) the variability of the earnings stream, (c) the mix of debt and equity, (d) the balance between dividends and growth in market value. These guidelines presumably help a company to gain the maximum in market value of its shares for the total company effort within the limits of its management, product, and market circumstances. The question raised here is not whether Company C was following someone's normative concepts of value maximization but rather whether it had some sensitivity to the goal of protection and growth of stockholder value and if so how this sensitivity related to the company's strategy of mobility. In general, guidelines on value maximization tend to impose certain rigidities or boundaries on action and would appear to imply a potential conflict with a strategy of mobility. It is significant to note that the chief executive of the company and his family had a substantial equity position in the company and so presumably cared as much as any chief executive would about the stockholder interest.

The critical investment decision was, of course, the commitment of long-term reserves to plant expansion, a decision made by the chief executive retiring at the time. This presumably enhanced the earnings potential of the company by promising cost savings but did nothing whatever to change the extreme variability of sales and earnings. By adding a new burden of overhead and by consuming key reserves it added to the vulnerability to unexpected change. In order to accomplish this investment the company deliberately pushed to the limit of long-term institutional lending and accepted the debt-equity mix dictated by the lender, which prescribed the amount of matching equity that would have to be issued to obtain the debt. Thus a strategic make-versus-buy decision largely guided by operating considerations determined the financial policies. Considerations of both value-maximization and mobility were secondary and did not appear to act as major constraints on the nature of the decision.

With the advent of the serious recession, considerations of financial mobility and survival came to dominate the thinking and behavior of top management. Cash dividends were an early casualty. Debt-equity mix was what the maximum debt available, short-term and long-term, would allow. As indicated previously, considerations of mobility backed up to the point where all new investment was banned — however profitable — and attempts were made to reverse previous investment decisions.

Two key constraints on mobility were in evidence:

(1) Management was unwilling to relinquish its control, through merger or the intervention of lenders or stockholders.

(2) Management was unwilling to "give away" common stock. Just what this meant is unclear. There is no way of knowing whether there was a price at which sale or exchange of common stock was acceptable, although continued interest in merger suggested that there was. Thus it can be argued that there was a value-oriented constraint on mobility and on the price management was willing for the stockholders to pay for the company's and management's survival.

The key source of mobility and survival came to be short-term borrowing power. Financial management went to great lengths to nurture this relationship and to be responsive to the wishes of the bank. Corporate financial policy came to be that policy which represented the bank's interests. The negotiations taking place at the end of 1963 showed clearly that time was rapidly running out on the gamble to preserve management and the equity position of the stockholders.

6

Company E: The Response to
Secular Change

1950 TO 1957: BACKGROUND

Company E is one of a substantial number of producers of basic metals for American industry. These metals are produced from raw materials obtained from natural sources both inside and outside the company and require a heavy investment in plant and equipment to extract, process, and transform the materials into various specified needs of industrial users. The industry is subject to cyclical variations in demand, secular pressures from competing materials, and secular changes in demand. There are also strong and sustained competitive pressures, particularly on the smaller firms in the industry, one of which is Company E.

At the time we break in on the stream of events in Company E — the early 1950s — the company had made a key decision on a basic shift in product mix requiring substantial new capital expenditures. The company at this time was doing reasonably well in terms of rising sales volume and profit but had shown considerable cyclical variation attributable to the previous product mix, which it now intended to change. During the five-year period leading up to 1955 the company made substantial investment in plant for the purpose of bringing about new proportions in product output. This required major changes in the financial structure. In order to make the most of internal sources, cash dividends were eliminated from 1951 to 1955 and replaced by stock dividends. A modest cash dividend was resumed in 1955. Long-term debt was increased by a series of negotiated arrangements with insurance companies and banks to a level of 28% of capitalization. Arrangements were made to obtain substantial amounts on a short-term basis from two major customers. Finally, certain operations considered of peripheral value were disposed of for cash.

Capital expenditures for the period 1949–1955, covering the first phase of company reconstruction, the diversification stage, were as follows:

1949	$ 3.4 million
1950	2.3
1951	11.2
1952	30.7
1953	22.4
1954	6.4
1955	3.8

The next step was undertaken in 1955 at a time when demand in the industry began a strong upward trend. This phase of the reconstruction program was aimed at increasing the company's basic capacity and reducing its cost of production in order to improve its general competitive position. The capital expenditures for the three years 1956–1958 were as follows:

1956	$ 9.1 million
1957	14.1
1958	5.4

The year 1955 recorded a 42% increase in sales volume and a tripling of net income. Under these circumstances a modest cash dividend was resumed (1956 payout: 32%). The high level of operations continued through 1956 and half way through 1957. Profits continued strong during this period, though the level of profitability in 1956 and 1957 dropped somewhat from 1955 primarily because of the expense and dislocation of the capital expenditure program. Financing during this period for plant and working capital was provided from internal sources, some increase in term debt, and a revolving credit arrangement with the company's commercial banks. The revolving credit, however, was not used until 1958.

Our examination of events in detail begins with 1958. After heavy expenditures of capital and management effort to bring about certain basic changes in production and market orientation, the company could not yet be said to be in a strong competitive position. Further stages in the reconstruction program were ahead of it. In addition, in the first quarter of 1958 the company appeared to be facing a serious industry recession. By the end of 1957 the company's long-term debt capacity had been put to considerable use (26% of capitalization). A reserve of marketable securities amounting to $6.5 million at the end of 1956 was now invested in working assets. Earnings had declined sharply. Exhibit 6A charts the fluctuations of several important aspects of the company's operations from 1958 through 1964.

1958: YEAR OF RECESSION

The recession, which began in the fourth quarter of 1957, continued through most of 1958 as indicated by the following statistics on operating rate as a percentage of capacity.

1st quarter	56%
2nd	58
3rd	57
4th	70

Sales for the year were off by 26% from 1957 levels.

As a result of the decline, first-quarter operations showed a substantial loss and in February the decision was made to suspend the cash dividend. Although the decline was the justification offered in the annual report, it was also apparent that (a) there was a need to conserve cash and (b) the terms of the revolving credit agreement, negotiated but not used in 1957, placed a net working capital restriction on dividends, and actual net working capital at the end of 1957 was only slightly above the point where the restrictions would become operative. Indeed, the company was obliged in April 1958 to obtain a waiver of these restrictions in order to continue to pay dividends on its preferred stock. At the same time there was a drive to reduce losses and conserve cash, singling out expenditures for maintenance and improvements for special attention.

In April 1958 the board of directors made a comprehensive review of the company's long-range capital expenditure program. It noted with satisfaction that the efforts at diversification of the

EXHIBIT 6A

COMPANY E: GRAPHS OF SELECTED FINANCIAL DATA
FIRST QUARTER 1958–FOURTH QUARTER 1964

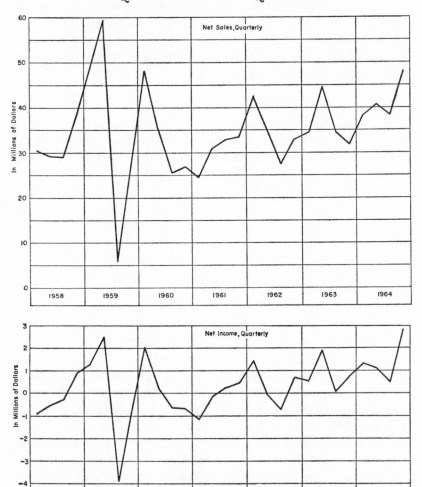

EXHIBIT 6A (continued)

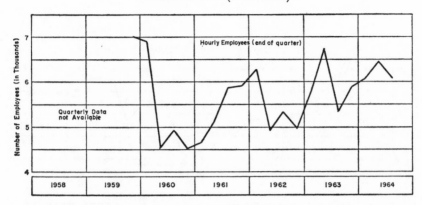

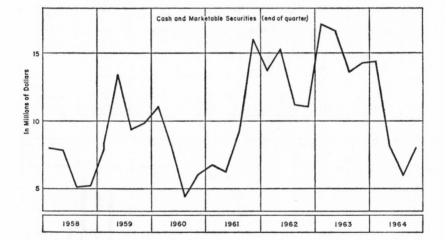

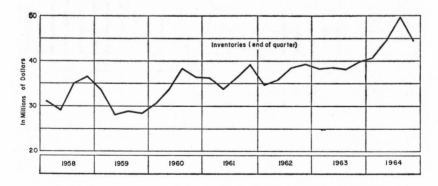

EXHIBIT 6A (concluded)

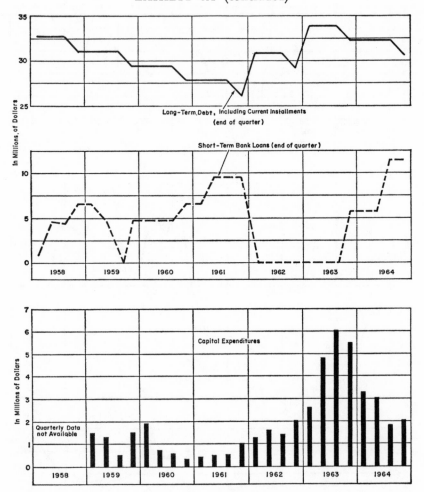

NOTE: No common dividends were declared during this period.

product line appeared to be paying off since the company's 1957 decline lagged somewhat the decline in the industry average. It also stressed, however, that there continued to be a great need to improve competitive position by capital expenditures aimed at reducing costs. Plans had been developed along these lines and "will be pursued within the limits of the company's financial capabilities while still keeping stockholders' faith in the company." This last reference presumably cautioned against financial policies that would be interpreted as excessively risky or damaging to market values. Capital expenditures were therefore continued in 1958, though at a substantially lower level than that of 1957.

In order to meet its financial commitments the company took down some $6.5 million of the $9.5 million revolving credit agreement in 1958. Further indication of the cash bind is seen in the fact that in October the company arranged a short-term $1 million loan from a wholly owned subsidiary. On the other hand, by year end sales were improving and the company was once more in the black on earnings. As a result, a 12½% cut in compensation for nonunion clerical personnel was restored in November. Such cuts were not unique in the industry, but this company was the first to cut and the last to restore.

1959–1960: The Struggle to Reduce Current Outflows

The year 1959 opened with discussion at board level of a possible merger with another company of about the same size in the same industry as a means of achieving a new level of profitable performance. Talks between the two parties, however, revealed so great a gap in objectives that they were abandoned a month later. The discussion on the part of Company E's management did reveal a willingness at least to consider the inevitable shifts in responsibility and control that a merger of such magnitude would involve.

The recovery of the last quarter of 1958 continued into the first half of 1959. Positive benefit was being held back by what the management regarded as an inflated wage level relative to competitors. The management was determined to bring wages into line, as labor negotiations loomed. In the meantime (April) management throughout the company carried out a major review of its expenditure commitments and rededicated itself to the cost reduction program started in 1958 with particular emphasis on raw material procurement and production costs. Another action taking place at this time was a decision to drop an unprofitable product line which had been severely hit by foreign competition.

Anticipating continued pressure on the balance of funds flows, in April the treasurer explored with the company's bank an extension of its line of credit, and in due course obtained a two-year extension of the credit line through June 1961. At the same time the company was drawing on internal sources of cash to the full extent possible.

In August, both company and union being adamant, labor negotiations broke down and a strike began which lasted four months and turned the profit gains of early 1959 into a net loss for the year. However, the impact on the company's funds flows was positive as well as negative. The immediate effect of the strike was release from certain major expenditure commitments, notably payroll, while inflows from outstanding receivables continued. As a result, short-term bank borrowings could be reduced. They reached the zero level briefly in September. Even by year end, bank loans stood at a level $2 million less than the previous year and cash balances were up by over $4.5 million. As a footnote, however, the loan's net working capital covenant had proved once again to be excessively binding and the bank had to consent to a reduction from $27 to $24 million, for 1960 only.

The remaining significant event of 1959 concerning funds flow position was a follow-up on the goal of reducing long-term material procurement costs. At the end of October the company entered into negotiations for new raw material sources. It is interesting that the general approach taken by the company was to use joint venture arrangements whereby the initial capital outlay was small or nonexistent. Potentially the funds requirements in this area were huge and the company was in no position to assume a major investor role no matter what long-term gains might follow.

The year 1960 turned out to be another year of struggle. Sales declined 5% from the 1959 level. It was becoming increasingly apparent that basic improvements in efficiency of operations would require a major investment of external funds. Although these were hardly the circumstances for presenting a bold face to the investing public, management was convinced that an essential preliminary step to an approach to the capital markets was to "set its own house in order." One major element of this was the issue of wage structure, which was eventually negotiated in 1960 after the lengthy strike of 1959 and with some general improvement in competitive position.

A second step taken in early 1960 was a sharp cut in "normal" capital expenditures, designed to conserve cash and to present a better image to the outside world. This heavy restraining hand is seen in the chart of capital expenditures (Exhibit 6A), though the precise effects are not clear from these aggregate figures. The restraint continued for two years beyond 1960. It was felt that with major "innovative" expenditures an absolute essential, all other capital expenditures except those having the most obvious income benefits must be deferred.

In spite of these steps there was no immediate improvement in the cash and working capital position, which at the end of May was at the same level as in 1959. Actually the cash position began to decline in April and continued to do so through September, the point at which the company's cash balances reached a historical low. Expenditures at the end of June were reported to be "at a minimum" after cutbacks in personnel and raw material purchases. The company continued to pay preferred dividends but to suspend the common dividend.

By year end the results of these efforts showed a small profit in contrast to the loss of 1959. On the other hand, through the last quarter of 1960 short-term debt began to rise as the company decided on a major capital expenditure program designed to enable it to break out of its weak competitive position tied to high-cost production facilities. There was a "do-or-die" mood. The house was not really in order but the guests were about to arrive in any case.

1961: YEAR OF CRISIS

In January 1961 the company launched a major investment program aimed at cost reduction, a lowering of the breakeven level of production, and profits to permit a resumption of dividend payments. This Plan for Profitability called for spending nearly $40 million in excess of normal capital expenditures over the period 1961–1965. The reader is reminded that this surge in capital expenditures had been preceded in the 1950s by a major commitment of funds designed to change the product mix to a more profitable combination. The new expenditure was also regarded as vital to the company's existence: "These new facilities are absolutely essential to preservation of security of shareholders' investment and employees' jobs during the intense competitive years ahead."

It was clear that major external financing would be required. The company had worked hard at squeezing as much as possible out of the funds already invested in the business. It was employing a consultant on cost control; it had enforced what it regarded as "tight" budgetary controls; and it had begun to shut down hard on "normal" capital expenditures. Normal capital appropriations declined in the first three quarters of 1961 to about one-third of the 1960 level. One major potential source of funds, inventories, resisted efforts because it was argued that it was "hard to bear down on inventory when business is bad." The views of the sales force appeared to prevail, at least momentarily. It is also worth noting that in January the net working capital covenant of the short-term credit agreement with the banks would prevent payment of any dividends. When negotiations showed the banks unwilling to relax these covenants, the decision was taken to suspend the dividends on the preferred stock.

The first step toward major external financing was to approach the company's existing long-term lender, an insurance company, to request half of the funds needed ($19 million). In anticipation the company prepared its case carefully and in great detail and approached the lenders at the highest level of management. The result was a "bitter disappointment." The management felt that it had gone with hat in hand. To be turned down flatly left a strong feeling of resentment, which was still apparent several years later. The insurance company's answer was that it had loaned all it was going to but would consider opening up its prior claim on assets for an additional $9.5 million from another lender, and it suggested a specific lender. A key condition was a substantial increase in the interest rate on the outstanding debt, from $4\frac{1}{8}\%$ to 5%. The insurance company also suggested supplier financing as an alternative.

This rebuff took place at the end of March 1961. At this point the company reviewed its Plan for Profitability and reaffirmed the vital necessity of spending these funds. Engineering costs were checked and rechecked to assure soundness, and cost savings estimates were confirmed as "realistic." The four phases of the plan were:

    (1) reduce labor costs
    (2) reduce raw material costs
    (3) reduce production costs
    (4) maintain and improve market position

Reductions in the first two phases were already well under way, and expenditures in phase (3) were next to move forward.

Through April the finance committee reviewed the financing alternatives, including a re-examination of an internal source of funds. The company had a profitable subsidiary considered to be separable from the main stream of the business. Sale of this subsidiary was now explored actively as the company's one remaining hope of finding a large sum of cash quickly. Potential purchasers were found who were prepared to pay a price considered acceptable but no one appeared able or willing to pay a lump sum cash settlement. Since this was the only basis satisfactory to Company E, the idea of sale was dropped, and the company turned its full attention back to the external capital market.

The next step was employment of an investment banker to aid in the search for outside funds, looking toward the possibility of a new equity issue as well as further debt from private placement. One of the first matters taken up by the investment banker was the possibility of recapitalizing the outstanding preferred stock, now two quarters in arrears. Unfortunately this was not a good time for the company to consider an equity issue for two reasons. One was the performance of the company's common stock. High and low prices were 26½–18 in 1959; 21–9½ in 1960; 16–8½ in 1961. These prices were obviously related to the problems the company was having in making a profit. The other reason was that at this time the market was considered to be "off the industry," that is, to feel that it lacked any particular glamour or interest.

While these explorations were slowly moving forward, management continued its relentless pressures on available liquid funds for day-to-day operations. During 1961 sales gradually increased and inventories went up along with sales. The company's cash position had recovered somewhat from the serious low of mid-1960, but it was held at the slightly higher level of about $6.5 million only by running up short-term borrowing to the maximum of $9.5 million available under the current credit agreement with the bank. The maximum was reached in June, and at that time a six-month extension was negotiated through December 31. A slight relaxation of the minimum net working capital covenant was also negotiated at the same time.

It is interesting that through this period the company continued to move steadily forward with its plans for assuring long-term sources of raw materials. Since these developments were all made on arrangements that avoided heavy initial ownership outlays, the serious financial bind in which the company found itself did not hinder planning or action. The arrangements included joint venture arrangements, future purchase contracts, and guarantees of loans, none of which affected the current balance sheet substantially. They did, however, involve future commitments and contingent obligations and the approval of the company's principal lender.

In July 1961 the exploration of new long-term debt came to a head, a major turning point in company financing. The complex negotiations required the resolution of four essential parts of the plan:

(1) Gain agreement of senior creditor to permit an increase in senior debt in the amount of $9.5 million. This was already promised.
(2) Obtain a commitment from a new source of long-term credit to supply the required $9.5 million of new debt capital.
(3) Secure approval by the board and stockholders of a new $9.5 million common equity issue demanded by the new long-term lender as a condition of its participation.
(4) Obtain from the bank an increase in the line of short-term credit to $15 million for working capital needs.

This plan would provide about $25 million of the nearly $40 million required for the planned capital expenditures. It was hoped that the remainder would come from internal generation over the next few years.

The terms show clearly that this was "back to the wall" financing. The price for opening up the existing debt contract was a rate increase from 4⅛% to 5%. The new debt money was to be supplied at 6% for 15 years and the lender was to receive warrants to purchase 200,000 shares (1,500,000 shares then outstanding) at $16 a share, exercisable at any time during the life of the debt. The final blow, however, was the required issue of common stock. At the end of 1960 the common stock had a book value of $37 a share, but the market price in the first half of 1961 was down in the $12 range and gradually sliding downwards. To raise $9.5 million would require the sale of over a million common shares, almost doubling the number of shares outstanding.

With no valid alternatives in prospect the plan went to the board of directors in late July and was approved. Details of the stock increase were worked out in August, and in late September the stockholders voted their approval. By then the price on the stock market was as low as $10¾. The new stock was offered on a preemptive rights basis to stockholders of record as of October 25 and priced at $9 a share. As reported in the annual report of 1961, the issue met with an "enthusiastic reception," indicated by a 97% exercise of the rights. It is clear that this level of subscription greatly eased management's position. What is unclear is whether the stockholders saw any real alternative to a major defensive investment at this stage. The offering is noteworthy as one of those rare cases when a new infusion of equity was made under circumstances usually regarded as intolerable to both management and stockholders.

The remaining segment of the plan was negotiated in September, when the banks agreed to a new credit agreement permitting borrowings up to $15 million. Thus by year end the immediate pressures were off to the extent of $25 million of new money available as needed. In addition, tight internal controls on inventory buildup and normal capital spending had started a gradual improvement in the cash position in July, which picked up some momentum by September. The net effect of all these activities was a year-end cash balance of $16 million, to be compared with $6.1 million at the end of 1960, and assurance of $15 million of unused borrowing power. In sharp contrast, the income statement for the year showed a significant sales decline and net loss.

1962–1963: SHORT-RUN VS. LONG-RUN SURVIVAL

The two years following the funds crisis of 1961 were a period in which the focus of funds management turned inwards and during which the continuing need for a choice between the issues of short-run and long-run survival was readily apparent. At each annual review of the company's explicit program for long-run profitability, customarily held at the beginning of the second quarter of the year, there was a re-examination of the financial requirements and a rededication to get on with the job. At the same time, however, the quarterly sales volume hovered about the breakeven level of profitability and moved agonizingly back and forth between modest profits and losses without developing a firm trend. A report to the board early in 1963 indicated that the management regarded the company as under some kind of competitive disadvantage in almost half of its markets. Thus constant attention to the short-run financial need to service current income was also necessary.

During the period in question sales fell off from the first quarter of 1962 to the third quarter, increased modestly in the next two quarters, rose strongly in the second quarter of 1963, and again fell in the third and fourth quarters of 1963. Because of an inability to foresee accurately and to adjust quickly to these changes and because of a sensitivity to marketing considerations in existing circumstances, inventories swung significantly. Work in process and finished goods inventories rose sharply during periods of declining sales. Financial management was acutely aware of the way in which such funds flows rapidly consumed capital earmarked for long-run purposes and of the difficulty of gaining its release once embedded in the working capital base.

In response to the problem, which was clearly one of ultimate survival, financial management developed control and reporting mechanisms designed to keep the issue constantly before management. Capital expenditures were clearly differentiated between "normal," which were held down to an absolute minimum, and "major," which were the investments necessary to establish a stable competitive posture in the market. The latter were the expenditures for which external financing was arranged in 1961 but which, because of construction lags, were not made until 1962 and 1963.

Along the same lines, and of greater significance, was a program instituted in 1962 and variously described by management as "cash rationing," "cash segregation," or "touch-and-go financing." The goal was to stop any further net flow of cash into productive facilities and working capital related to the generation of current income beyond bare maintenance levels. The device adopted, admittedly arbitrary, was to screen normal capital expenditures severely, and to permit growth in inventory and receivables only to the extent of existing cash and unused short-term bank loans. New external funds previously negotiated, net income, and depreciation beyond amounts taken up by normal capital expenditures were then allocated to major capital expenditures. By this means it was hoped that major capital needs beyond the funds raised in 1961 would be found internally.

The practical effect of this allocation was to stress the direct competition between current working capital pressures and long-term objectives and to make it clear that new working capital was being "borrowed" from the improvement program; and the point was driven home on a monthly report to the president and top operating executives. It was indicated by financial management that by 1964 cash flow had become the number one reporting language for top management and the board.

In spite of the fact that the primary focus of expenditure for long-term objectives was in the construction of certain specialized capital assets, which were a part of the company's Plan for Profitability and necessitated full cash financing, other long-term goals were also advanced in 1962–1963. These related to a continued interest in tying down access to low-cost raw material sources for the long-term needs of the company and to overseas expansion of productive and sales capacity. In each case means were found to minimize the immediate cash outlay. In the case of the raw material sources joint participation with other users was coupled with payment over a five-year period tied to tonnage. Overseas operations, too, were financed as a joint venture, with a substantial use of foreign debt sources extending the modest initial equity outlay. These investments required and received approval from the company's long-term lenders. In the case of the foreign ventures the lenders required that the officers of the company not commit it for expenditures in this connection in excess of $500,000.

After the long-term financing arranged in 1961 the company was able to retire short-term debt completely by March 1962, but only because of the lag in the spending of this money for long-term purposes. The treasurer knew that by the end of 1963 the money would be spent. Consequently, by July 1963 the company took steps to renegotiate the credit agreement with the commercial banks and extend it for one more year from December 31, 1963. This agreement, originally in the amount of $15 million, had called for conversion into a 5-year term loan. The new agreement also called for such conversion but payments would not begin until June 30, 1965. Borrowing under the old agreement was resumed in October 1963 and by December 31 had reached $5.7 million.

The following figures show the rate of capital expenditure for long-term goals:

1961	$ 475,000
1962	4,750,000
1963	17,750,000

In March 1962 the company took down the first $4.75 million of its 1961 term loan. It took down the remaining $4.75 million in March 1963. Thus by the end of 1963 the company had taken delivery of the long-term funds negotiated in 1961 and was now eating its way into its short-term borrowing power and cash balances.

During the years 1962 and 1963 dividends on both preferred and common stock remained suspended in spite of the fact that both were years of some recorded profit, 1963 being definitely better than 1962. The dividend action was taken, as the company reported, "after very careful consideration of the heavy cash demands and additional borrowing required in 1964. . . . It does not appear prudent to jeopardize the completion of the capital improvement program and our relationship with the lending institutions by a premature resumption of dividend payments."

The company continued to give thought to the sale of the profitable subsidiary that could be separated from the main business because it was a self-contained physical and sales unit. However, there was always the problem of the immediate loss of sales and profits to be made up. In any case, no action was taken.

1964–1965: RENEWED PRESSURES

If financial peace of mind is to be judged by the conventional yardsticks of growth in sales and profits, the year 1964 should be regarded as a positive step in that direction for Company E. Sales were up significantly, 14%, over 1963 and profits were up 80%. In addition, because of the heavy investment in new plant, operating cash flows hidden by rising depreciation charges were moving up significantly. Total internal generation amounted to over $14 million in 1964.

In spite of this very desirable result and the apparent success of the Plan for Profitability, the year developed as a major challenge in the continuing battle to balance funds flows. The reasons for the renewal of funds flow pressures were as follows.

(1) By 1964 the company had invested or otherwise spent the external reserves tapped in 1961 through the equity and term-debt markets. Major capital additions initiated in early 1962 came to the point of completion in late 1963. Thus the temporary relief which the external reserves brought to the cash flow system was now exhausted.

(2) Although a major portion of the 1960–1961 Plan for Profitability had been completed on schedule, important segments of the plan, requiring additional capital outlays above and beyond normal capital outlays, were still to be completed. Further, as events showed, management was beginning to think about a new program to consolidate and increase the gains from the 1960–1965 expenditures. This clearly signaled a continued imbalance in funds flows.

(3) The years of belt-tightening were beginning to show up in pressures for increased spending for normal operations. The company had substantially shortened its expenditure horizon and strains were beginning to develop.

(4) The inevitable peaks and valleys of current investment related to unexpected events continued to complicate current funds requirements. An example is the increase in inventories in 1964 due to the rising volume of sales and an unusually high raw material position in anticipation of a shutdown related to plant construction. As it worked out, this shutdown was delayed, resulting in the delayed release of the funds tied up in raw materials. The inventory position became a major preoccupation of financial management during this period as it became more and more evident that inventories represented one of the few remaining opportunities for funds reallocation.

At least for the time being major capital expenditures appeared to be tapering off in 1964. Gross quarterly expenditures were as follows:

2nd and 3rd quarters, 1963	$11.4 million
4th quarter, 1963	5.7
1st quarter, 1964	3.4
2nd quarter, 1964	3.5
3rd quarter, 1964	1.8

They were clearly not finished, however. The annual report for 1964 reported planned major expenditures for 1965 at $8.5 million to complete the 1960–1965 plan. Late in 1964 the board was advised that a new plan would be developed for 1965–1970.

At the same time pressure to hold down normal capital expenditures was beginning to meet increasing resistance from operating management. By 1964 financial management conceded that the best it could hope for after several lean years was to hold expenditures down to about half of the depreciation charges. The hard line on operating outflows became increasingly difficult to hold as the profit performance improved beyond the earlier breakeven situation.

Another source of pressure on management was the arrearages in preferred dividends, which would amount to nearly $5 million by the end of 1964 and presented an ever-increasing barrier to ultimate resumption of common dividends. As a result of the improved profit performance, the board was finding continued suspension of dividends hard to justify to stockholders. The first step was to seek a waiver of dividend restrictions under the Credit Agreement with the banks. This was obtained toward the end of 1964 and action came in January 1965. The manner in which preferred dividends was resumed was interesting because of an obvious intent of preserving flexibility. The company announced a lump-sum payment on arrearages, carefully explaining that this did not imply an early resumption of quarterly preferred dividends, but that if conditions continued to be favorable, another lump-sum payment would follow at some later date. The company was wary of any new fixed cash outflows when cash pressures remained so uncertain.

That these and other pressures on the careful control of outflows were disturbing to top management is evidenced by a special report presented by the controller to the board in late August 1964 to review a list of abnormal expenses. The reason for the concern was obvious, for the company was facing the immediate future with only two basic sources available to it — the remainder of the funds that could be borrowed under the Credit Agreement and the reallocation of internal flows. During 1964 internal sources, while substantial, proved inadequate to meet all expenditures. The company took up an additional $5.7 million under the Credit Agreement in the third quarter of 1964, leaving only $3.6 million unused under the $15 million limit.

As the end of 1964 approached, the company once again sought and received a one-year extension of the Agreement, which postponed for one more year the conversion into a 5-year term loan with the inevitable repayment schedule. Although this study of the company does not extend beyond early 1965, it may be reported here that the Agreement was finally converted into a term loan at the end of 1965, at which time the remaining $3.6 million was borrowed.

In early 1965, however, the company treasurer saw the remaining balances of $3.6 million under the Credit Agreement as a key reserve against uncertain needs. It was his hope, in fact, to end the year with bank loans at $10 million, which he planned to convert into the 5-year term loan, leaving a line of credit of $5 million for inventory accumulation. He believed that the banks might be persuaded to go above $15 million if necessary, but he preferred not to have to test that limit.

FINANCIAL MANAGEMENT'S VIEW OF SOURCES OF MOBILITY

With all existing external sources apparently at their limit of availability, with internal sources apparently incapable of handling alone the rising flow for current operations, and with new capital expenditures needed to consolidate gains made so far, the company appeared to be facing a difficult future in the battle for balanced funds flows. Early 1965 is a highly significant point in time, therefore, to review the existing sources of mobility recognized by financial management. First, as the treasurer looked forward to the remainder of 1965 and 1966, he saw this as a period for "beefing up the balance sheet" by ploughing back as much of the new earning power as possible. There was every intention of keeping costs low and continuing the ban on common dividends. It was felt that improved balance sheet ratios following a couple of "get well" years would open up access to additional senior debt sources (long-term), which were essential for the future. The management hoped that by 1966 it would have proved to the creditors the wisdom of its capital expenditure program and its capacity to make a profit. The goal was to lower the breakeven cost of operations in order to be better off defensively and offensively. Either 1966 would be a poor year, in which case the company would show breakeven ability at low volume, or it would be a good year, in which case profits would be strong. This kind of evidence, it was hoped, would be regarded as at least as important as the debt-equity ratio and would encourage lenders to go the next mile with the company.

In this connection it is interesting to note that the treasurer rejected the idea of reducing the burden of the preferred stock by replacing it with after-tax debt charges. The substitution of new debt for old preferred stock would in his mind lead to a "frightful" debt ratio and preclude new debt sources needed in the near future. (It is only in those cases where the debt-for-preferred substitution comes out of unused and unneeded borrowing power that the action has a practical appeal.)

The importance attached to the improved debt-equity position by the financial management can be seen in its insistence on cleaning up the balance sheet even at the expense of some slow-down in the Plan for Profitability. In this we see the evidence of a shifting bargaining position between financial and operating management. The degree of success produced by the new investment program tended to make it more difficult for operating management to press the urgency of further spending in new directions and easier for financial management to advocate the buildup of new reserves. It was abundantly clear that the financial officers had no appetite for a return to the creditors in a weak and humiliating bargaining position. They wanted to go only when they could deal from a position of strength.

In addition to suggesting a slowdown in the Plan for Profitability, financial management was turning with renewed interest and vigor to what were regarded as excessive inventory levels. These were high not only because of the temporary rise in raw material inventories cited earlier but also because over recent years inventory had been used as a competitive tool by the promise of quick delivery. Thus the circumstances that had developed the need for heavy capital expenditures were also the circumstances tending to resist a transfer of funds out of inventory. Customers were in a position to insist that the company carry their inventory for them in warehouses close to the point of use.

One avenue for substantial reduction was discontinuance of lines combining high inventory commitments and low profit margins. This, however, gave rise to a problem similar to that associated with the possible sale of the profitable subsidiary — what management referred to as the "phase in-phase out" problem. It was recognized that over time the company should be adding new profit-making products and phasing out those that had become unprofitable. The problem was one of timing. The officers felt that the present period was one when the company could ill afford any reduction in sales volume and profits. They hesitated to drop a line without the assurance of another to fill the sales gap immediately. Continued overall growth was seen as critical to the acceptance of management's performance. Undoubtedly this problem was aggravated by the industry characteristic that capital investment could not be made in small increments but rather involved big "bites" of irregularly spaced (and therefore sometimes overly concentrated) capital input.

Thus, despite the rather limited range of alternatives open to the company at this point, inventories were not regarded as an easy or a predictable source of capital.

The following uncertain but potentially important sources may be listed as means by which funds flows could be balanced in the future:

(1) Slow-down of Plan for Profitability
(2) Reduction in inventories
(3) Sale of subsidiary
(4) Increase in long-term borrowing power as profits improved and equity grew

Of greater certainty were the following more immediate sources of mobility:

(5) Unused short-term bank loans
(6) Cut-back in raw material purchases
(7) Leasing of assets
(8) Factoring of receivables

So far the last two had not received active consideration although they were recognized as a secondary line of defense. Left out completely at this point was the possibility of going back to either long-term or short-term creditors with a request for more funds. It was believed that some funds might be arranged but only under intolerable conditions.

As we terminate the account of Company E at this point — breaking off as abruptly as we began — it is apparent that the problem of balance in funds flows had not yet been solved but went on from one uncertainty to the next. The final chapter will be written only if financial ruin or loss of independence through merger brings the story swiftly to a close. In conclusion I quote a comment from a company official. He said in part:

> Every move along the way, as you will see, required approval from our various lending agencies. Therefore, to convince so many, so often, with what was done, was being done, and will be done, showed more than faith in Company E; rather it proved

through action in following our stated objectives that we were in effect doing through long- and short-term borrowing what must be done and in the only way left open to us.

Academically, we speak of financial mobility, timing, market trends, broad outlook, alternative choices of funds; however, in reality, a company in a tight liquidity position, beset by equipment, labor, product-mix problems — all hitting at once — has little maneuverability. The company must act now — in this interest market, in this strike period, in that downward turn of business — if it is to stay in business and meet competition at all. These factors, I hope, will emerge clearly from a review of the record.

THE ELEMENTS OF STRATEGY

The preceding narrative of events in the experience of Company E during the period of 1958 to 1964 will now be examined for evidence of a general strategy for dealing with undetermined deficits in funds flows. It should be apparent that the overriding consideration that dominated decision making during this period, including financial decision making, was the desire to change, modernize, and enlarge the productive facilities so as to have a secure competitive position in the industry and make a satisfactory, though undefined, rate of profit. To repeat an earlier quotation: "These new facilities are absolutely essential to preservation of security of shareholders' investment and employees' jobs during the intense competitive years ahead." The goal thus stated was subject to a financial constraint expressed as follows: to pursue this objective "within the limits of the company's financial capabilities while still keeping stockholders' faith in the company."

The financial implications of corporate strategy materialized in the form of successive waves of investment in property, plant, and facilities in large amounts relative to the existing investment and internal funds flows. Neither the amount nor the timing of the need was easily forecast, and even when the outlines of the immediate future had been hammered out there remained the great uncertainty of what lay beyond. Complicating the picture were other events with a material effect on funds flows, primarily the year-to-year fluctuations in demand, the strike, and other seemingly random occurrences such as production break-downs.

Undoubtedly there was a large element of randomness in the particular sequence of events during this period. On the other hand, there is reason to believe that the weakened competitive position of the company not only brought on the capital requirements referred to above but also increased the burden imposed by normal fluctuations in business. It also heightened the chance of and need for the pressures that led to a severe labor dispute over wage levels. Thus adversity was to some extent correlated and reinforcing.

In speaking of a strategy of mobility for dealing with the needs of this period, the first thing to be said is that evidence of an explicit strategy is extremely limited. There was no formal statement of policy for handling uncertainty in funds flows, nor did management ever verbalize anything approaching guidelines for use of the resources that were in fact employed. Strategy had to be inferred from action over time. Thus the summary of acts displayed in Exhibits 6B and 6C is the starting point of an attempt to develop a strategic pattern out of a series of overt acts in balancing funds flows over time.

In identifying overt acts as the clue to strategy it must be said that the evidence is necessarily incomplete. Lost to view are the important but imperceptible influences of the everyday conduct of the financial and other executives on the trend of events. Consistent patterns of behavior can have a strong effect on action taken by others. Thus a vigorous line of questioning by the financial officer on investment proposals could over time lead to a substantial lessening of new requests for funds when it became known that the V.P. Finance was a hard man to get by in investment committee meetings. This posture could shift over time depending on the financial officer's expectations regarding funds availability in the future.

Another aspect to be kept in mind when examining the record of this or any period in a company's history is the perhaps obvious fact that each action taken in the balancing of funds flows has an antecedent action and a subsequent action, to both of which it is inevitably connected. The various resources available are inherently finite in nature and so, for example, the use of debt today is conditioned by whether it was used yesterday or may be used tomorrow. To break in on the history of a company at

EXHIBIT 6B

DECISION TREE REPRESENTING COMPANY E's STRATEGY OF MOBILITY

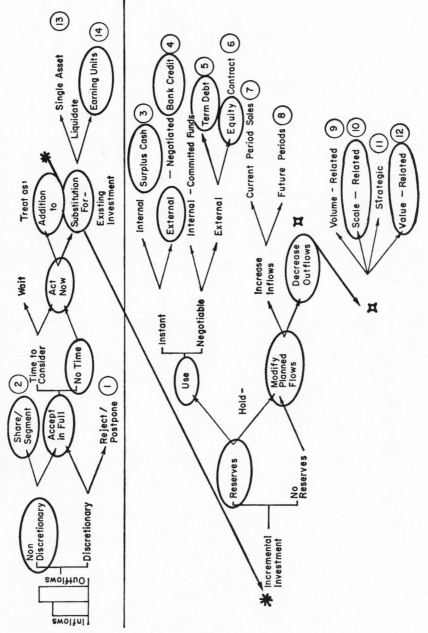

EXHIBIT 6C

SEQUENCE OF COMPANY E's RESPONSES TO EVENTS

Events →

Reaction to the Need	Source of Mobility	1958 Recession 1 2 3 4	1959 Raw materials policy / Strike 1 2 3 4	1960 New investment program 1 2 3 4	1961 Reaffirm inv. / Board-stockholders approve stock issue / New investment program begins 1 2 3 4	1962 Sales hover at break-even profit 1 2 3 4	1963 Sales up strongly / Capital expenditures heavy / Sales decline 1 2 3 4	1964 External funds now exhausted / Sales and profits up for year 1 2 3 4
I. Modify Amount or Timing	Reject/Postpone Share/Segment	U	C C U	U	U	U U C	C U	C
II. Accept as Incremental:	Instant: Internal	U	R R R U	U U R U	U R R R	R U	R R U	U U
(A) Commit Reserves	External—Bank Line				C C U]			
	Negotiable: Term Debt	U U R R			C C U]			
	Equity				C C U] ↑			
(B) Modify Flows	Increase Inflows: Current							
	From Future Periods							
	Decrease Outflows: Volume-Related	U U	U	U U	R R R	R R U	R R R	R R
	Scale-Related	U	U	U	U U	U	R R U	R R
	Strategic		U		U		R	R(C)
	Value-Related							
III. Accept, but as Substitution for Existing Investment	Liquidate: Single Assets Earning Units		U		C			C C

Symbols: C—Consider U—Use]—Limit R—Restore

any point inevitably picks up the constraints of the action taken in the immediate past.

An examination of Exhibit 6C shows that most of the action to balance funds flows was operating under the assumption that the needs as defined by corporate strategy had to be met regardless of near-term cost and that the investment would be "additive" — that existing bases of sales and earnings would not be curtailed in order to provide the new capital requirements. Within this assumption the primary balancing mechanisms, which played a more or less continuous role over the entire period, were the pre-negotiated reserve of short-term borrowing power and the ability to reduce or postpone certain regularly planned outflows. In addition, bank balances played a part though secondary to the bank line of credit.

Without question the bank line of credit played a pivotal role in Company E's strategy of mobility. Its most immediate function was to take care of the continuous fluctuations in volume-related outflows caused by industry fluctuation in demand — the short-term upward movements in outflows when orders began to pick up sharply and direct labor, raw materials, and other expenditures followed suit. Negotiated two years at a time, it relieved management of pin-point forecasting of these changes. Experience showed that renegotiation was not difficult. Although there was the possibility that at the end of any given two years the amount borrowed would be converted into a terminal term loan with serial repayment, this prospect did not appear to worry management. The bank loan was a solitary island of relative certainty in a sea of uncertainty. The amount of any unused balance was always a comforting fact.

Nor was the role of the bank loan confined to short-term swings in inventory and receivables. Since there was no prescription by the bank as to the specific use of the funds, the line of credit could be used in the very critical function of buying time in which to activate other resources for balancing the major deficits that the bank could not or would not finance. These were the resources that required time to negotiate either externally or internally or required time for the actual release of the funds. Evidence of the bank's role is found in the fact that the company was continuously in debt to the bank regardless of the level of sales except during the period when there was a major infusion of external funds and before these funds could be invested.

Under these circumstances the part played by cash balances was secondary to the bank line. It is evident that cash reserves represented the point of initial impact of changes in the balance of funds flows and as such moved up, down, or sideways depending on the relative rates of inflows and outflows month by month. However, with more or less continuous pressure on the cash position and with the bank line of credit as the most obvious source from which to derive immediate supplements of cash, the free bank balance was not the primary resource in a strategy of mobility. Further, the financial management did not in fact know except through actual experience how low the operating balance could go without embarrassment. Thus the unused line of credit was a clearly defined number, whereas the size of free or available cash reserves was not. It would be most accurate to say that the company's instant reserve position was thought of as a combination of the unused bank loan plus a vaguely defined amount of cash on hand. At these levels of cash balance the commitment of some of the remaining balance to specialized investment was an action reserved for more remote and more desperate circumstances after other higher priority resources had been brought into play and exhausted.

Next in line of priority were two further means of funds flow balance, which proved to be interrelated: (1) the manipulation of the established structure of outflows and (2) acquisition of additional external capital by means of long-term contracts. Both of these sources had the common characteristic of requiring time to activate or negotiate and both had significant elements of uncertainty as to the amount of funds available and the timing.

The internal source through modification of the established flow structure will be considered first. In this case the acceleration of inflows did not offer significant opportunities. Exhibit 6C shows a breakdown of outflows into broad categories relating to the basic determinant of the outflow. These are the categories discussed in Chapter 3: volume-related, scale-related, strategic, and value(time)-related outflows. Because variations in volume-related outflows were largely determined by changes in customer demand, Company E's ability to use declining demand as a basis for a reallocation of funds under a general strategy of mobility was severely limited, a matter of coincidence rather than plan. However, volume-related outflows such as direct labor had certain discretionary dimensions which management might use when demand declined. The existence of inventory meant that potentially at least the extent of the layoff in an industry recession and the rapidity of re-employment in the recovery were matters of choice.

In the case of Company E the buffer of inventory was not regarded as a major potential source of funds (saving payroll by running down inventory) and therefore did not appear to be a part of the strategy of mobility. The management felt large inventories to be a major element in competitive strategy; and since the company was considered to be in a relatively weak competitive position, marketing considerations dominated financial considerations. Stated differently, marketing mobility dominated financial mobility.

Another category of outflows that did not become a part of the strategy of financial mobility was strategic outflows — those regarded as playing a key role in the stability and growth of the corporate entity. The definition of a strategic outflow is admittedly subjective. The category might be defined merely by listing those outflows that were protected under pressure. In the case of Company E the narrative indicates what capital expenditure categories were periodically reviewed and reconfirmed as of high priority even when the costs of financing were obviously great. Only toward the very end of this period of review was there some indication by the chief financial officer that the competitive pressures had eased enough to permit consideration of some postponement of these high priority capital outlays in the interest of balanced funds flows and a tidier balance sheet.

The categories of outflows that came in for careful control as a balancing mechanism in funds flows over this period were those that have been described as scale-related and value(time)-related. The scale-related expenditures covered a wide range of expense categories, including payroll, expenditures on marketing, and certain classes of capital expenditures. These kinds of contractions in the flows were typically negotiated once a year, about the end of the first quarter, when the management looked ahead one

or more years and made judgments about the probable overall
need for funds. The reference to such reductions on Exhibit 6C
is intended to indicate the timing of the decisions rather than the
timing of the cuts themselves, which generally took place over the
entire year. The restoration of the cuts in 1963 and 1964 sig-
nified a gradual creeping upward of these expenditures after the
company had reached the limit of pulling in the expenditure
horizon over the preceding four or five years.

Into the remaining category of outflows, referred to as
value(time)-related expenditures, have been put all the expenditures that were basically a trading of dollars over time solely or
primarily in the interests of creating value and did not directly
concern the organizational purposes of the business. Into this
category would go the outlay for ownership of a building when
it can be leased, certain kinds of cost-reducing capital expenditures such as substituting machines for men, and dividend payments. Under the circumstances of Company E at this time these
expenditures appeared relatively vulnerable. It is an overstatement to suggest that dividend payments were entirely at management's discretion. Loan agreements restricted dividend payments
under the circumstances in which the company found itself.
However, these covenants could have been modified through negotiation if high enough priority had been assigned to them. In
fact there was no evidence that management was prepared to pay
a price to maintain common dividends. Greater efforts were exerted to continue the preferred dividend as long as possible and
to resume it before earnings really warranted it.

It may seem contradictory to assert on the one hand that the
company was engaged in a major effort to become more competitive and profitable and on the other that it was prepared to
sacrifice expenditures that were "merely" designed to increase
value, such as certain substitutions of machine for labor cost.
The decisions made in this category were in fact judgments reflecting management's priorities in the face of sharp limitations
on available capital. Certain expenditures were regarded as critical to the basic corporate objectives. Other outlays, however attractive their return on investment, did not fall in this category.
Postponement was considered to be merely putting off inflows

from the present to the future. Dividend payments could be regarded as merely a matter of the timing of adjustments in the debt-equity mix and this too could be regarded as highly postponable.

For the concept of the overall strategy of mobility, adjustments in the outflows to scale-related and value-related expenditures must be paired with the company's approach to external sources of long-term capital. In Company E it was considered an essential prerequisite to an approach to long-term debt sources that there be clear evidence of need after strenuous efforts to squeeze out all available capital from internal sources. This meant close scrutiny of operating and capital budgets. Only then could the management go to the lender with a clear conscience and defend the estimates of funds requirements and the capacity to repay.

As the narrative indicates, the approach to the lenders was slow and uncertain and in the end very costly. However, at that point the remaining alternatives were few and even more uncertain and costly, at least to management. When eventually the funds were forthcoming by a combination of debt and equity, there followed a period of one to two years of relaxation of funds flow pressures while the capital so raised was gradually absorbed into investment. Then the internal pressures on the established structure of flows began to build up again. Unfortunately, by this time the expenditure horizon on many scale-related outflows had been so shortened by years of tight budgets that the room for mobility was greatly reduced. The result was pressures in other directions.

The remaining resource of mobility, which has not been discussed yet and which played a major part in the sequence of events, was the opportunity to share the capital outlay on certain major investment needs. These arrangements were primarily in the area of raw material sources, where a substantial investment was required in order to assure a long-term source of cheap raw materials. For the company to finance these sources itself, on top of the other investments considered vital, would have been an impossible burden at this time. Fortunately other companies in the same industry were in similar strained circumstances and the idea of a shared investment in the sources was appealing to several companies at about the same time. Therefore, Company E was able to make the series of arrangements during this period previously described.

Much lower on the priority list was the opportunity to share the investment by merging the total operation with another large producer. Since the timing of the opportunity was obviously only partially subject to the initiative of Company E, merger as a part of a general strategy of mobility had very limited usefulness. Of course, if successful it was one of very few alternatives offering the prospect of sudden and complete relief from cash flow pressures. However, the price was likely to be very high in terms of possible loss of control and loss of value. Consequently merger tended to be placed in the "last resort" category of alternatives beyond the range of normal action. On occasion, when pressures got severe, the company edged up to consideration of this way out, but it backed away again as the real cost became apparent and other alternatives remained.

Another low priority resource was the option of financing one investment by liquidating another. This was in fact an alternative frequently under consideration but rarely acted upon. During the period in question there were three instances of proposed withdrawal of investment brought on in large part by the pressures on funds flows. In one instance a product line was dropped with the explanation that it had become unprofitable because of foreign competition. Thus the evidence is unclear as to the extent to which short-term cash pressures influenced the decision.

In the other two instances — the sale of a profitable subsidiary and the abandonment of a line of products with a heavy inventory commitment — the reasons for consideration were clearly cash-related. Here again there is a problem of uncertainty over timing, especially regarding the sale of the subsidiary. However, the real dilemma in which these alternatives placed the company was what management called the "phase in-phase out" problem. This translated into the idea that in order to get cash in this way for new investment opportunities there would inevitably be a short-term discontinuity in sales and earnings which would embarrass management in those quarters or years when the old source of sales dollars was gone and the new source was not yet developed to its full potential. Sales and earnings targets, typically cast in the form of an unbroken upward trend, would be hard to meet. For this reason liquidation of earning assets, however low the rate of return might be, was not an attractive alternative to management. Nevertheless, financial management continued to eye it as a way out of its cash flow problems.

The final element of strategy to be mentioned is the interaction of the constraints of funds flows with the original pressures that brought funds flows into an unbalanced position, namely the program of updating productive facilities and product mix. Not until the end of the period under study were there indications that financial management might be exerting its influence to slow down these strategic investments in order to restore some financial mobility. The interaction is very difficult to identify. Only by living with the people involved and observing their behavior in decision situations could one sense the extent to which financial management "leaned against" the policy decisions that dictated the rate of investment and the pressure on funds requirements.

All that can be said is that the investment program over these years appeared to have unanimous support at the executive level and that the opportunity to "buy a little mobility" by holding things back was not really available. This, however, is a matter of degree. Certainly the evidence is that when the sales and profits situation began to ease a bit toward the end of the period, the financial people saw a chance to get a little more margin back into the company's reserve position. This suggests the need for some "evidence" before the financial viewpoint could hope to negotiate a little more freedom for itself at the expense of those who wanted to press forward with the investment program, presumably with other ideas as to where corporate mobility should be located.

Part III

Observations of Practice: The
Common Elements of Corporate Behavior

Introduction

It is an inevitable criticism of case histories used as research evidence that, although interesting, they offer no basis for the identification of similar patterns of experience in other companies or for the prediction of behavior by business firms as a whole. While this is true, at least so far as "scientific method" is concerned, the individual case history reveals a major ingredient of decision making that is missing from generalized experience, namely, the constraints imposed by time, place, environment, and human frailty as seen in a specific stream of events and responses to events. Through an effort to capture the full atmosphere of decision making some of the rationale of the decisions made may become more apparent.

There remains, however, the need to look to a broader sample of experience and to try to identify common characteristics of experience suggesting some tentative generalizations about business behavior as a whole. This is the purpose of Part III. These generalizations, drawn from close observation of less than two dozen companies, cannot be said to represent American business as a whole. On the other hand, strong similarities observed in a number of cases within the sample lead to meaningful hypotheses about the phenomenon of financial mobility in general.

The first of these chapters deals with how the companies perceived the future and used the resource of time to minimize uncertainty about future funds requirements. The second chapter deals with the nature of the resources of mobility as seen by the managements concerned. The third chapter deals with the evidence of a strategy of mobility; that is, evidence of a predetermined pattern of response to unexpected change in funds flows related to the timing and sequence of use of resources.

7

Financial Planning and the Unexpected Need for Funds

INTRODUCTION

A good deal of descriptive information is now available on the processes of financial forecasting and planning in business, though in my opinion much of what has been written is more concerned with the visible form of planning than with understanding what is actually being accomplished. The purpose of this chapter is to report on evidence of exploration of the future found in the research sample of companies, with particular reference to the problem of financial mobility.

The reader is referred back to Exhibit 3D, where a hypothetical set of funds inflows and outflows was charted for a four-year period. This is the shape of the future which, if available, would guide financial management in arranging the balance of funds over time.

Presumably the goal of the information search concerning future inflows and outflows is to minimize the uncertainty about their magnitude and timing and to provide the time for an orderly response to future needs. Presumably the less is known about the future, the greater is the chance of an unexpected need arising with little or no time to marshal resources, the greater the burden on resources available without notice, and the greater the hazard to the intended purpose of the expenditure. The goal of a strategy of mobility is to avoid the situation where the essential purposes of the corporation are frustrated for lack of funds, and to do so in a manner to minimize idle or unproductive resources.

THE INCENTIVE TO PLAN

Few if any important financial decisions can be made solely in terms of considerations relating to the moment in time at which the choice is made. Invariably current acts have direct implications for future acts, and future possible acts or events have direct implications for the present. Every investment choice modifies the future pattern of funds flows and changes the investment choices of the future as well as the remaining choices in the present. Every financing decision is related to the next financing decision and alters the options open the next time around. Every evaluation of the options open in the present will be made with an eye to the probable events and circumstances of the future. The interrelatedness of events and acts is a fact of business life, as it is of life in general, and in its broadest sense financial planning is the effort to identify and evaluate the significance of this interrelatedness.

As indicated in the introductory chapter, this research study was designed with the thought that formal financial planning could be used as an objective source of information about business expectations against which events after the fact could be checked. Information on the field sample of companies soon indicated a wide range of practice regarding the extent to which expectations of funds flows were systematically recorded and analyzed. The evidence suggested that several factors might explain this diversity, including the size and maturity of the company, the size of the financial staff, the age and background of the chief financial officer, and the simple fact that careful cash or funds flow forecasting has not been widely practiced for very long. Particularly noteworthy for this study was significant evidence of correlation between the extent of financial planning and the size of the company's financial reserves.

In the process of getting a cross section of companies reflecting a range of need and capacity to respond, a few companies were included which, from public records, appeared to have a history of ample liquid reserves. One of these may be used to illustrate the state of financial planning under such circumstances. This company operates in a very cyclical capital goods industry. It is a well-managed and profitable business with a product line highly regarded by its customers. At the same time its board of directors was characterized as "conservative," as were the current and past presidents, and the goal of the company was stated as "slow but solid" growth. New investment or acquisition representing sudden change was to be avoided.

Both the current and the past president had been with the company through the 1930s. The company had had a long and difficult depression experience lasting up to World War II. The current president had been the company's financial officer prior to promotion, and both he and his predecessor had conservative financial views. This meant a steady ploughback of a substantial portion of earnings and the avoidance of debt obligations. Because of the policy of slow and steady growth this had resulted in a gradual build-up of liquidity so that at the time of this study cash and marketable securities were in excess of 20% of total assets and had been as high as 50% in the post-World War II period.

The effect of this liquidity was to provide a thick layer of insulation against the uncertainties of funds flow variations. Although the extent of the cash reserves had gradually diminished, leading to some vague thinking about the next steps if the reserves were to disappear, the general atmosphere of funds flow control was one of watchful but relaxed supervision. It is interesting to note that this circumstance permitted financial management to turn its attention exclusively to the job of profit maximization on the earning assets. Attention at the time of the study was centered on minimizing labor costs, on pricing policy, and on the cost of the engineering function.

Under these circumstances funds flow or cash planning in any formal sense was almost nonexistent. Management was somewhat apologetic about this, but the facts were that the only formal forecast was a two-month cash forecast for purposes of managing the marketable securities portfolio. Little was being done about keeping channels open to outside sources of funds, though the financial officer did welcome contacts made by commercial banks, which he thought gave him a feel for his "line of credit." Internal controls over flows, particularly flows into inventory, were considered sound, but it was admitted that it was very difficult to exert financial pressures on operating executives when cash was obviously plentiful.

The inference to be drawn from this and other cases where resources were abundant relative to current need is significant, if obvious. It is that an organized concern for the future, which takes the form of an information search, cultivation of alternatives, and development of an explicit or implicit strategy of mobility, develops only when the future represents a serious threat to the balance of funds flows. Financial planning is an organized response to such a threat, designed to maximize and utilize the resource of time. I found that little could be learned about concepts of mobility from companies, such as the one described above, that had not been required by recent experience to deal with the problem. Officers of the company in question could and did make some responses to a "what if" kind of questioning, suggesting the direction if and when cash balances became minimum operating balances; but such thinking had little depth or conviction.

This is not to say that financially strong companies do not do long-range financial forecasting and planning. Many do. Such planning, however, is more concerned with the realization of corporate goals under the most favorable financing terms than it is with the problems of mobility per se. The form of the planning and forecasting bears this out. The need to interrelate current acts and events with future acts and events has much to do with the intimacy of the relationship, depending on whether the relationship is merely based on broad financial policy guidelines or whether it involves a closed and tightly knit system where a change in the position of any one part directly affects every other part.

THE CONCEPT OF A TIME HORIZON

I believe that the substantial gap between financial theory and financial practice is largely explained by the difference in attitude toward the appropriate time horizon. Financial theory assumes a significantly longer time horizon for the data of decision making than most companies use in practice. Further, financial theory views the future as much more continuous than it is in

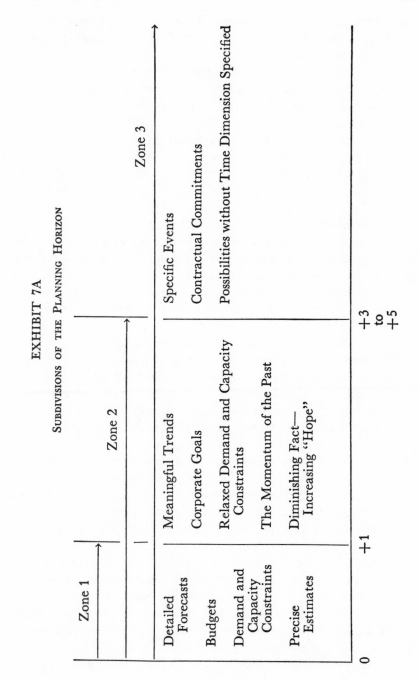

EXHIBIT 7A

SUBDIVISIONS OF THE PLANNING HORIZON

Zone 1

Detailed
  Forecasts

Budgets

Demand and
  Capacity
  Constraints

Precise
  Estimates

Zone 2

Meaningful Trends

Corporate Goals

Relaxed Demand and Capacity
  Constraints

The Momentum of the Past

Diminishing Fact—
  Increasing "Hope"

Zone 3

Specific Events

Contractual Commitments

Possibilities without Time Dimension Specified

0   +1   +3
                                             to
                                             +5

fact. This book suggests that the business horizon may usefully be divided into three zones with significantly different characteristics. These are illustrated in Exhibit 7A.

Zone One is the immediate future, which is almost universally limited for industrial companies to the period one year hence. This is the period with which detailed business planning is largely if not entirely preoccupied. From general economic forecasting right through the lowest level of company budgeting procedures, the horizon is a moving six months to a year, with visibility subject to variation within that period depending on such factors as the timing of seasonality in customer consumption and the conventions of internal budget negotiation.

In general, this is the period for which the company's productive capacity is fixed and the parameters of customer demand relatively predictable because consumption capacity also is fixed within narrow limits. Changes in share of the market are not likely to be large within this period except in those cases where sales are concentrated and loss of a major customer is likely to occur suddenly and without warning.

On the funds outflow side, the conventions of annual operating and capital budgets mean that at least once a year top management will conduct internal negotiations as to how the anticipated operating inflows will be spent. Funds are parcelled out and each expenditure unit agrees to abide by the budgeted figures until the next negotiating time comes around, at which point it is again free to attempt some change in the distribution of funds flows for the various corporate purposes. Thus, barring unusual circumstances, behavior on outflows is relatively predictable up to the date of the next annual budget submission. Of course, the predictability depends much on the discipline of the organization and the controls exercised by top management in the interim.

In conformity with these characteristics of business practice, near-term corporate goals are set on an annual basis. Depending on sales forecasts, targets are set for the year in terms of sales volume, profit, return on investment, and earnings per share. These targets then become an overriding short-term preoccupation of management until the corporate year is over and a new set of targets is established. Adding to the importance attached

to the Zone One horizon is the frequent practice of compensating higher levels of management according to how well they perform against the annual goal. Thus management is inclined to live and think one year at a time rather than on the sort of continuum assumed by financial theory. Unquestionably this has great significance for the strategy of mobility in practice.

The second zone of the business time horizon, called Zone Two in Exhibit 7A, is a period of time customarily described as three to five years hence. Here the characteristics of planning are distinctly different from those of Zone One. Having exhausted most of their efforts on the next six months or a year, general business forecasters have little to say about the business cycle profile beyond that period. Certainly business does not make a practice of building a cyclical profile into its "long-term" projections. At the same time the restrictions of capacity on both producer and consumer are substantially relaxed by the end of this period and the possibility of shifts in consumer demand, competitor action, and the company's own ability to respond to new opportunities is greatly increased.

With a greater range of internal options as well as external possibilities, budgeting constraints lose much of their meaning and it is legitimate intracorporate practice for the various corporate groups to propose major reallocations of resources and to promote these vigorously. The specification of corporate goals becomes much less precise for most companies for this period of three to five years. Goals frequently boil down to a dedication to the universal desire for continued growth in sales and earnings, holding or improving share of the market in key areas of endeavor.

In general it may be said that Zone Two is largely perceived in terms of trends rather than specific changes. As time extends beyond a year these trends become increasingly a function of goals rather than of known constraints — of hope rather than of fact. It is not too uncharitable to say that the period of many a long-range forecast (three, five, or ten years) is more a function of the length of the ruler used to extrapolate the past than it is of any specific limit to corporate vision. Long-range forecasts have real meaning only as there is justification for a trend line based on the momentum of the past — in customer behavior,

market position, productive capability, technology; and the precise time horizon of Zone Two should be set by a realistic assessment of how far ahead this momentum has a substantial influence on funds flows. In fact the point in time when the constraints of the present cease to dominate expectations for the future may be subject to considerable uncertainty, and it undoubtedly varies from one factor to another. As a consequence the five- or ten-year horizon commonly associated with long-range business forecasting may be misleading if taken literally. Unquestionably it should vary from one industry to another and possibly from one company to another.

The last zone into which the time horizon is subdivided, Zone Three, is that period stretching indefinitely into the future beyond the range of significant trend data for the company. Some things are known about this period, deriving primarily from contractual commitments made in the past. There are some vague expectations as to where the industry and the company may be at that time. However, information about this period, to the extent that it exists, is likely to be in terms of possible events without a specific time dimension and with probably only a general notion of financial magnitude. Thus, for example, the loss of a major customer and the development of a new product by a competitor are events that are recognized as well within the realm of possibility, but there is little usable knowledge as to when they might occur or what the impact on funds flows would be.

It will be noted in Exhibit 7A that the arrows indicating the three zones into which the time horizon has been divided all begin at time zero and therefore overlap each other. The characteristics of the zones are not mutually exclusive and they do in fact interrelate. Thus the random events or contractual commitments characterizing Zone Three are also present in Zones One and Two. Similarly the trend considerations dominating thinking about Zone Two are also present in Zone One.

One of the key questions in getting a good descriptive "model" of the practice of financial mobility is: What is the operational horizon of the strategy? The foregoing breakdown of the shape of the future for the average business firm into three rather different zones can be helpful in trying to answer this question.

It will also be helpful to look at the formal procedures of planning in common use for additional insights on mobility. This is the subject of the next section.

THE EXPECTED NEED FOR FUNDS

It is now general practice for the managements of business firms to go through the periodic ritual of committing to paper their best guess as to what the future holds financially. Of course, companies can and do get along without formal forecasting and financial planning. On the other hand, even in repetitive businesses, willing to take life as it comes and be guided by the order schedule, some lead time is required for the accumulation of funds against seasonal or random peaking of funds requirements. The exception is the company with so much cash or short-term borrowing power that variation in the funds requirements can be ignored. For such companies forecasting is largely an exercise in satisfying curiosity.

For the large majority of companies there is constant change (partly environmental — partly self-induced) combined with limited instant reserves, so that the impact of change must be anticipated so far as possible. Further, most companies of any size have a major problem of coordinating and communicating expectations, which the formal forecasting and planning procedures serve to accomplish. Financial planning commonly serves several purposes. It is instructive to try to identify these purposes.

(1) To anticipate the economic and financial environment within which the business will operate during the planning period and to identify the magnitude and timing of significant deficits in funds flows.

(2) To translate corporate goals into specific financial objectives for the planning period and gain a group commitment to the achievement of these objectives.

(3) To motivate management in the pursuit of specific financial objectives, to measure performance in this direction, and to control funds management so as to be consistent with these guidelines.

(4) To coordinate the entire corporate entity with respect to plans for the future, a process that involves communication,

negotiation, integration. Finance serves the unique role as
the common denominator of planning.

It is apparent that the practice of financial planning, for
the short or long range, is much more than predicting events
of financial consequence and taking steps to deal with an
anticipated imbalance in funds flows. To enlarge on the implications of the several considerations listed above we can undertake
a brief review of the typical routines involved in producing a
one-year financial plan. Every financial forecast begins with a
sales forecast. The data of the sales forecast generally come from
the salesmen, although more or less independent market research
groups may serve as a check on the estimates of the sales organization. This sales estimate is a composite of expectations about
the industry and competitive environment over the next year,
the plans of the sales force for operating in that environment,
and the expectations of the degree of success it will have. The
estimate is likely to be a single number or "best guess" of sales
volume, which at some point, possibly after some negotiation up
or down, will be accepted by top management. It then becomes
the basis for all further financial planning.

The sales forecast as an objective judgment of the trend of
future events is influenced and modified by the knowledge that
this number becomes the means by which the sales force will be
motivated to greater effort, the yardstick by which actual sales
performance will be measured and praise or blame meted out,
and ultimately the cornerstone of detailed corporate plans for
the year. The number is inevitably an indistinguishable blend of
what management expects and what it plans to do.

The sales forecast then forms the basis of a plan of expenditure designed to achieve this sales volume as profitably as possible. Initial estimates made on a sector-by-sector basis must be
assembled and fitted together into a picture of the whole. These
estimates are in due course refined into operating and capital
budgets with the sanction of top management. Such budgets
become the official rules of the "spending game" until they are
redrafted at the next budget period. Because the freedom of
action of responsible executives in the various areas is so dependent on control over corporate purchasing power, the nego-

tiation of budgets becomes a critical phase of planning in the subsectors of the corporate entity. This negotiation will be easy or difficult depending on whether major shifts in the balance of spending power are being proposed and whether the company is anticipating difficulty in achieving its profit goals during the period in question. Where negotiation is difficult, there is a natural tendency to hold rather rigidly to the planned expenditures during the budget period and to institute careful controls to this end.

Because in the larger business unit the preparation of a financial forecast and plan, together with the related budgets, is time consuming and at times difficult, involving considerable effort on the part of top management, there is good reason not to repeat the process more often than necessary. Once a year appears often enough to most managements. Provided there is no drastic change in the game itself during the year, the rules are unlikely to be changed. The forecast can of course be updated and there is a frequent practice of moving the one-year forecast ahead quarter by quarter or month by month — dropping one month and adding another. This procedure may not be significant, however, for those industries where the future changes considerably from time to time because of seasonal or other factors.

So far we have been talking about the "expected need" for funds in terms of the one-year forecast (Zone One in our time horizon diagram). What is the nature of the expected need in the conventional five- or ten-year industrial forecast (Zone Two)? Observation of these forecasts for the companies involved in the study plus other companies to which I have been exposed suggests some significant differences from the Zone One forecast.

Let us assume a long-range forecast made by a medium-sized, aggressive, well-managed company, typical of the best of its kind. This ten-year forecast, represented by a fat volume of back-up data, took months to assemble. It works carefully from external forecasts of Gross National Product and industrial production, through customer forecasts of demand, to a company sales forecast taking account of such issues as share of market trends and possible loss of major customers. The forecast was prepared against the background of an explicit statement of corporate goals in terms of growth in equity value and the related corporate growth objectives.

A careful reading of this document, plus knowledge of management attitudes related to it, would indicate the following objectives behind its preparation:

(1) To communicate long-term corporate goals in explicit financial equivalents.

(2) To stimulate management thinking about the long-term implications of current policies and activities.

(3) To stimulate thinking about what needs to be done to achieve corporate growth objectives.

(4) To explore the broad funds implications of a chosen strategy or alternative strategies; e.g., foreign expansion or domestic acquisitions.

Only the last of these can be regarded as a purely financial purpose of the planning. The main purpose is to communicate and to coordinate general management via the common language of finance. The two major inputs of information, which form the basis of the "expected" financial need, are the corporate goals and the trend lines of the immediate past. This is illustrated by the accompanying graph (Exhibit 7B), which portrays an actual ten-year sales projection by one company. This was characterized by the company as its "realistic" forecast (in contrast to an "optimistic" and a "pessimistic" alternative) and is dominated by a target growth rate that the company takes very seriously.

It is important to emphasize how this type of forecast differs from the Zone One or short-term forecast previously described. The long-range forecast is obviously much more generalized and deals with broad aggregate estimates. It is a continuous line over the period in question but really does not purport to say exactly where the company will be at specific points along the line. It is primarily interested in evaluating the end position five or ten years hence. It is not designed to set specific operating targets by specified dates and is not normally used as a yardstick for evaluating or compensating management. Finally, the Zone Two forecast does not have the related budgetary controls on expenditure that are a characteristic of the Zone One forecast. It is, rather, a planning device pure and simple.

EXHIBIT 7B

A Ten-Year Sales Forecast

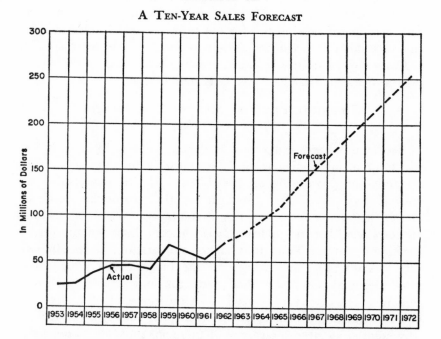

The financial implications of the Zone Two forecast and plan are relatively simple and obvious. Estimates of the trend of profit indicate what funds are going to be available internally. If approximations of plant, working capital, and other expenditures called for by corporate plans and expectations exceed internal generation, then there is an expected deficit of funds to be provided for externally by an approximate date. Plans must be laid as to the source of funds. Alternatively, the growth rate would have to be slowed down to be consistent with available funds. Of course, everyone realizes that in fact sales, profits, and fund requirements will not follow a smooth trend and the forecast is useful only in indicating a possible need, as yet undefined. Precise negotiations for external sources are normally left to within six months to a year of a well defined need.

It is hardly necessary to say that there is no such thing as an expected funds requirement for the Zone Three time period. Information about Zone Three is completely fragmentary and there is no basis except pure aspiration upon which to hang an integrated and comprehensive funds flow analysis as business now performs that task. There are too many unknowns and too wide a range of possibilities for the business practitioner to take any such forecast seriously. Indeed, even five-year forecasts are at times viewed lightly by businessmen accustomed to the sharp swings of events that have marked their careers.

FINANCIAL PLANNING AND THE UNEXPECTED NEED FOR FUNDS

The actual funds surpluses or deficits month by month for which financial management is responsible are the net result of many forces working on funds flows. If this net result was entirely foreseeable, then financial mobility would be merely a matter of spacing the maturities of company investments so that outflows would match inflows. It is the complexity of the forces working on funds flows that makes the attempt at prediction very difficult. The one thing that the businessman knows "for sure" about his forecast is that prediction and actuality will not coincide. The unexpected need is an obvious fact of life in the business world and this, as has been asserted before, is the reason why companies need a strategy of financial mobility. The question raised in this section is: Since it is known that forecasts and plans are likely to be in error, does formal financial planning attempt to take account of the unexpected need? If it does, how does it relate expected and unexpected needs for planning purposes?

Perhaps the first point to be made in this connection is that in most companies the actual amounts of funds flows in any given period are never accurately known until the period is past. The uncertainty in the near future derives primarily from the flow of funds into and out of the several elements of working capital. With collections from customers subject to uncertainty, especially if some large accounts are involved, and with spending power for day-to-day operations dispersed and flexible so as to promote operating efficiency, the net result remains in doubt until after the fact. This means of course that Zone One forecasting, even for the few weeks that lie ahead, contains considerable chance of the unexpected need. Zone Two forecasting is even more uncertain.

Here an illustration is introduced to indicate the problem in more specific terms, but not to suggest the typical state of the art. The company involved manufactures industrial machinery. At the time of the research the company made two types of forecasts — one by quarters, one year ahead, and the other by weeks, four weeks ahead. The problem of the unexpected need can be illustrated by examining the performance of the company's four-week cash forecast. Exhibit 7C shows over a two-year period *differences* between the actual cash balance at the end of any given week and the balance as forecasted one week ahead, two weeks ahead, three weeks ahead, and four weeks ahead. Over this period the actual balances varied between $1.5 million and $3.0 million.

Certain conclusions are evident from the charts. Perhaps the most significant is that, even with only seven days to go, the forecast frequently had substantial errors as, for example, for the week of August 3, 1963, when the balance as forecasted one week ahead was $1.9 million and the actual proved to be $2.8 million. Other conclusions are that the magnitude of the errors both over and under the estimates appeared to increase as the time gap increased and that over the two-year period forecasting appeared to improve somewhat. A somewhat less reliable observation is that there appeared to be a pessimistic bias to the forecast, which was more often under than over the actual results.

The major point to be made here, however, is that in this company substantial uncertainty persisted over the entire forecasting horizon. Another way of illustrating the same data is given in Exhibit 7D, which shows graphs of successive four-week cash forecasts plotted against the actual cash balances for a twenty-week period. This graph gives a better picture than the previous exhibit of how successive "shots" at the target value moved toward, away from, or randomly around the actual value. Those engaged in cash forecasting could not draw much comfort from this kind of experience.

In this company major causes of forecast error in the short-term cash forecast were matters of timing — of receivables, payables, and on occasion capital expenditures. In the collections area alone the error could be as much as 50% to 60% of the

EXHIBIT 7C

AN ILLUSTRATION OF SHORT-TERM CASH FORECASTING ERRORS
(in millions of dollars)

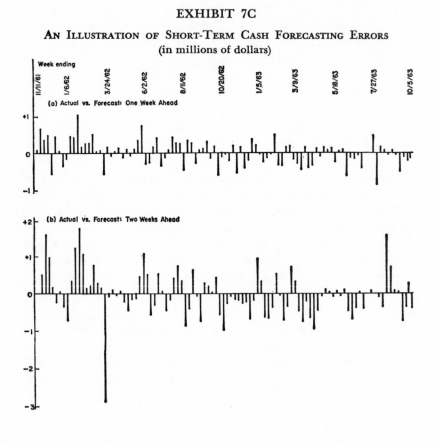

EXHIBIT 7C (continued)

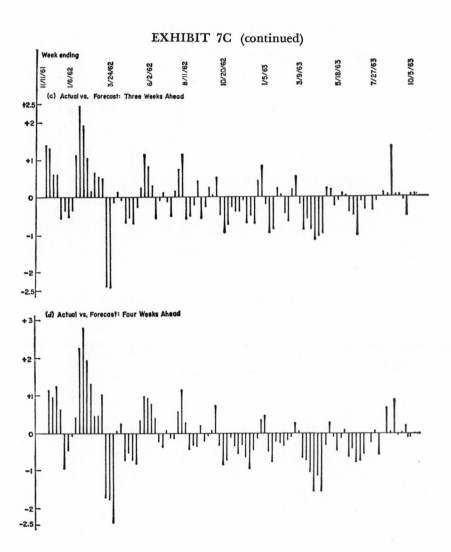

EXHIBIT 7D

ILLUSTRATION OF PROGRESSIVE MODIFICATIONS IN A FOUR-WEEK CASH FORECAST

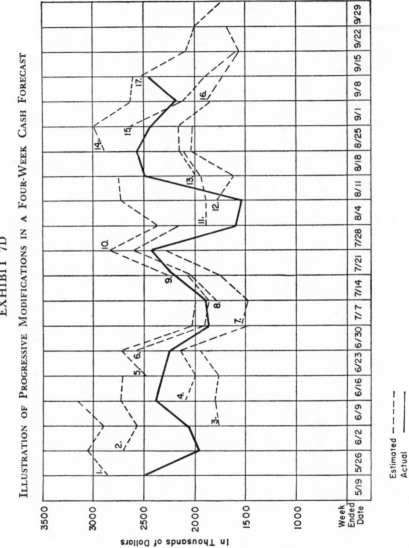

Estimated – – – –
Actual ——————

amount involved. Obviously this kind of error would not occur in a company where receivables were widely dispersed over a large number of customers. It is also apparent that errors in forecasting payables resulted to some extent from the lack of tightness of control over the timing of payments. Thus circumstances and behavior had much to do with the problem of short-term uncertainty.

It is of interest to note that the financial officer in this company used the cash forecast (1) to identify possible shifts in the cash balance "of a substantial nature" and (2) to keep himself "informed." Presumably the difference between (1) and (2) related to the question of whether overt action was called for in the event of a major deficit of cash. It is also interesting that the financial officer appeared unconcerned about the serious errors in forecasting. This casual attitude appeared to follow from confidence that the company's instant reserves other than cash were equal to any "normal" deviation in the balance and "major" sharp deviations — deficits — would be the result of events or acts known far enough in advance for adequate response.

It is not our purpose at this point to consider the response to the unexpected need, but merely to illustrate the nature of the problem. Similar problems existed in the company's one-year forecast of balance sheets and income statements, quarter by quarter. The immediate question is how such companies modify their formal procedures of "search" respecting the financial future, living as they do with the knowledge that these kinds of errors are a continuing fact of life.

As to the Zone One type of forecast, it seems a fair generalization to say that the usual response to uncertainty about future funds requirements is to keep repeating the forecasting exercise over and over in the general belief that as the date gets closer the forecast becomes more accurate. So each quarter a new four-quarter forecast is produced, which predicts the precise values for each item on the company's balance sheet and income statement. The quarter that has become history drops off and a new one is added for a first look at that period one year away. Any new information that has come in over the past three months becomes integrated into the new forecast. The company then has the latest "best guess" or "most probable" value. The adequacy of this way of dealing with information about an uncertain future in regard to a strategy of mobility must be judged in the light of a goal of maximizing the time and the capacity for response to a defined need.

The problem of uncertainty about the future is also recognized in the methodology of forecasting in quite a different way in some Zone Two, or long-range, forecasts. The reader is referred back to Exhibit 7B, illustrating a ten-year sales projection. This was characterized as the company's "realistic" projection. Recognizing the great uncertainties about events 10 years out, the company took two additional formal steps. One was to develop additional projections based on an "optimistic" and a "pessimistic" trend line, a very common practice. These presumably defined the boundaries of expected sales and profit performance. The other step — a less frequent practice — was to superimpose on the trend a cyclical fluctuation with a uniform period and amplitude. The company had no basis for the timing of alternating periods of recession and prosperity and did not pretend it had. The purpose was rather to give explicit recognition to the cycle as a fact of life and to test out its impact on sales and profits.

Thus even within the same company there often appears to be a sharp distinction between the one-year and the five-year or ten-year forecast. The former appears to treat the future as a certainty and the latter explicitly if rather vaguely recognizes substantial uncertainty. The rational observer would say that this is an unrealistic distinction and that uncertainty is always a matter of degree and not of kind. In my opinion the difference as it exists is largely the result of the distinctly different purposes behind the two levels of planning. For the purposes of managing and coordinating an ongoing business, a time comes when the future must be taken as a certainty and action initiated as if the predicted events will actually occur. Further, as explained before, there will be a major effort to *make* them occur regardless of unexpected change. The typical Zone One forecast — usually one year out — is such an action document. The inclusion of possible variations from the most probable outcome would be an impediment to decisiveness and action. On the other hand, the Zone Two forecast seems to be largely an exploratory exercise with fewer immediate action implications. Here a consideration of a range of events is more tolerable even though it may come into conflict with corporate goals.

It is worth adding that the various budgetary constraints set up to support the Zone One forecast are part of the effort designed to make the next few months work out as planned. It is usually recognized that if a major change unexpectedly occurs, the budgetary "contracts" may be called off and new ones substituted. So long as this is not done very often, the option to revise budgets in midyear is an important element of preparing for the unexpected need.

There is another important dimension to the manner in which the unexpected need impinges on financial planning. Early in the research on how businesses make use of their resource of time through forecasting and planning, it became apparent that the formal forecast did not contain all the information inputs available to the financial officer. Conversations with financial officers indicated awareness of a number of contingent events of which there was not the slightest hint in the formal funds or cash forecast. Examples of this are a capital expenditure at the discussion stage and a payment for damages resulting from legal action currently before the courts.

In general these contingencies affecting funds flows tended to fall into one of four categories: (1) events of such a nature that public disclosure at the time of the formal forecast even within the company was inadvisable; (2) events with a low probability of occurrence at the time of the forecast; (3) events the probability of which was under substantial disagreement within the management group; (4) events recognized by the forecast for which a substantial range of values had about the same chance of occurrence.

The reason why events of Type (1) do not appear in formal forecasts is self-evident. Events of Type (2) are excluded because the decision to make formal plans for certain expenditures forces management to draw a precise line between "certain" and "uncertain" needs. The forecasting procedure commonly used makes no provision for varying degrees of certainty. Just what level of probability classifies an event for the uncertain and therefore undefined category is never specified. The reason for excluding events of Type (3) — those where probability assessments are in dispute — is that the forecast and plan is a group document, which normally implies group agreement on what expectations must be acted upon. If such agreement cannot be obtained, the event is likely to be excluded unless the financial officer imposes his own judgments on the document. Finally, there is no doubt that though the conventional forecast demands a single "most probable" value for each element of funds flow, when that number leaves the financial planner uncomfortable he will take account of a wider range of values on an informal basis.

To further emphasize a point made above, the formal forecasting and planning procedure, which produces guidance for group action, may be only a partial picture — perhaps even an incorrect one — of the expectations of the person or persons responsible for keeping funds flows in balance. They have their own perception of the future and their own probability assessments, and these in the last analysis are likely to dominate their preparation for the future.

In view of the possibility of substantial differences between the formal and the informal procedures for digesting information about the future, it is apparent that the original intention of this study to use formal written forecasts as an objective document of management expectations was bound to be frustrated. Response and expectation as shown by the formal forecast could not be logically related.

Financial Mobility vs. Financial Planning

Financial mobility was defined earlier in this study as "the capacity to influence the rate of change of economic resources from one form into another and hence to determine the mix of resources at a point in time." Because profit making usually demands a commitment of economic resources to specialized use with restrictions on and uncertainties about the event of withdrawal from use, and because optimum investment behavior in the future is uncertain, time is a critical element in any strategy of mobility. Ideally, changing needs should be identified in sufficient time to permit an orderly transfer of resources to new uses without loss of their revenue potential.

The principal obstacle to achievement of this ideal is the unexpected event. The word "unexpected" has been recognized as relative in nature, with few events of such suddenness that payment is demanded the instant the need is identified. Some reaction time is usually available. The goal is to make the available reaction time as long as possible so that the widest range of alternative responses — sources of mobility — is open to management. In order to facilitate a strategy of financial mobility and make the most of the resource of time the following steps would be necessary.

(1) For that future period for which precise forecasting is meaningful, develop a funds flow projection for the most probable combination of external events and internal responses.
(2) Develop an "early warning" information network to identify possible causes of deviation from projected flows (unexpected events), to assess their impact on funds flows, and to maintain an up-to-date estimate of probability of occurrence.

This section will attempt to evaluate the relevance of current practice in forecasting and planning for these two prerequisites of a strategy of financial mobility. As the title of the section suggests, the current practice of financial planning in many respects works against the needs of mobility.

It can be argued that the principal goal of modern financial forecasting is precisely step number one above. However, the circumstances under which formal forecasting and planning take place contaminate the results for the purposes of mobility. For mobility it is desirable that the forecast be as objective as possible in estimating the company's position X periods hence. But in fact the formal forecast as a part of a plan for group action in the immediate future is strongly influenced by the goals management sets for itself and by efforts to motivate people to achieve these goals. Since the forecast is made up by those whom management seeks to motivate and to measure, an awareness of this inevitably creeps back into the estimates and makes a clear distinction between objective judgment and subjective response impossible. One is left with the question: Is the formal forecast a measure of what is likely to be achieved, or what top management would like to be achieved, or what operating personnel are willing to accept as achievable during the period?

Another concern respecting the usefulness of the formal forecast for purposes of mobility relates to the meaning of the phrase "most probable" used in describing step number one above. It will be generally agreed that a single number forecast of cash position one year from now is a number that describes the most probable or most likely cash position at that time — the best guess. But whose best guess? The forecast will be a group document with many people involved in generating the numbers. Inevitably there will be differences of opinion on the "most probable" sales level, for example. Such differences can only be resolved by one judgment overriding another or by some compromise value in between two or more estimates. The process by which such differences are resolved is important to the interpretation of the final number, but invariably the process is unspecified and frequently haphazard.

So far, then, formal forecasting does not appear well suited to the purpose we have in mind. However, a second look at the process as it actually takes place suggests that the results are more useful than they might appear at first sight. A forecast may be considered to have three key elements: (a) an estimate of the economic and competitive environment within which the company will operate, (b) an estimate of how the company will respond to that environment, (c) an estimate of the probable success of that response. What we see in the formal planning procedure is the interaction of (a) and (b) going on simultaneously. As the forecasters are looking at the future, they are formulating plans of how to deal with it. Further, in the setting of specific targets and the rewards and penalties associated with them, top management is expressing a judgment as to what is attainable. In accepting these targets, divisional managers are conceding that the probability of reaching the targets is high enough for them to be willing to stake their compensation and reputation on achieving the forecast.

The "most probable" value also has meaning. Normally the financial officer will be deeply and continuously involved in the forecasting and planning procedure and will be aware of where the numbers came from, who made the "best guess," and whether any major compromise values were involved. It is standard procedure for budget people to "second guess" their internal sources of information. Years of working with the same people develop knowledge of how individuals estimate and whether they tend to have an optimistic or a pessimistic bias. This knowledge of how the system works and of the people who make up the numbers comes only from experience. It is a vital element in the interpretation of the estimated values.

Thus a case can be made that as a practical matter a well organized forecasting and planning procedure—carefully interpreted by those intimately familiar with how and by whom it has been developed — can be a reasonable first step in developing a strategy of financial mobility. The great problem arises in taking the second step: in dealing with the unexpected events or the variations from the "most probable" outcome. Here formal group procedures of forecasting and planning seem to break down. Indeed, it would seem as though planning and mobility designed to deal with the unexpected are mutually exclusive concepts.

As it commonly works, a group-sanctioned forecast of sales and net earnings is taken as a "certainty" for purposes of planning and coordinating group action during the forecast period. Because this now becomes the corporate goal every effort is directed toward making the forecast come true, even to the extent of adjusting the books a little at year-end by pulling in some revenues from or pushing out some expenditures to the next period. Many a financial officer, with or without the knowledge of his president, keeps a few cents of discretionary earnings per share tucked away out of sight for the year when goals are hard to attain. So long as the forecast and plan are in effect, it approaches disloyalty to suggest that the plan will not be achieved. If actual results fall short, then the new forecast and plan will start from a realistic evaluation of the ending position of the old planning period and proceed to develop a new objective, which once again is taken as "certain."

In this atmosphere it is difficult if not impossible to build answers to "what if" kinds of questions into the formal group forecasting procedures. To identify the possible deviations from the most probable ("certain") outcome and to develop formal contingency plans for dealing with them signals uncertainty, distracts attention from the stated goals, and erodes the drive to achieve or surpass those goals. It is almost as if the person involved in action respecting the future must for decision-making purposes take the future as "known," and only the observer of action can afford the luxury of dealing in probabilities.

On the other hand, any realist knows that things may not work out as planned, and he will be doing some thinking about his course of action in that event. Thus the practical effect of the conflict suggested above is to force contingency planning "underground" — to make it informal rather than formal, individual rather than group. Step number two for facilitating a strategy of mobility — identifying possible causes of deviation from the expected value, assessing funds flow implications, and estimating the chances of occurrence — clearly goes on, but in the main it goes on in the mind of the man responsible for balancing funds flows and not on paper. What goes on paper appears to be those events that management consensus says have a "high" probability of occurrence.

The one observed practice approaching formal contingency planning was testing variations in some long-range planning. However, these tests were more concerned with magnitudes than with timing and more associated with achievement of financial goals than development of alternative financial strategies. In general it may be said that the formal planning process serves the very important role of getting certain group expectations and probable responses out into the open. These important pieces of information improve the capacity of informal planning to meet contingencies as they arise.

It is worth noting that one of the likely effects of leaving contingencies out of the formal planning system is to fragment the strategy of mobility. Throughout the organization there will be bits of planning going on which are not likely to be communicated well, if they are communicated at all, and not likely to be coordinated. Certainly the observed informal contingency planning in the financial area was related to similar planning in production or marketing only to the extent that the financial officer guessed how his colleagues would respond under certain circumstances.

It is also observed that the informal planning with respect to variations from expected funds flows was largely if not entirely confined to the time horizon of one year. This may be due in part to the fact that specific and detailed corporate planning is usually confined to one year out and the shape of the future in a total funds flow sense beyond that point becomes very vague. As a consequence, specific thinking about alternatives does not have much meaning. The time limit on contingency planning may also relate to the fact that formal negotiations on funds flows, internal or external, are not normally initiated more than a year ahead of the specific need. To repeat a statement made earlier, there is a distinct break in the planning horizon of most industrial companies at the six-months-to-one-year mark and this has a great deal to do with how management thinks about and plans for the future.

As one looks at a potential strategy of mobility in terms of the resource of time, there appear to be limiting considerations at both ends of the time span. At the far end (the Zone Three end) there is a serious lack of information around which to build an adequate expectation of funds flows and possible deviations therefrom. In the immediate future serious limits are imposed by the need to be committed to a chosen course of action regardless of doubts. In other words, at the far end of the time span there is much potential mobility but little information. At the near end there may be much information but little mobility. A strategy of mobility must operate within these facts of life.

8

A Review of Corporate Behavior: The Unexpected Need and the Resources of Mobility

INTRODUCTION

The three chapters in Part II described in considerable detail the pattern of response to changing funds flows in three companies. The purpose was to give some feel for the day-to-day environment of decision making in a specific business organism at a specific period in its history. The chapters do this very imperfectly. It is hoped, however, that the reader can recognize the evidence of dynamic uncertainty and the sequential nature of the decision-making process, in which actions taken in the past and the perception of actions and events in the future condition the response in the present.

The next two chapters are an attempt to generalize about behavior as observed in the 15 companies that I studied in detail during the three-year period over which I pursued the research. This sample of observation is not presented as necessarily representative in any precise statistical sense. At the same time I know of no major characteristic that would lead to the conclusion that the sample of companies is atypical. Under these circumstances the observations are presented as a basis for generating hypotheses of behavior in the total business population rather than as a test or validation of hypotheses.

There are four major subdivisions to the two chapters taken as a whole. The first deals with the nature of the unexpected need for funds as perceived by financial management. Here the characteristics are explored in order to identify implications for the response to these events. The second section deals with the resources of mobility as perceived by management — the way in which these were identified, measured, and deployed. The third section describes the evidence of "strategy," the ways in which the people involved responded to variations in funds flows over time, always aware of the undefined need just beyond the planning horizon. The fourth and final section deals with the evidence of interaction between the ongoing responses of financial mobility and the set of financial policies representing guidelines toward long-range financial goals.

The Nature of the Need for Funds

Among the research sample of companies the source of pressure on the balance of funds flows varied considerably, as one might expect. The situation is always to some extent unique for each company and industry. On the other hand, it is possible to classify the immediate events confronting these companies at the time of the study according to the basic impact on the pattern of funds inflow and outflow. The following breakdown has been found useful:

(1) The isolated and apparently random event causing a sudden change in inflows or outflows of definable limits in magnitude and duration — a strike, a model change-over, a damage suit, a fire, an unplanned expenditure decision, death or withdrawal of a major stockholder.

(2) The interrelated and at times cumulative changes in the volume of sales and operations deriving from changes in a company's demand environment — fluctuations *around a trend line*. These changes have rough boundaries in magnitude and duration related to the economics of the industry but the precise effects at any point of time are uncertain. The degree of uncertainty is itself subject to change. These changes are typically summed up as the business cycle but are likely to be a combination of change in industry demand and competitive position. The investment implications are largely confined to working capital needs.

(3) A basic change (increase) in the required scale of expenditures, either because the business has moved to a higher trend line of sales and operations or because a higher level of ex-

penditures is demanded to maintain the existing trend line.
The best examples of the latter situation are two companies
in the study which, because of a major change in production
technology, had to make major commitments to new plant in
order to stay competitive. The new conditions demanded that
they grow substantially in scale of operations, and the first
step was a much heavier investment per dollar of sales based
on the hope that growth in sales would follow.

(4) Belated recognition of a seriously deficient competitive position, which now demands major strategic outlays in order to
restore the desired profitability and growth.

It is significant to note that these four basic causes of pressure
on funds flows have differing dimensions of uncertainty. In
general, the first category, the random adversity, has the characteristic of happening with little or no warning but, once it has
been identified, its magnitude and timing are known within
reasonable limits. It is possible that the financial demands of
one of these random events would be overwhelming and pre-
cipitate cash bankruptcy. In the companies in the study these
events were more in the nature of temporary embarrassments
and not seriously threatening in and of themselves. If in fact
the event was essentially unpredictable, it was not regarded as
a reflection on managerial competence. This, coupled with the
limited nature of the need, had much to do with the willingness
of others to help the financial officer over a rough spot.

The second category, the continuous fluctuations of sales
volume around a trend line, is by contrast an ever-present fact of
life in business but, despite keen awareness of its existence, a fact
that is very difficult to translate into its funds flow implications.
For the companies in this study the effective planning horizon for
investment decisions in support of sales volume (working capital
requirements) was at most a year and often six months or less.
This has major implications for the strategy of financial mobility.
It is also true, however, that a cumulative reinforcement of
evidence supporting a certain direction for sales (up or down)
could lead to a lengthening of the planning horizon — at the
increased risk of misjudging a turning point. All company
officers stressed their limitations in forecasting the turning point
and the resulting tendency to keep the horizon of plan and

action short. Thus, although the events were obviously sequential in nature, the companies tended to treat them in discrete time segments.

Longer time horizons for planning and action are inherent in the third and fourth categories of events. Some might question the inclusion of these events in a listing of "unexpected" needs for funds since they tend to be more knowable and to come about more gradually. However, "unexpected" is a relative term, and for practical purposes it must be defined as applying to a need that has not been fully anticipated by any given financial plan. What these events lack in sudden surprise they make up for in magnitude and duration of impact. There is no doubt that in this sample of companies the categories three and four represented the most serious challenge to the skills of financial mobility.

Take category three, the need to increase the scale of expenditures in support of a given level of sales volume. This could come as a need to step up marketing expenditures, to increase research and product development, or to make drastic changes in productive facilities. Once the need is recognized, these new outflows can be expected to continue for some time and indeed may be open-ended until evidence of the results in improved sales performance, new products, or lower costs can be observed. Obviously the response of the financial strategist to the need, once identified, will be different from the response in the first two categories. A longer time horizon may permit some choice, some room for difference of opinion, as to the rate of response. Clearly the nature of the response is influenced by the knowledge that further response without apparent limit will be needed.

In the case of Company E in Chapter 6 the reader may recall the "Plan for Profitability," a five-year plan and a program of heavy expenditure to overcome the effects of change in production technology. Once a course of action was defined by management, the need became known to the financial officer and its cash flow implications for several years were spelled out. What was not known was how effective the program would be and when the effects would be felt. At times the demand for capital expenditures appeared to be a bottomless pit.

In the first three categories of need the company in question may be in a basically strong competitive position with good internal generation of funds and on a strong growth trend. The fourth category separates out those companies with serious competitive problems as evidenced by such indications as sales trend, share of market, declining profits. Six of the 15 companies in the sample studied could be readily classified as having serious competitive weakness to which the company was at least partially alerted during the period under examination. The problem of an effective strategy of mobility under these circumstances was substantially different from the problems in the first three categories. The alternatives were not the same. A position of competitive weakness tends to increase the pressures to spend and reduces the ability to defer.

These categories of pressure on funds flows were not mutually exclusive and in fact tended to overlap during any given planning horizon. Cyclical fluctuations were complicated by random events simultaneously with a shift in the scale of expenditures or a weakening of competitive position. In fact, the sample included two companies where all four pressures existed at once. This raises the question as to whether the various forms of financial adversity are in any degree correlated. In general, management appeared to believe and behave as if they were not; it tended to face and solve problems one at a time.

An argument can be made, however, that some of the so-called random events tend to be more likely under conditions of competitive weakness: strikes and model change-overs, for example. Likewise cyclical swings may be more exaggerated under such circumstances. Thus adversity may breed adversity, and vulnerability to a series of financial shocks may increase the likelihood of the series. The only recommendation here, besides the obvious one of avoiding competitive weakness, is to recognize the possibility of correlated adversity in formulating a strategy of mobility and not to blindly assume that, once the current crisis is over, all will be well.

In all these areas of uncertainty there is no doubt of the strong conditioning effect of past experience. If our understanding of financial decision making is to make any headway, it must be seen not as a series of isolated rational choices but rather as a continuum in which each decision is conditioned by what has gone before and by what is expected to come after. One cannot break in on this stream of choices and have an adequate understanding of the choice made today without looking at the choices made yesterday and the day before and the manner in which experience appeared to validate or question those decisions. The "track record" of decisions and the decision maker are highly relevant.

Along the same lines, the reader is reminded that this book adopts the view that financial resources (alternatives) for any given company over any normal planning horizon are finite; they can be exhausted. The standard argument that funds are always available "at a price" ignores the fact that there are distinct limits on the price that can and will be paid. The limitation on resources is only partly a question of how recently the same resource was used and what the experience was. There is a strong precedent against going back to the same well — external or internal — too often, and particularly so if there were problems associated with the most recent trip.

In contrast, the rational view of this sequential decision making would tend to accentuate the constraints imposed by the current choice on future choices. Reason says that, by definition, the past is beyond influence and attention should focus on the choices yet to be made. One can characterize the contrast between the so-called rational perception of time and the one observed to exist in practice as follows:

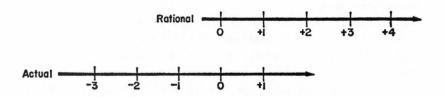

This contrast relates both to the differing emphasis on the constraints from the past and to the observed limitations on management's effective planning horizon.

When managements discussed the kinds of events that gave rise to unexpected needs for funds, it was apparent not only that the causes of uncertainty differed from situation to situation but also that there were marked differences in what may be called the "climate of uncertainty." Although the following observations are highly subjective, they may be useful. Of the three companies that appeared to be at the comfortable end of the scale of the climate of uncertainty, the common underlying characteristic was a firm competitive lead in their industry deriving from technology, product leadership, efficiency, and market dominance. This was reflected in profitability, and when it was matched, in varying degrees, with a narrow definition of industry (the range of appropriate investment alternatives) and a conservative payout ratio, the result was a strong or "conservative" financial position, reflected in low or no debt and strong liquidity. It cannot be determined whether the financial peace of mind thus created was a primary goal of top management or a by-product of other policies. It was a fact that in all three companies the chief executive was a man of advanced years whose business experience spanned the difficult period of the 1930s. In two of the companies there was a strong emphasis on quality rather than size or rate of growth. In the third the restrictions on growth within the industry were more a function of indirect governmental restraints on share of the market. In all of these companies there was evidence of awareness that the relaxed financial atmosphere could, and likely would, change with a change of top management.

At the other extreme of the climate of uncertainty — the uncomfortable range — were companies that had been buffeted about for some time by various financial shocks which gave no evidence of letting up, had not given the companies time to catch their financial breath, and had left them with seriously depleted alternatives. Here also, financial circumstances or financial mismanagement were not, per se, the explanation. Rather there was the common characteristic of underlying competitive weakness, which had not been fully corrected. As one might expect, these were the companies with the most explicit strategy of financial mobility, however belated and imperfect it might be.

Under these circumstances it is difficult to evaluate how much of the financial consequences of unexpected events were beyond the control of management and thus attributable to randomness or luck. It is true that characteristics inherent in the industry had something to do with the timing, magnitude, and predictability of financial shocks. For example, the re-equipment problems in one industry were of such a nature that the cash impact could not come any earlier than a year and a half to two years after serious consideration of the re-equipment decision had begun. Again, some industries had notoriously poor leading indicators of demand, so that turning points had been passed for several months before they were clearly recognized.

On the other hand, the evidence of hindsight is strong that events beyond management's control were a less critical factor than poor judgment by management in bringing about uncertainty of funds flows and its attendant problems. This points up a potential dilemma in developing a strategy of mobility: a conservative position and abundant reserves, offering apparent safety, could in the long run be a risky strategy if it denies these resources to investment that would strengthen the company's basic competitive posture. However, it is not investment per se that assures competitive strength, but wise investment. No financial strategy can protect against bad judgment or inefficient management.

THE RESOURCES OF MOBILITY: (1) INSTANT RESERVES

Cash

In the conventional reporting of corporate values the balance sheet is essentially an inventory of assets recorded at historical cost and an inventory of liabilities recorded at contractual repayment values. The residual difference that has accumulated over time between these two sets of values is recorded as owners' net worth. Thus there is one concept of a residual in terms of ownership value defined by accounting conventions. Another kind of residual, which is more immediately relevant to management action, is the accumulation of uncommitted funds (cash) in the possession of the company. This residual results from differences in the rate at which assets are converted into liquid form and are then reconverted into specialized earning assets. The first point to recognize with regard to a cash balance is that at any point in time it is the residual effect following from a wide variety of events and acts concerning the inflows and outflows of funds. Thus, only to the extent that management is in complete control of these events and acts can it hope to have a precisely defined and predetermined cash balance. The facts are that a company is rarely if ever in complete control. The extent of the control of cash balances depends very much on the predictability of external events and internal acts over which the financial officer has no control.

It follows that to the extent that cash balances (cash plus marketable securities) are in fact a residual effect of financial uncertainty, their role as a key element of a strategy for dealing with uncertainty is diminished. Financial officers do not talk in terms of target or optimum cash balances but rather in terms of *minimum* cash balances. In practice, cash balances broadly defined as above are made up of (1) a desired minimum balance as defined by some objective yardstick, (2) specific accumulations toward known large lump-sum payments (e.g., dividends), and (3) transitory residual excesses produced by circumstances. There may, in addition, be deliberate seasonal accumulations to the extent that the company finances seasonal swings in working capital internally. At times, not only the residual excesses but also some of the desired minimum balance may disappear as the company moves to overcome an unexpected excess of outflows over inflows.

The point of interest to us here is the role of the minimum balance and the unplanned residual in the strategy for dealing with uncertainty. By definition the latter component of the cash balance is merely a fact which exists and is known at a point in time and therefore enters into the forward thinking at that point. For example, many companies emerged from the circumstances of World War II with large cash surpluses brought on mainly by profitable performance and restricted investment opportunities during that period. Such balances clearly influenced their posture on financial mobility in the immediate postwar period, and in some cases for a time represented the entire strategic reserve.

It is interesting to observe how financial officers can soon rationalize even large residual reserves in terms of a variety of financial contingencies. One company in my acquaintance had for a period of time 25% of its total assets in cash and market-

able securities. The treasurer of the company had a formal justification of the liquid position, which I have organized into the
format of Exhibit 8A.

EXHIBIT 8A

XYZ Corporation — Form for Analysis of Liquid Balances
(In millions)

Current liquid position — cash plus marketable securities		$46
Less: Frozen balances: cash for day-to-day transactions and compensating balances		10
Usable liquid balances		$36
Less: Current forward commitments not covered by operating revenues		8
Current free balances		$28
Less: Cash for seasonal working capital		6
Contingency balances		$22
Less: Identified contingencies		
(A)	$2	
(B)	8	
(C)	4	14
		$ 8
Add: Bank financing of seasonal needs		6
Liquid assets available without visible risk		$14
Liquid assets available with risk*		$28

* Dependence on external funds or liquidation of earning assets for
contingent needs.

The obvious criticism of this justification is that the probability
of all of the identified contingencies occurring at the same time
was extremely remote. None of the specific identified contingencies had any known correlation to the other demands. One
of those contingencies was an undefined defensive investment in
a recession period. To me the figures presented were essentially a
pure rationalization of a residual cash position that had resulted
over the years from a highly profitable operation in a narrowly
restricted range of investment under conditions where larger
cash distributions to stockholders were undesirable for tax reasons. At the time of observation the pressure to break out of
traditional products and markets was becoming irresistible and
a diversification program was being mounted.

Returning to the question of minimum balances, it is useful to

review some of the guidelines by which these targets were established, in the hope of shedding some light on how they relate to
the unexpected need. In some cases a bank making a loan had
required or suggested a compensating balance. At best this was a
highly generalized measure of "normal" liquidity needs. It was
quite unrelated to the special circumstances of the individual
case. It had the advantage for the financial officer of being very
specific and being backed by an external authority generally
acknowledged to be conservative.

There was also the company with the rule that minimum
liquid balances should equal the sum of the federal tax liability
plus the normal contribution to the profit-sharing fund. The
superficial justification for this guideline was the fact that these
two outlays were the two major lump-sum cash outflows faced by
the company during the year and the two needs that could be
most embarrassing if the cash was not on hand. Yet, of all the
needs bearing on cash reserves these were two of the most easily
predictable not only as to magnitude but also as to timing.
Thus, cash would be accumulated in anticipation of the specific
dates of payment, and to have a minimum balance equal to these
amounts would seem to be double-counting. What the rule really
amounted to, therefore, so far as unexpected needs were concerned, was that with these two payments assured by a minimum
balance, all excess cash *over and above this amount* could be
counted as a reserve against the unknown.

Another type of rule specified a minimum dollar amount
without any rational or objective explanation given. Undoubtedly
these rules had their roots in past experience. Time had "proved"
amounts of cash of this magnitude to be "safe," and on occasion
amounts less than this may have caused embarrassment. Such
guidelines are subject to upward revision if experience proves
them inadequate and to downward revision if pressures demand
some experimentation with lower levels and no trouble occurs.

Several of the companies under study did not have, or would
not admit that they had, specific guidelines on minimum balances.
It is difficult to believe that the financial officers had no idea of
the cash level that would make them uncomfortable. So long as
cash balances were significantly in excess of this amount there
would be no need to specify the level. With contingency planning

in the large majority of companies an informal and implicit process, rather than formal and explicit, there was no reason to publish what this minimum level might be. If cash could be held above that level, so much the better.

Before concluding this section on observed practice with respect to minimum cash balances it is of interest to refer to a tax court decision concerning the Bardahl Manufacturing Corporation[1] in which the judge, required to rule on whether the company had excessive accumulations of cash, went through a lengthy rationalization of the amounts that could "legitimately" be held as a cash reserve. In the opinion of the court a reasonable cash balance would be represented by the sum of the following amounts:

(1) An amount equal to the normal amount invested in working capital over one operating cycle, the time it took for cash to flow *into inventory* and ultimately to be recovered as cash by the collection of an account receivable.

(2) An amount equal to the expenditures on new plant and equipment specifically approved and in process of being implemented at the time of the examination.

(3) An amount equal to the sum needed for a stockpile of such inventory as was in scarce supply.

(4) An amount equal to certain overseas expenditures in the process of being implemented.

It is interesting to note that items 2, 3, and 4 all relate to known needs, amounts, and timing and that their certainty was the condition of approval by the court. Item 1 can be explained as the contingency reserve but can be rationalized only on the expectation of a complete stoppage of the working capital flow for one cycle — a very unlikely event. This example is included because it is a common decision rule to relate cash somehow to working capital levels, for instance to such a number as one month's sales.

Looking back over these various decision rules one can sum up as follows. Cash balances are recognized to be made up of:

---

[1] Commerce Clearing House, Inc., *Tax Court Memorandum Decisions*, Vol. 24 (1965), pp. 1030–49 (*Bardahl Manufacturing Corporation* v. *Commissioner*).

(1) Current transactions balances locked into the transactions system and related to current volume of sales and operations, *plus*

(2) Minimum reserve for contingencies, *plus*

(3) Specific accumulations toward known lump-sum outlays, *plus*

(4) Residual surpluses.

When management speaks of minimum balances, it is usually referring to 1 and 2 above. Typically, financial officers lack both the basic data and the means of analysis for an objective determination of the amount. This is partly because the precise relationship between the volume of transactions and the transactions balance of cash has not been clearly identified. More importantly, what to reserve for contingencies appears to defy rationality, and no generally accepted system exists. As this book contends, if uncertainty in cash flows is correctly viewed in the broader context of *all* alternatives to deal with it, there is no rational solution in terms of cash balances *alone*.

In the face of this confusion and recognizing the desirability of *some* reserve of cash for contingency needs, financial officers will do the instinctive thing by seizing on an arbitrary rule which has three essential characteristics: (1) it is clearly in excess of the minimum transactions balance — though by an undefined magnitude; (2) it is simple and objective; and (3) it appears to others to be a rational rule related to cash needs. (Closer examination generally proves these arbitrary rules to be questionable, but if they are accepted by nonfinancial management, the purpose is served.) The result of all this is that the company may be assumed to have some amount of cash earmarked for a role in a strategy of financial mobility, but the precise amount remains vague even to the financial officer. One of the men interviewed summed up the whole process of cash balances by referring to it as an "artistic" decision, obviously implying that real objectivity was unattainable.

Commercial Bank Borrowing

Perhaps one reason why minimum cash balances have not been more carefully defined is that in many companies the cash balance is the tip of the reserve "iceberg." The larger, unseen

portion is the latent borrowing power at the commercial banks
with which the companies have a long-standing relationship.
There is no doubt that commercial bank debt played the key
role in short-range strategy of financial mobility so far as the
substantial majority of companies studied were concerned. In
contingency planning up to one year — the period that absorbs
most of the financial officer's attention — the available bank
borrowing was widely regarded as the primary defense against
the unexpected. Many financial officers placed considerable emphasis on the importance of cultivating a close relationship that
would be clearly advantageous to both parties. Further, this relationship was usually regarded as a highly personal one between
the financial officer and the lending officer — a relationship involving mutual trust and continuous communication of relevant
information.

In considering the problem of response to new information
suggesting a change in the allocation of resources — the basic
problem of financial mobility — it is helpful to contrast the
business corporation with a portfolio of blue chip securities. In
the latter case, new information about either a deterioration in
investments now held or an improvement in investments not now
held can and often does result in a virtually instantaneous change
in the mix of investments. There is no need to hold a portion of
the funds in liquid form since reallocation can occur without time
lag and at a precisely determined cost. In contrast, an operating
business demands a temporal identification with specific earning
assets. It cannot be continuously on the move. The withdrawal
of investment from specialized operating use has dimensions of
scale, circumstance, and time that make the outcome difficult and
uncertain.

Consequently, if the response to new information should be or
has to be immediate, the only answer would appear to be a liquid
reserve. As a result, resources are not fully utilized and the
"working assets" have to work harder. Short-term bank loans,
however, present the alternative to a liquid reserve by providing
what may be described as a temporary and reversible liquidation
of current assets while leaving those assets in active employment
by the borrower. In an extreme case the liquidation process may
go so far as to physically segregate the assets in question from

other assets, as in the case of inventory in a field warehouse, but normally the process is not carried this far. With a short-term loan the borrower is able to respond immediately to the investment opportunity but is given time to effect the needed reallocation of funds from existing investments — funds that may or may not come from the particular assets standing behind the bank loan.

Thus a bank loan offers the prospect of instant mobility of resources without the cost of holding idle resources. The size of this potential liquidity depends, of course, on many factors but is ultimately limited by the size and stability of the value of the assets that actually or potentially secure the loan. Its magnitude tends to be defined for the borrower by formal contracts, informal verbal commitments, or generalized guidelines drawn from the financial officer's own or another's experience. At one end of the scale of size would be the relatively small but certain amounts available under a line of credit on a standby agreement. At the other end would be the relatively large but uncertain amounts available if the company is willing to offer an explicit pledge of its more valuable current assets. In between are the amounts that the borrower has been "assured" are available through periodic discussions with a loan officer.

A highly important question for this study was how the financial officers related free cash to short-term borrowing power in developing a strategy for dealing with totally unexpected needs —the "instant deficit" to be covered by "instant reserves." In many companies short-term debt capacity was actually or potentially larger than free cash balances. If that borrowing power is in fact related to the values of current assets (inventories and receivables) as previously asserted, then one would expect it to be the larger of the two reserves in the normal case since total cash is usually dwarfed by the investment in inventory and receivables.

In addition to being perhaps larger than free cash balances, short-term debt capacity also appears to be more certain, though that may seem surprising at first sight. The reason advanced for this is that, first of all, many financial officers are not entirely clear on how much of their cash balance is free. Second, the encroachment on this balance from normal working capital variations is essentially beyond the control and perhaps the prediction of the financial officer. Consequently he may even be disposed to abandon these visible free cash reserves to operating managers as a part of *their* strategy of mobility and place more reliance for his own financial mobility on the off-the-balance sheet resource, which he alone knows best, which he personally negotiates, and the use of which he must therefore be advised of in advance. The importance of this point can hardly be overemphasized: of all the resources of the business, the banking relationship comes closest to being a personal and private resource of the finance function rather than of the corporation as a whole. This gives it unique characteristics for its role in a strategy of *financial* mobility.

It is possible that recent events in the money markets during tight money conditions have shaken the confidence of some financial officers in the relative certainty of this reserve. However, most financial officers who have worked hard at cultivating a banking relationship and have a record to justify confidence have not been seriously disturbed. In any case, normal contingency planning works on the basis either of established lines of credit or of borrowing limits on unsecured bank debt allowing a comfortable margin of safety. These are the kinds of limits customarily cited in discussions of where contingency needs might be financed. Borrowing short term on specific pledge of assets is recognized as a potential emergency source, but it is sufficiently distasteful to be usually eliminated from a defined strategic role.

No clear picture was obtained of a perceived difference between the cost of cash reserves and unused bank debt. In general, explicit costs are taken more seriously than implicit costs. On the other hand, management is more conscious of idle resources *on* the balance sheet than *off* the balance sheet. In this sense the temporary use of bank debt is regarded as cheaper than the permanent commitment of a comparable amount of idle cash. However, while the financial officer will undoubtedly try to negotiate any loans at what is regarded as a favorable interest rate (relative to what others are paying), it is my opinion that cost is one of the lesser considerations in the use of strategic instant reserves. Certainty as to the magnitude and timing of available funds and the degree of personal control are far more critical in the minds of those who make these decisions. This may be illustrated by one of the companies concerned, which for a period relied on commercial paper rather than bank borrowing because it represented a low-cost source of temporary funds. Because of competitive and managerial deficiencies the company's credit rating slipped and eventually the company was no longer able to sell commercial paper. At that point the financial officer deeply regretted that he had not cultivated a close relationship with a commercial bank which he believed would have endured adversity. After the fact, at least, the saving obtained by the use of commercial paper appeared inconsequential.

In addition to the obvious linkage to cash reserves, short-term debt capacity with commercial banks has a connection with long-term debt capacity, whether through a longer term contract with the same institution or with another and different type of lender. Perhaps the most significant thing to be said here is that there is no clearly defined relationship among debt contracts of differing maturities and institutional connections. The normal tendency is to treat commercial bank debt as one pocket and term debt with insurance companies as another pocket. Each has its defined capacity, which appears unrelated to use of the other. They play distinctive roles in the overall strategy of mobility.

The roles played by these two sources of funds may be contrasted by reference to their use in covering unexpected funds flow deficits that persist for more than one year and thus are outside the class of loans for which short-term bank debt has by tradition been intended. The normal initial response to an unexpected need is recourse to liquid reserves or short-term bank debt. This provides the quick response and also the time necessary to assess the magnitude and duration of the need. When it is apparent that the need will persist for some time, short-term debt is replaced by long-term debt and short-term debt capacity is restored by consumption of long-term debt capacity. Presumably the company is then in a position to respond to the next unexpected deficit. Thus long-term debt capacity represents the back-up for inadvertent misuse, so to speak, of short-term debt capacity. A good example of this was the cyclical behavior of Company A in Chapter 4.

At times, however, this "misuse" will be quite deliberate. This was the case with Company E in Chapter 6. Here the company repeatedly sought and obtained one- to two-year extensions of its line of credit agreement with the commercial bank and in effect converted borrowing on a line of credit into a term loan to cover what was manifestly a long-term need. Eventually the bank insisted on a conversion into long-term debt, but in the meantime the company was able (or believed it was able) to expand its long-term debt capacity by this means.

The question naturally arises: are these really separate contingency reserves or are they merely temporal subdivisions of one finite debt reserve? In this descriptive section this question is not primarily one of rational definition but rather one of how they were perceived in practice. I have suggested that they were usually seen as independent of each other, in the belief that independent negotiation with two or more lenders is likely to generate more borrowing power than negotiation with one. However, the appearance of independence may, in a number of cases, have simply been the result of under utilization of both sources of debt capital. It is only when short-term or long-term debt is pushed to the limit that the restrictive clauses regarding other forms of borrowing begin to take effect as lenders sharpen their definition of limits on prior or equal claims to earnings and assets.

On the other hand, lenders' concepts of debt limits are sufficiently vague, their concepts of risk sufficiently different, and the negotiations sufficiently separated in time and space that borrowers have a genuine opportunity to expand debt capacity by separate negotiations and are therefore justified in seeing them as at least somewhat independent of each other. Certainly their differing nature means that apart from the amounts involved they play distinctly different roles in dealing with uncertainty.

Reference has been made to the close personal relationship that often develops between the financial officer and the bank loan officer. One must not underrate the importance of this in the game of financial mobility. In the modern corporation with its widely dispersed and impersonal ownership group it is hard for the financial officer to find a predictable and reliable ally on the outside who is in a position to respond to a need for funds quickly and in magnitude. The banker may be the only one who can fill that role. Indeed, the banker may be the financial officer's best ally inside or outside the company since those on the inside in a position to help financial mobility are likely to have conflicting interests. In the extreme case, as we saw in Company C, the alliance reaches the point when the financial officer becomes its captive and is behaving, at least in part, as an extension of the bank's interests in the company, representing the loan officer as much as he does the company itself.

THE RESOURCES OF MOBILITY: (2) MODIFICATION OF BUDGETED FLOWS

A second major resource of mobility, in addition to the instant reserves, is the option of responding to an unexpected need by modifying the existing plan and avoiding a deficit by substituting the new need for a planned expenditure in the current budget. The ability to avoid cash flow deficits by manipulating the expenditure horizon for various categories of expenditure is a widely and continuously used resource of mobility, if the research sample of companies is any indication. The process may be described as the continuous re-examination and revision of outflow priorities as new information is received, a fundamental consideration being the trade-off between short-term cash "solvency" and long-run profitability. (Solvency is placed within quotation marks since the question is normally not a legal but rather a policy issue.)

The range of alternatives for the substitution of one outflow for another open to a particular management at a particular point in time will be conditional on the nature of the unexpected need and on the circumstances at the time of need. It is therefore impossible to generalize on the specific choices open for the purposes of financial mobility without first specifying something about the class of uncertainty. For example, the cash flow deficit arising in the early period of a business recession because of a misjudgment of sales trends may be and probably will be countered in whole or in part by layoffs of direct labor and reduction in other outlays related to volume of production. Cash flow problems related to a strike are obviously qualified by the fact that payroll will be drastically reduced so long as the strike lasts.

Cash needs related to a strong uptrend in sales are affected by the fact that external sources of funds are in part determined by the economic environment of the time. Clearly a strategy of mobility must differentiate between resources of mobility that are unspecialized as to use and those that are specialized or limited as to use. In addition, a specific strategy or strategies will be developed to meet the specific contingencies that are the dominant concern of the business at a given time.

Most of the action with respect to funds flows centers around reallocation of outflows. In the sample study the options to modify the inflow stream by accelerating the timing of inflows appeared relatively few and inconsequential. In the main, companies took their cash inflow from sales as a given, which was not subject to significant short-run manipulation. The two basic possibilities were: (1) to separate the cash receipt from the shipment and sale date through some sort of negotiated prepayment arrangement; (2) to reach out to the potential sales of the period beyond the planning horizon and bring these into the planning period by such devices as a price cut or an announced price increase to take effect in the future. The latter actions were most relevant to the sale of goods such as machine tools, which are purchased at irregular intervals and allow considerable discretion as to the timing of the purchase.

Neither of these alternatives was looked on with favor as a part of normal mobility of funds flows, the first requiring a confession of financial weakness and the second involving serious disturbance of market relationships and possibly serious effects on income. Nevertheless, there were examples of both of these actions in the study. The negotiated prepayment was obviously connected with cash flow needs, but management denied that postdated price increases were a part of cash flow management.

Chapter 3 suggested a classification of expenditures (volume-related, scale-related, strategic, and value-related) which may be helpful in a consideration of the periodic modification of expenditure horizons. This breakdown of cash outflows suggests that there are significant differences in the discretionary powers of management over the magnitude and timing of flows and therefore that the various categories may be expected to play significantly different roles in a strategy of financial mobility. *Volume-*

related outflows are obviously closely tied to the expected level of sales in the planning stage, the expenditure horizon being largely dictated by customer orders, the nature of the product, and the productive process. Given the expected sales level, which for most companies is considered beyond their control within normal planning horizons, the outlays for such needs as direct labor and materials afford little if any room for discretionary modification. If the unexpected change includes a decline in sales level, then of course there is an opportunity to drop volume-related outflows, and a choice exists as to whether the decline in outflows is more or less than proportional to the expected level of sales in the future.

The discussion of change in the volume-related outflows is usually phrased in terms of control over inventory levels, the buffer between production levels and sales or shipment levels. Physical inventory, however, is the resource of mobility for dealing with uncertainties in production and marketing decisions. Uncertainties in these functional areas are covered in part by buffer stocks. Whenever the financial officer attempts to use changes in inventory levels as a resource of financial mobility, therefore, he must realize that he is involved in a trade-off between financial and operating mobility. Discussion of inventory levels so far as cash flows are concerned is merely shorthand for summarizing action on the multitude of expenditures relating to production levels. It is possible, of course, to change the level of production without a change in the sales level. The combination of a reduced level of cash inputs and a sustained level of cash inflows makes funds available for alternative use. However, there are distinct physical and practical limits on such action and, more importantly, there is strong resistance on the part of those concerned with operating mobility. The evidence of the field study is virtually unanimous in indicating that inventories as a source of funds for alternative use are in practice extremely difficult to control and to predict.

Even when sales decline there may be difficulty in lowering the level of volume-related cash inputs. Uncertainty as to the duration of the decline argues against cutbacks, and there is always the question of the rate at which production will be scaled down. Thus, depending on how drastic the response is, the inventory may decline, remain level, or even increase. Cash flow considerations conflict with cost and profit considerations, and the variables in the equation are numerous and difficult to measure. This is clearly an area in which management of funds flows involves difficult, time-consuming, and unpredictable internal negotiation. The reader is reminded of the experience of Company C in Chapter 5 and the resistance of operating heads to the president's directives in this area.

In addition to a reduction in the number of units produced, volume-related outflows may under special circumstances be reduced by a negotiated reduction in the payment per unit of product or service. This applies to scale-related expenditures as well. Reduced wage rates or payments for raw materials, for example, are normally possible only when the company or the economy is manifestly suffering financially to the point where other participants in the operation, such as workers or suppliers, can be induced to bear some of the shock of the event. They then become a source of mobility to the corporation. This requires clear evidence of an industry recession or a deteriorating competitive situation in an individual firm. The study included examples of both situations. The groups affected were generally immobile themselves — captive suppliers or established employees — who therefore had a major stake in the financial survival of the business entity. These situations must be regarded as the exceptions (certainly management would prefer to think so) and generally unit costs for volume-related outflows are assumed to be on a persistent inflationary trend.

Scale-related expenditures offer a much wider range of discretion as to the magnitude and timing of the cash outflows for several reasons. Basically, these expenditures are not prescribed by the process of production or sales on a unit-by-unit basis. The volume of work that can be handled by an accounting staff can vary considerably. A warehouse is designed for an approximate volume under "normal" conditions and maximum efficiency of handling, but its actual physical capacity may be substantially larger. A machine often has a range of output per unit of time and the units of time are variable: one, two, or three shifts. There being no precise definition of scale, there is a range of choice as to whether administrative staff, for example, at any given time leads or lags the scale of operations then in existence. In other words, the expenditure horizon may be extended or retracted substantially as funds pressure or other considerations dictate.

Because the cash outlays for these purposes buy a range of output that is inherent in the nature of the product or service purchased, they tend to be "lumpy" and discontinuous. A related but somewhat different dimension of some scale-related expenditures is a choice in the degree to which management anticipates future growth. In such expenditures as land, buildings, equipment, management development, and preventive maintenance the expenditure horizon is variable within wide limits. As these choices come up, the circumstances of cash flow balance can and do significantly influence the expenditure horizon.

Furthermore, the relationship between the amount spent and the prospective sales and earnings is sufficiently vague that there can be honest differences of judgment as to how much to spend. Institutional advertising and new product research are cases in point. The payoff is so difficult, or even impossible, to measure that it is easy to rationalize cuts in these outlays when a cash deficiency manifests itself. Under such conditions financial pressures may change judgments in favor of smaller outlays. The comment was frequently made that such budget items as advertising and maintenance were always "fair game" when pressures developed.

Another reason for management discretion lies in the fact that these are for the most part negotiated expenditures — negotiated within the management group or directly with the source of the good or service. Changing bargaining position may alter the needed outlay. For instance, negotiation may involve production management over the extent of plant maintenance or may involve salaried executives over the extent of a salary cut.

In general, significant reductions in scale-related expenditures as a response to anticipated deficits in funds flows are subject to a considerable degree of management discretion but they take time to negotiate, are somewhat uncertain as to the size and timing, and have definite time limits on the duration of the "saving."

As previously explained, the category of *strategic expenditures* is, by definition, relatively secure from short-run cash flow pressures arising because of unexpected needs. It is impossible to identify this category by specific example since what is of strategic importance varies among companies, managements, and time periods. The category will include the volume-related and scale-related outlays that appear vital to the company's future as management currently defines it. Exceptions to the inflexibility of these outlays are related to two principal situations: (1) where circumstances are so extreme that corporate or management continuity is threatened by cash deficiencies or (2) where the unexpected need occurs against a background of new information, which makes existing strategy out of date and in need of revision, including a revision in outlay priorities. Thus, a high priority expenditure on new product research, tooling, or market development could be drastically affected by an unexpected change in a competitor's strategy. Even in extreme circumstances strategic expenditures, for example, for engineering staff, are defended for as long as possible in the hope that the pressure will be relieved before a cut is made.

The last category of expenditures covers those described as *financial* or *value-related*. Their distinguishing characteristic is that they do not relate directly to the operating activities of the business, and therefore the decision to spend or not to spend does not affect strategic or tactical action respecting, for example, production, technology, or customer service. These expenditures are primarily concerned with the manner of payment for assets over which the company wishes to exercise control and with the methods by which the company chooses to obtain its funds. In addition, there are certain choices of action, as in cost-reduction capital expenditures (e.g., a make vs. buy decision), where the operating result is essentially the same but the timing and perhaps the magnitude of the cash outlays differ. Thus a part can be obtained by means of a major outlay for tooling up and equipment within the plant or by means of a higher cost per part from a supplier. The part is essentially the same; the outlays differ.

These expenditures are particularly significant from the viewpoint of this study since the basic choice is close to a purely financial one, though it is not always seen that way. Typically a larger current outflow is traded for a series of smaller outflows in the future, or vice versa. The incentive to choose the increased near-term outflow is the prospect of improved future flows and earnings and therefore improved value of the firm. Thus the decision is in essence a choice between short-run cash flow and long-run profitability. The option to delay or abandon these outflows and thus obtain greater financial mobility is at the expense of earnings per share.

The evidence of the study is that this category of expenditure, along with the scale-related category, plays a significant role in financial mobility. It would be a mistake to generalize very broadly about the priority given the value-related expenditure, since there was some conflicting evidence in this regard. However, some tentative reasons can be advanced as to why many financial officers regarded these outlays as open to reallocation. One reason was that operating management had comparatively little sympathy for expenditures that "merely" increased earnings per share, if this meant denying funds to operating objectives. Another reason was that they were often regarded as postponable (e.g., a machine-for-labor substitution) without loss of the investment opportunity, whereas other expenditure opportunities were regarded as more perishable. A third reason was that the expected return on the investment was often a matter of judgment and therefore open to question. Finally, the benefit might stretch over many years and the year-to-year gains might be small in relation to the initial outlay.

The opportunity to defer or abandon value-related outlays would appear to depend substantially on the *trend* of earnings at the time of the decision and on whether the outlay would make a material impact on that trend. The general concern for *some* improvement in earnings from year to year as a key measure of management performance would strongly influence any choice that had the prospect of changing the trend significantly. However, if the trend was so clearly down that nothing could change it, there would be less concern about a decision that merely made the trend worse by postponing a benefit to earnings per share. There might even be a preference for such postponement if it meant that the earnings of future periods would, by contrast, look that much better.

THE RESOURCES OF MOBILITY: (3) LIQUIDATION OF ASSETS

One management concept with unusual acceptance within the study sample (and very few concepts could qualify) was that the sale of specialized, earning assets could not and should not be a significant part of a strategy of financial mobility. The arguments were most persuasive. Assets should not be sold (disinvestment decisions made) at the random impulse of unexpected needs for funds. Rather, such decisions should be based on a deliberate evaluation of long-term earnings potential measured against alternative opportunities. This choice was characterized by the officers of one company as a "business" rather than a financial decision. At times of financial stringency the company's bargaining position is weak and it is unlikely to get the best price. Finally, the process of liquidation of real assets is so uncertain as to timing and magnitude of funds released that it cannot be a part of any plan for mobility.

However, these statements, the logic of which can hardly be disputed, express a view of business practice as it should be rather than as it is. Observation of several companies experiencing serious and sustained financial pressure demonstrates clearly that under these circumstances the liquidation of assets becomes a part of consideration and action in the strategy of mobility. Inevitably when free resources are shrinking and needs are abundant, thoughts turn to the matter of priorities in the funds already committed. This is apparent in the detailed cases already outlined. The process may be considered as an attempt to reverse earlier investment decisions, if possible without loss of the investment value, and redeploy the resources to uses now considered of higher priority, either defensively or aggressively.

Evidence suggests some reasons why liquidation of assets often appears to coincide with periods of financial strain, as opposed to a more orderly process distributed over time. One practical reason is that so long as an asset is contributing something to earnings or to sales there is a reluctance to give up that contribution. Further, hope springs eternal in the managerial breast and there is always the prospect that conditions will improve in the future, and hence a tendency to hang on one more year. Even in the case of assets that are a drain on resources, such as idle plant, there is this hope for an upsurge in sales to require the assets. The net result is a pressure to defer action until a financial emergency forces action.

Different categories of assets are likely to receive different treatment. Those given up most willingly are assets such as land or surplus plant facilities, which are contributing nothing to earnings and cash flows and may even be a drain. Idle or redundant assets are likely to be the first to go. There is a preference for avoiding book losses, and inevitably the specialized assets such as plant are harder to sell and more likely to involve a loss. A second category of assets are those that contribute to earnings but not to sales dollars, typically investments in real assets peripheral to the main business, such as an investment in employee housing or in a supplementary industry or service. The category excludes a liquid portfolio, which is more properly thought of as part of the cash reserve. Finally, there are those assets the sale of which means a loss of both sales dollars and earnings. These are typically the most difficult to give up.

The common characteristics of all these assets are that they must be separable from the mainstream of business without serious damage to the remaining earning power, that they can be sold for a substantial amount of cash available immediately, and that they do not involve serious loss of book value, thus suggesting financial weakness and errors of judgment. This third requirement may have to be abandoned in time of stress. By far the most difficult to separate are segments of the business that in the past have represented part of the mainstream of managerial activity and employment and of sales and earnings. The problem is of course the discontinuity that results in employment, sales, and earnings and may persist for several years until the funds so released are returned to full productivity in some other area. This problem, referred to in Company E as the "phase in-phase out" problem and observed in other companies as well, is a real issue for management preoccupied with year-to-year measures of performance.

In the last analysis, liquidation of assets is a very unsatisfactory element of mobility primarily because of the great uncertainty surrounding both the amount to be realized and the time when it will be realized. Hard choices have to be made between the most salable assets, and therefore the most certain as to inputs to cash flow, and the most expendable assets from a strategic viewpoint, which are likely to be the most difficult to sell at an acceptable price. It may be recalled how Company E periodically toyed with the sale of a profitable subsidiary and then backed away again as the pressure eased. It may also be recalled how Company C tried in vain to dispose of a major facility which, although relatively new, had become a financial millstone around the company's neck.

THE RESOURCES OF MOBILITY: (4) INCREMENTS OF LONG-TERM CAPITAL

It is not surprising to find that the long-term or "permanent" capital contract did not play a dominant role in the strategy of mobility. This is particularly apparent in the light of the normal emphasis on a planning horizon of one year. In the typical industrial company such contracts are infrequently used, perhaps no more frequently than every three to five years, and are typically the product of a perceived imbalance in the long-term trend of funds flows. Consistent excesses of outflows over inflows and the expectation of continuation in the foreseeable future would naturally lead to a desire to increase the "permanent" debt or equity base.

In spite of this basic logic, however, long-term debt and even equity played a support role in the various strategies of mobility. The use of equity was very infrequent. It was universally true that the sale of new common stock was regarded as undesirable because of its immediate dilution of that prime measure of performance, earnings per share. Consequently the few companies that used common stock were "forced" into it, either because lenders made an issue of common stock a prerequisite to new debt or because it was literally a last resort. In only one instance did an issue of common stock appear to be a free and deliberate choice as a means of gaining "flexibility" for the future. In fact the substantial lead time required on issue and the general unpredictability of the common equity market — the sudden, unexpected changes of market value — make this resource rather unreliable as a defense against unknown fluctuations in funds flows. It is much more attractive, in theory at least, as a source when there is a strong upward trend of earnings and market value and this is expected to continue for some time.

The long-term debt contract is looked on with considerably more favor for purposes of dealing with uncertainty. There is widespread acceptance of the concept of a reserve of long-term debt capacity. By definition this reserve is a restraint on the rate of current spending in order to protect against an unidentified high priority need, which may be either an opportunity or a defensive act. The debt contract, which is commonly assumed to involve direct negotiation with a single term lender with whom previous contracts have been made, is much more of a known quantity than equity and therefore a much more reliable component of a strategy of mobility. It does not represent the same degree of close, personal understanding as the commercial banking relationship but is nevertheless a situation in which there can be considerable confidence in expectations of availability. Further, previous contracts may and normally do spell out explicitly the upper limits of such borrowing, leading to a belief that funds will actually be available in these amounts if needed.

Under normal circumstances long-term borrowing is expected to be the result of formal planning for specific needs, the identity of the need being an important consideration in the lender's willingness to lend. In this sense it cannot be considered an unexpected need. On the other hand, it is obvious that the stated purpose for the use of such completely unspecialized funds may be far from the actual use and in any case the use is impossible to trace after the fact. The circumstances under which long-term debt played a role in financial mobility were those cases where either (a) the company was "funding" one or a series of unexpected needs financed initially by internal trade-offs or from short-term borrowing or (b) where the company was anticipating an unspecified possible need ("for general corporate purposes"), and was adding to its current liquidity, usually by tacking this borrowing on to some specific financing.

In either case the general intent and effect are the same: an improvement in the resources that can handle a need quickly and without time delays. Thus the reserve of long-term borrowing power is valuable not so much as a resource in itself but rather as a means of restoring or increasing other resources of mobility. This was well illustrated in the case of Company A. The possible limitation of the long-term debt contract as a means of fast response to unexpected needs is illustrated in the case of Company E, where the careful preparations for an approach to the lender consumed as much as a year or more in getting the company's financial house in order and preparing the approach. This is probably more indicative, however, of the company reaching its borrowing limit than of a company with a large reserve. The larger the reserve, obviously, the faster the response and the more likely it is that long-term debt can play a direct role in a strategy of mobility.

9

The Evidence of Strategy

It is impossible to place a valid interpretation on action without being aware that these decisions do not take place in an intellectual vacuum but are strongly influenced by a variety of conditions, both external and internal, of which some are unique to the time and some are of more enduring influence. One condition, which was prominent in the three case histories, is that decision making is a sequential process and each decision relates to the past as well as the future. The linkage among the separate components in a series of decisions and acts is a key characteristic differentiating a dynamic from a static situation. This is usually discussed in terms of the future; for example, when it is recognized that the use of debt financing today may preclude its use six months from now and therefore the present decision must take account not only of present but also of future needs and how they will be financed. This study, however, brings out very clearly that in a variety of ways past actions and events have a strong bearing on current choices and future strategy. This is not simply a matter of having used up certain resources as of any point in time. Obviously, the financial action over any time span depends on the inventory of financial resources at time zero. Beyond this is the fact that the availability of certain resources is often conditional on certain precedent actions or conditions. A general observation about the use of financial resources is that they are rarely used continuously but more normally have alternating seasons of use and comparative idleness.

Several examples can be cited to show that the availability of certain resources of mobility was dependent on the circumstances in the preceding period. One of these is the observed fact that pressure on an organization to use funds more efficiently (free up some resources for alternative use) cannot be sustained indefinitely but tends to take the form of economy "drives," which are followed by periods of relative slackness. Another example relates to borrowing. Previous chapters have shown that lenders expected that new borrowing, particularly at the limits of debt capacity, should be preceded by evidence that the company had been trying to make the most of what it already had. Also, there is a tendency for lenders to want a period in which to observe how investment financed by past advances has worked out before they make further advances. On the corporate management side, there is the need to develop a bargaining position for those resources that must be negotiated. A drive to find funds internally may require "proof" to operating management that normal external sources have been exhausted. Finally, we can mention the common notion that to go back to the capital market frequently, particularly to the same source, is evidence of lack of planning and weak financial management. All of these considerations mean that in order to understand the reasons why a given series of mobility responses was limited to certain resources one must explore the past as well as the present and future.

Another and obvious constraint on action is the existing set of financial policies relating to the maximization of profit and value. These policies, which are presumably stockholder-oriented, develop out of past experience and are reflected in current management convictions. As such they may be expected to have a strong influence on the way in which cash flows are balanced over time. By definition, such policies presumably reflect long-run financial standards and goals and set boundaries on short-run action, including cash flow management, so that it does not violate these standards and goals. One of the conclusions of the study is that there is in fact considerable interaction between financial policy and strategies of mobility. Thus financial policy must be regarded as a constraint but not necessarily an inflexible one.

A third limiting consideration is the people involved. Apart from the obvious fact that people are involved in every decision process and the actual judgments reflect the limitations of these people, there are particular aspects in which personalities enter the management of funds flows. Generally speaking, the financial viewpoint on the coordination of funds flows is represented by one man, the chief financial officer. His capacity to influence the flow of funds and the choices he makes will be dependent on three factors that he, as an individual, brings to the job and would take with him if he left. These are: (1) confidence in his competence and trustworthiness on the part of external sources of funds, particularly lenders; (2) bargaining strength when resources under the full or partial control of others are under negotiation (and this is at least as much internal as external); and (3) attitudes toward risk bearing in the financial sector, including both corporate and personal risks. A related consideration is the influence the financial officer has in the president's office and the extent to which the president reflects strong financial viewpoints of his own. In managing funds flows there are certain actions that by custom the financial officer may take on his own authority and others he must deal with through the chief executive.

A fourth limiting consideration is the effective planning horizon of the company and the finance function. Chapter 7 has developed the characteristics of such horizons and their basis in industry characteristics and practices, customer buying cycles, budgetary practices, and resource commitment. Observation of practice indicated that the dominant period for funds flow management had a moving 12-month horizon. It is apparent that this approach has an important bearing on the resources of mobility since different resources require varying periods to bring them into active employment.

A fifth constraint is the general economic and business environment of the time. The climate within which resources are sought, both externally and internally, has much to do with the ease of access to those funds and the cost involved. Periods of tight or easy money have their effect. In addition, the evidence of trends, for example in interest rates, would lead to expectations that would inhibit or encourage the use of certain external resources. Even internal resources are easier or more difficult to release for alternative use depending on whether the industry or the economy is considered to be weak or strong. Economy drives are much easier to launch in a period of increasing competition or declining demand. On the other hand, strong prosperity makes it almost impossible to reduce the level of expenditure and improve the inventory turnover.

Finally, the nature of the specific needs impinging on the company at the time under consideration has much to do with the response. This relates not only to the sense of the urgency of the need but also to the form of the response. For example, the need may be one that is frequently handled as a joint venture with competitors or it may be one that is easily financed with mortgage debt. While the longer term future can only be defined in terms of generalized uncertainties and generalized measures of risk, the near term horizon is filled with specific needs and specific risks, the nature of which conditions the plan of action. *In general, management cannot react to the future until uncertainty does begin to take specific form:* for example, in order schedules, budgets, contracts let, competitors' acts, governmental directives. Collectively these "certain uncertainties" *define the planning horizon for funds flow management.*

An illustration of all these constraints was seen in the case of Company C, described in Chapter 5. The constraint of past acts and events was very apparent. Recent long-term debt and equity issues had left these two sources effectively used up for the near future. An industry recession had set in, bringing sharply declining sales and earnings. The planning horizon was reduced to near zero as orders booked became the only reliable index of the future. The alternatives by which funds flows could be balanced were effectively reduced to control over volume-related and scale-related expenditures and such assistance as could be provided by a committed commercial bank. The basic issue became one of priorities among internal funds flows with protection afforded as long as possible to those outflows regarded as of strategic significance. The entire period represented constantly narrowing alternatives in the effort to keep flows in balance until at the darkest stage the bank limit had been reached and a dwindling cash balance promised only a few months of solvency.

A Generalized Descriptive Model of Strategy

To undertake to describe the nature of a typical or normal strategy of financial mobility is both presumptuous and hazardous. Observation brings home the wide range in perception of the problem of uncertainty and in response. There are in fact many different strategies, as evidenced by the responses of the people involved to variations in flows. At the same time, and in spite of the obvious dangers of oversimplification, it has been the mission of this research to attempt to identify common characteristics among the cases examined and from them to attempt to piece together a model or description of behavior for use as a frame of reference in discussing individual variations. This section will present the model, which is perhaps best characterized as a hypothesis about average or typical behavior.

The problem of financing the future is commonly viewed in academic discussions as a sequence of specific financing needs (a new plant, an acquisition, working capital to support increased sales) for which specific sums are required of known amount and maturity. This type of "one-shot" financing of specific needs is of course part of business life and "one-shot" responses can be developed to match the expenditure neatly. In the dynamic situation, however, the company's financial future is unfolding in an environment of many-sided uncertainty respecting wage rates, prices, sales volume, capital costs, timing of financings, and so on, all of which have their ultimate impact on funds flows to produce a net deficit or surplus quarter by quarter. The hypothetical company we wish to consider, therefore, is constantly probing the future through a moving one-year forecast. The forecast attempts to identify the net effect of many elements of change and is supplemented by a three-year to five-year probe designed to pick up whether a near-term deficit or surplus foreshadows a more persistent funds flow disequilibrium.

This never-ending series of probe-event-response will be described in terms of an assumed set of circumstances giving rise to a problem of financial mobility, namely, a series of deficit positions that test management's ability to cover the deficit and keep the company moving forward toward established goals. The responses are described as a series of phases through which the company passes as a result of a conscious strategy of response. In order to illustrate the entire range of action, funds flow deficits are assumed to persist without relief from quarter to quarter and year to year. In actual situations there is more likely to be an ebb and flow — several quarters of deficits followed by quarters with a net surplus of funds flows, followed by deficits again. Even the company with a long-term negative funds flow position is likely to experience periods of relief from pressure and retrenchment.

Assume that we are looking at a company that in the beginning is in a steady state condition: a stable competitive environment, satisfactory sales volume and profits, funds flows in basic equilibrium, no major policy violations, and a minimum of initial constraints on the alternatives of mobility open to management.

Now assume an event that disturbs the financial calm. The cash or funds flow forecast has picked up the likelihood of a significant deficit, probably the result of several factors at work on funds flows. We have ruled out the specific, clearly defined one-shot need. The deficit is considered certain enough to require that a plan of action be placed in a state of readiness.

Response: Phase I

When deficits begin to emerge under conditions where their duration and magnitude are unclear, the initial response is likely to be an attempt to contain the effects entirely within the financial area of the business and thus to insulate operations from the shock of this event. This is a kind of wait-and-see, business-as-usual approach founded on the hope that the deficit will be only temporary. If the deficit is clearly identified as a major financial shock well beyond the ability of normal financial reserves to handle, other action would likely take place.

To contain the deficit within the financial area means to leave budgeted expenditures unchanged and investments intact and to consume reserves or modify flows that are entirely within the discretion of the financial officer. In this way the operating management is unaware that a funds flow deficit exists. The alternatives open to the financial officer consist of (a) free cash balances; (b) discretionary payments (amount or timing: e.g., pension fund, accounts payable); (c) short-term bank loan.

In using these alternatives to balance funds flows the financial officer is likely to follow an almost instinctive and universal rule of behavior, which is never to use any resource to its limit before the next resource is employed. For this purpose the financial officer has a set of rule-of-thumb limits which trigger a shift to the next alternative. The origins of this element of strategy appear to derive from the following considerations: uncertainty as to the need for funds, uncertainty as to the funds available from a given source, a need for an objective criterion setting the limit from which to negotiate the use of another source of funds. Thus there will be an arbitrary minimum cash balance, an arbitrary limit on short-term debt, an arbitrary limit on long-term debt.

These limits will be particularly in evidence in the early stages of a deficit phase. At one time it seemed to me that the apparent indifference of financial officers to a more refined definition of, say, short-term debt limits and to more aggressive utilization of this resource was irrational. I am now persuaded that this is a basic response to uncertainty designed to preserve a part at least of the more predictable and readily available sources of funds. Thus at this stage the financial officer may willingly collaborate with his banker in supporting moderate loan levels, entirely avoiding secured borrowing or other forms of high risk debt. Generally applied, this strategy of preserving pockets of unused resources appears as a kind of squirrel instinct for tucking various financial "nuts" away in different locations against the chance of a long cold winter of need, when some at least will still be accessible.

Whether other action accompanies the Phase I response depends on environmental conditions at the time, particularly:

(1) the economic environment — prosperity or recession;
(2) the definition of the cause of the deficit as basically offensive or defensive.

If the funds flow deficit is associated with defensive action, and particularly if it occurs at a time of declining sales and earnings, then Phase I action is likely to be accompanied, with varying time lags, by a concerted effort to reduce volume-related and scale-related outflows (for example, payroll and capital expenditures). Whether or when this occurs will be influenced by how recent the last economy drive was, how much financial slack is believed to exist (a function of the length of the preceding prosperity period), and how visible the evidence is of weakening business conditions. In a recession the strength of the first-line financial reserves will have an important bearing on whether the drive for greater internal efficiency will center on expenses or expenditures; that is, whether it will have an earnings or a cash flow emphasis.

If it happens that the balance of flows reverses in subsequent quarters, then there can and likely will be a gradual restoration of the reserves previously used, paying down bank loans first and then accumulating cash balances and restoring discretionary payments to normal. However, we have already assumed for our model situation that this is not to be and so, with further funds flow deficits in prospect, we reach Phase II.

Response: Phase II

At some point the decline in instant reserves approaches the limits set by the established norms of the company and its bankers. The response is then likely to be the negotiation of a long-term loan. The immediate purpose may be either to restore reserves of commercial bank borrowing power or to add new resources while rolling over the existing bank loans. It is of course necessary to do more than continue the funding of past deficits if current deficits are to be met. As part of a general strategy of mobility this step is designed to continue to insulate the organization from the causes of the funds flow deficit and avoid a confrontation between old commitments and new (unexpected) needs. The negotiation of external reserves buys time, either to clarify future needs without jeopardizing present plans or to prepare for the inevitable reallocation of resources if and when these reserves run out.

Here again it is likely that the company will stay well within accepted debt limits, so that a reserve of long-term debt capacity is retained as a part of the financial officer's kit of alternatives.

If after this action deficits persist, then it is likely that the company will face up to the fact that it can no longer put off some hard choices among alternative uses of funds. So long as reserves existed, new needs could be treated as additions to existing investments, but particularly when these needs are defensive in nature the necessity of substitution of the new needs for existing investments sooner or later becomes apparent. The period of insulation from financial shock is at an end.

Response: Phase III

At this stage the company will turn in on itself with a vigorous program to increase efficiency, minimize costs, and make sure that every invested dollar is actively employed. It may be argued that this should be a constant concern of management but the typical large business needs to organize itself for maximum efficiency and finds it hard to maintain a sustained emphasis indefinitely. There is likely to be an attempt to improve the turnover of working capital and in particular to reduce the investment in inventory per sales dollar, but if the experience of this study is any indication, this attempt is likely to meet with indifferent success. Higher standards will be demanded of capital expenditure proposals, and horizons on scale-related expenditures will be pulled in. At the same time, however, current sales and earnings will be carefully protected. This is the main reason why inventory controls are unlikely to be very effective. Outflows considered of strategic significance to the future of the business will of course also be protected.

The steps described in Phase III will be difficult to take in a buoyant economy where the cash flow deficit results from offensive action. If the company shares in this buoyancy, however, a sustained deficit of funds is likely to result from rapid growth, which usually can be readily financed by additions of external capital. The problem is therefore more likely to be associated with industry or competitive weakness. If this is so and the condition is recognized by the organization, cooperation along the lines of Phase III is easier to obtain.

Regardless of circumstances, this is likely to be the time when the company re-examines past investment decisions that were purely value-related to see if they are reversible through failure to replace, sale, or sale and leaseback. This simply means that if the investment has no direct relation to operations or if use can be obtained without ownership, the investment of capital will be subject to challenge. Efforts will be made to liquidate any asset considered redundant. This is also likely to be the time when off-the-balance sheet "borrowing" comes in for active exploration as a means of getting more external financing without violating conventional norms.

Recapitulation

To recapitulate, persistent funds flow deficits have now consumed the company's instant reserves and long-term borrowing power, leaving in each area whatever reserves lie hidden behind conventional limits of use. Having gone to the conventional limits, the company has then turned inward to see what funds can be released internally without interfering in any serious way with corporate strategy or with current sales and earnings. The organization now knows that a financial squeeze is on and is beginning to examine the trade-offs among uses for funds.

If the deficit persists beyond this point then:

Response: Phase IV

The drive to make the dollar go farther within the company ("Operation Profits" or some similar slogan may be used) sooner or later will meet with increasing resistance as the effort to find *financial* mobility internally comes up against the organizational cushions designed to provide *operating* mobility. The investment in inventory is in part a deliberate act to provide production and marketing protection against unexpected events such as breakdowns or unexpected customer orders. Capital expenditures and research and development are designed to provide a lead as protection against unexpected moves by competitors. Depth in staffing provides protection against unanticipated demands on administration or sudden resignation or death.

The more this so-called "fat" is squeezed out of the organization in order to gain financial mobility, the less organizational mobility remains. This does not mean of course that there is no fat that can be eliminated without penalty but it is not always easy to distinguish the nonessential. In time the mounting resistance by the organization to further encroachment on *its* norms of mobility reserve forces the next step, namely a re-examination of the norms of financial policy which have set the boundaries on use of various reserves up to this point. Thus, for example, the traditional policy in long-term debt will be challenged and new levels considered. Lenders will be probed for the real limits of their willingness to lend and, if the customary sources resist, new lenders may be sought.

As this re-examination of financial norms and the utilization of remaining reserves begin, the sequence of use is likely to be reversed. Whereas originally the sequence was from cash to short-term debt to long-term debt, in this phase the approach is likely to start with long-term debt, the source that is the most uncertain and takes the longest time to negotiate. The intent is of course to protect the most predictable, reliable, and easily accessible reserves to the last.

The violation of historical norms on debt usage usually makes management distinctly uncomfortable. This awareness of increased financial risk may lead almost immediately to Phase V.

Response: Phase V

Whether or not flow deficits continue to occur, the existence of new highs in borrowing is likely to result for the first time in a serious examination of major reallocation of existing resources. New uses must now be viewed as substitutes for existing uses, not supplemental to them. This is likely to be a time for re-examination of strategic goals and strategic expenditures. Because liquidation of assets to provide major financial relief is likely to lead to loss of sales if not earnings, such action presents the major problem of at least a temporary adverse effect on performance until the released funds are again at work. What the management of Company E called the "phase in-phase out" problem makes it difficult to accept such reallocations.

In addition, as previously indicated, the liquidation of segments of the business, whether of redundant plant or of separable earning entities, is a highly uncertain process usually requiring considerable time. Often at this stage the urgency of need will force substantial sacrifices of value in order to induce a quick sale, if, indeed, sale can be realized at all.

Survival: Phase VI

If deficits persist beyond the stage of exhaustion of external reserves and liquidation of peripheral assets, then the only alternative left will be to curb outflows, inevitably reducing current sales and profits. The expenditure horizon has been pulled into the current year. Experience of some companies also indicates that the organization may have successfully resisted even to this point encroachment on operational mobility and there may still be substantial capital tied up — in inventory particularly. When the company's back is to the wall, these funds may be released. Some residual secured short-term borrowing may take place but this really amounts to a liquidation of the assets offered as security.

Summary Comments

As stated at the outset, this descriptive model of a strategy of mobility is an attempt at generalization of behavior in a sample of companies over a part of their history. There were, of course, many variations on the indicated pattern of response. There were wide differences in the degree and duration of funds flow pressure, and only two or three companies could be said to have approached the Phase VI limit. The remainder experienced an ebb and flow of need involving earlier and less extreme phases of response. Differences in the nature and timing of response were in part attributable to different environmental circumstances, but they also related to the attitudes, perceptions, and bargaining position of management. In particular, differences existed in the roles played by manipulation of expenditure horizons, inventory, and the liquidation of separable earning assets.

The description does not mention a common stock issue. This action was taken in so few cases and in these the circumstances were so different that no general statement can be made as to timing. In any situation involving persistent deficits there will come a time when this alternative is considered; but unless the need is explicit and clearly beyond the capacity of other alternatives, the issue of common stock is likely to be postponed as long as possible regardless of whether the need is aggressive or defensive. In the defensive situation there is obviously a delicate judgment to be made as to whether further postponement of the common stock alternative (in the hope that the need will disappear or be met in other ways) may bring circumstances under which the sale of common stock is no longer possible or acceptable. Most of the companies in the research sample did not put a common issue to the test of the market. They chose to find solutions in other ways.

Most companies were able to reverse the trend of funds flow

deficits at one of the intermediate phases of response, and thus had the opportunity to begin to restore the various internal and external, operating and financial reserves against uncertainty, which had been consumed in the process of response to the deficit flows. Since this study has not looked as carefully at the process of restoration under conditions of funds flow surpluses as at the process of response to deficits, its generalizations are more hesitant. One point that can be made is that the sequence of events in the period of recovery is not necessarily a literal reversal of the steps indicated for a series of deficits. The effect of a financial shock of substantial magnitude is likely to be a reassessment of priorities which may lead to a more conservative set of priorities at least until the memory of the shock fades. Thus, the effect may be adoption of more conservative debt limits, restrictions on the use of the more certain reserves, and maintenance of greater liquidity. The first reaction to relief from financial pressure may be to build up cash balances or short-term debt capacity rather than to restore the operating cushions of inventory or capital expenditure that were involved in the later phases. Much depends of course on the bargaining position of the various internal centers of interest.

The Role of Negotiation

For those who seek a rational explanation of behavior in the use of the resources of mobility, much of the answer lies in the process of negotiation which is necessarily involved in the use of both external and internal resources. Few of the resources of mobility are under the direct and undivided control of the financial officer. Cash and near cash, unused bank lines, and certain payments may be so regarded; but all other resources require the consent of either an outside or an inside party if they are to be reallocated as to use. This applies to future flows as well as to existing investments because financial plans and budgets assign these flows to various operational uses well before they are realized. To those who may argue that this understates the range of authority of the financial officer, since he is an extension of the office of the president, the answer is that the president is necessarily subject to many pressures in addition to financial matters and cannot therefore assign to such matters the same degree of emphasis as one solely preoccupied with them.

Observation suggests that in fact it is often easier for a financial officer to negotiate with external sources of funds than with those operating executives who are currently in control of existing resources. And this is understandable. The prospective institutional lender has something to gain by a sound investment and approaches a reasonable loan application in a receptive frame of mind. By contrast the vice president of production who is being asked to release some funds from inventory or the vice president of marketing who is being asked to cut back on his advertising budget has nothing to gain and much to lose by such action. The result will be to make his job more difficult, however worthy the intended use of the released funds may be. As a consequence operating executives are likely to put up a strong fight if the internal pressures are substantial.

Thus in the typical company, with most of its existing resources committed to specialized use, the financial officer is constantly engaged in a process of negotiating the release of funds as the company's requirements unfold. The ease and success of negotiation obviously depend on bargaining position, which is itself subject to change over time. In general, it is difficult to negotiate internally for a shortening of expenditure horizons when the sales trend promises continued growth; it is difficult to negotiate an economy drive when profits are holding their own or improving; it is difficult to argue for a reallocation of existing investment if internal or external reserves appear to exist. Previous examples have illustrated the unfortunate fact that all too often the internal bargaining power of the financial officer varies directly with the degree of financial adversity already in evidence: exhausted reserves, deteriorating sales, declining profits. He is strongest when adversity is deepest.

By contrast, his external bargaining power is strongest when the company is financially strong: good reserves, good sales trend, good profit performance. There is of course some bargaining strength at the other end of the scale, when creditors are so far committed that they cannot easily withdraw, but the easiest money to get comes to the company appearing least in need of it.

Ease of negotiation would direct that a company tap external sources first before turning to internal sources in order to cover a funds flow deficit.

Part of the problem of managing funds flows lies in the fact that most companies are unaccustomed to forecast and measurement in these terms. When emphasis is so heavily on sales and profits, there is a strong tendency to measure financial need by these yardsticks. It is apparent, however, that net funds flows and net profits do not necessarily move together. Major funds flow deficits may vary substantially in timing from a decline in profits, which is the customary signal for internal economies and sacrifices.

Some Variations on the Strategic Theme

It was possible in individual cases to identify a characteristic response to the pressures of financial mobility, and some of these variations on the general theme outlined in the descriptive model of strategy are worth noting. One of these can be referred to as the *strategy of least resistance*. Based on a primary concern for ease of negotiation this strategy, particularly in cases where the magnitude and duration of the need were uncertain, would first consume reserves directly controlled by the financial officer, then proceed to negotiate funds from familiar and "friendly" sources, such as a commercial bank, and lastly negotiate with unfamiliar or hostile sources external or internal.

Closely related to the concern for ease of negotiation, and tending to be found with it, is the factor of predictability and certainty of the source. When these two considerations are taken together they provide a powerful motivation in the sequence of use. Observation strongly suggests them to be a dominant force in shaping the specific responses to sequential deficits.

Another form of strategy is what might be called the *key resource strategy*. Some financial officers placed heavy emphasis on one particular source of funds as the primary defense against uncertainty. Frequently, though not universally, this was the commercial bank. Great care was taken to cultivate that source and terms of participation were followed religiously. Here the primary concern was for a "certain" source of quickly available funds of substantial magnitude. Where this resource involved negotiation with others, the financial officer might be said to have cultivated a trusted ally who stood ready to assist him in time of unexpected need. In turn the financial officer was prepared to pay whatever price that ally demanded for his potential assistance.

The most obvious key resource, of course, is redundant cash. A few financial officers based their strategy of mobility on the *big cash balance* approach. Few companies could afford the luxury of an amount of idle cash large enough to provide funds flow security by itself. The balance was more often than not a historical accident rather than a deliberate accumulation for this purpose, and it functioned in this capacity only for a period of time. While it lasted, however, it provided the financial officer with great independence and peace of mind. He had a powerful credit rating with unused external sources who constantly solicited his patronage, and he had excellent relations with his own management team who were free from the pressures of alternative use for the funds committed to their management. The big cash balance is the only sure road for the financial officer to be a friend to everyone, except perhaps the stockholder.

The great problem of the big cash balance approach is its visibility and the fact that stockholders and more particularly management turn hungry eyes on it and want to put it to use. This fact leads to the alternative of *secret reserves* under the control of the financial officer, with or without the knowledge of the president. These reserves are not so much secret as out of sight of the person untutored in accounting and financial practice. They largely take the form of prepayments or adjustable payments, which can be manipulated to provide considerable flexibility when occasion demands.

Finally, a few financial men claimed at least that they based their strategy of mobility largely on *accurate forecasting of funds flows*. They claimed that this ability allowed them to use resources freely in specialized use and to bring about necessary reallocation of resources through long-range planning of funds flows. Undoubtedly the opportunity to anticipate needs was substantially greater in some industries than in others, and accuracy of forecasting in some companies at least for certain periods was quite high. I remain skeptical, however, that present-day techniques of financial forecasting have the reliability that would permit a financial officer to neglect entirely the possibility of unexpected demands for funds.

Financial Mobility and Classical Financial Policy

An issue of lively interest to the reader, particularly the academic reader, is likely to be the relationship between an observed strategy of financial mobility and what might be called the classical concept of financial policies designed to maximize profit and the value of the stockholder equity. The question may be presented as follows: What was the evidence that management was concerned with maximization of value and with policies directed at value, and was there harmony or conflict between these policies and a strategy of mobility?

The reader may have been surprised that the description of strategy has made so little mention of cost as a consideration in the determination of priorities among resources. Theory would suggest that the proper approach to the use of resources under uncertainty would be to rank these resources in order of increasing cost and use them as required, starting with the cheapest first. The problem in practice lies in the fact that cost does not in itself relate to the needs of mobility, nor does it naturally coincide with characteristics of resources that do relate to mobility.

It should not be concluded, however, that management was insensitive to cost when developing its responses to funds flow deficits. On the contrary, it was very much concerned with the impact of its actions on reported earnings and earnings per share. This implies that the costs which mattered most were explicit, out-of-pocket costs rather than opportunity costs. It is further true that when a cost like the interest rate was in question, the rate usually was regarded as less important than the probable duration of the need and the desire not to prolong the cost beyond the period of need. Opportunity costs were recognized but normally as a secondary consideration and in terms of explicit and specific *internal* opportunities forgone. Management does not think in abstract or generalized terms. To speak of a redundant cash balance as having an opportunity cost to the stockholder would have little practical meaning, but to recognize that the funds could be invested in marketable securities or some capital expenditure promising cost savings is easy and natural for management.

It should also be noted that the large majority of managements carefully protected the stockholder interest by holding the number of shares outstanding to a minimum and thus maximizing earnings per share. The issue of common stock in either prosperity or adversity was unattractive because it quickly eroded the earnings per share that had been built up so laboriously over the years. The exception was the use of common stock for acquisition, where the acquired earnings could be expected to offset the increased number of shares without time lag.

In the light of these considerations there can be no doubt that the goal of cost minimization (or profit maximization) was a major constraint on applied strategies of mobility by tending to restrain the use of high-cost sources. An important qualification was that the costs of several alternatives were extremely difficult if not impossible to measure. Deferring capital expenditures, reducing research and development, and reducing inventory levels were examples of such alternatives. Here cost was reflected not by a number but by the degree of opposition that the proposed action generated on the part of those who would bear the sacrifice.

The point to be emphasized is that cost was *a constraint* and not *the determining factor* in financial mobility. Its role was essentially a negative one in restraining the use of sources that otherwise were desirable in terms of ease of access, predictability, reliability, flexibility in use, freedom from restraint on management action.

One of the more significant observations of the study was that in only a very few companies was financial management found to be entirely occupied with matters that could be described as the maximization of profit. The interesting point is that paradoxically these were companies with very large reserves of unused capital in the form of surplus cash or borrowing power. These resources so fully protected the financial officer from the risks of funds flow deficits that it was unnecessary for him to develop alternative strategies or to engage operating management in the internal trade-offs that a more fully committed situation would have demanded. Compromises of operating efficiency were unnecessary and the economies of extended expenditure horizons could be exploited to the full.

And yet it is obvious that what was being attempted was maximization of the return on only a part of the resources available to the company. Thus in a total resource sense these companies were not maximizing profit at all. *To drive to a full utilization of resources, however, would bring maximization of profit into conflict with the needs of financial mobility, and some sort of compromise between these two opposing objectives would have to be worked out.* As it happened, the two companies in the sample with heavy cash reserves were both expected to work out of this position in the foreseeable future. In each case it was apparent that the financial officer was already beginning to think about the needs of financial mobility and how they might be covered. It is at this point that an extension of the profit maximization goal into the minimization of the cost of the strategy of mobility runs into the nonquantitative considerations that make certain resources of mobility more attractive than others.

So far in this section no mention has been made of the link between earnings and market value that has become so all-important in discussions of financial theory — the price-earnings ratio. In theory it is the essential purpose of financial policy to protect the price-earnings ratio from erosion and if possible raise the ratio to its highest point so that improvements in earnings have the maximum multiplier effect on market value. Because of this it was one of the objectives of the study to try to observe the way in which explicit financial policies, particularly with respect to debt usage and dividend payments, interacted with a given strategy of mobility.

One of the first things to be said on the subject of the price-earnings ratio is that managements are as ill informed as anyone else as to what causes variations in the market prices of their stock. They are of course in possession of a good deal of inside information respecting change in factors that could affect market value and they have it long before the Street receives it. But they have no precise idea what the response will be, nor can they explain many responses that arise at a time unrelated to change in company fortunes. They can be as curious as a novice speculator about the trend of the market, and as frustrated in a search for hard information.

As a consequence managements generally tend to refuse responsibility for the behavior of the price-earnings ratio even though they are much interested in its improvement. Beyond a basic belief that a trend line of growth in earnings per share has a positive effect, there are no firm and universal convictions about how to influence the value of this ratio. Managements therefore tend to concentrate on improving earnings per share. Consistent with this I have found very little evidence that managements have in mind an optimum debt-equity ratio or an optimum dividend payout to generate the maximum earnings leverage on market value. This does not mean that they have no opinions about policies in these areas, where extremes would adversely affect market value. What it does mean is that there does not appear to be any target policy regarded as the ideal, contrary to what most theory would imply.

But these companies do have debt policies and dividend policies. What are they? In one sense a policy is merely a historical fact — what a company does now and has been doing — coupled with some sort of rationalization. A series of ad hoc decisions generally have some rational linkage which can be verbalized. Undoubtedly a great deal of "policy" is merely this. What we are interested in, however, is a concept that in some degree prescribes or circumscribes future actions for the purpose of increasing value or serving some other managerial goal. Of course, as this study has emphasized, the past does constrain the future in the precedents it sets and in the sequential nature of certain interrelated acts.

Speaking specifically of debt policy, this study has emphasized the role of the debt limit in providing a cushion against financial uncertainty and in calling for negotiation of the use of other internal resources before borrowing power is completely exhausted. Viewed in this way the preferred debt limit is one that is clearly less than maximum borrowing by standards of lenders, industry, or history. What appears risky to most managements is whatever exceeds anything done in the past. The stated debt policy is frequently the high water mark of successful past experience. The management will tend to adhere to this limit until events force it to consider a higher level, at which time it will cast around for industry precedent or lender approval in order to reassure itself that the risk is tolerable.

Thus debt policy is frequently a negative concept of minimizing a risk and assuring room for unexpected needs, rather than an optimum debt-equity mix designed to maximize value of the shareholders' equity. The pattern of events may force a new higher level of debt and, if the experience turns out safely, this may become a new guideline for future decisions.

Dividend policy has quite different implications, since for common stock there is potentially at least much greater freedom of adjustment to events. As other studies have brought out, there is a strong tendency for mature companies to hold to a relatively stable dividend payment, on the assumption that what the stockholder wants above all is regularity of payment. The result is a resistance to frequent cuts and also caution on increases in order to assure that the new level can be maintained. However, among the companies studied I encountered a surprising amount of willingness to cut back the dividend when the cash flow situation got difficult. In almost every case it was necessary for a deterioration of earnings to precede the cut in dividend in order to justify the action, but the incentive was in part to support the cash position. In addition, the reason might be advanced that fairness required everyone to share the sacrifices of difficult years. Usually a lower base of payment was established for the ensuing recovery.

The evidence of this group of companies is that dividend policy was only very roughly related to a concept of what determines maximum market value, the stability concept; and certainly there was no idea of what payout would produce this maximum value. The overwhelming justification of whatever payout obtained at a given time was the factor of precedent; the dividend was right because that was what had been paid in the past and there had been no significant protests from stockholders.

The interesting question for this study is the interaction of such policies, which have at least a general relationship to the value of the equity, and the strategy of mobility geared as it is to corporate and management needs. Financial policy, if it means anything, results in a certain consistency of behavior over time which may impose rigidity in response to new events. In this sense it is in conflict with the needs of mobility in the face of unexpected needs. The evidence of the study is that financial policies on such issues as debt and dividends were constantly interacting with the company's strategy of mobility. On the one hand, a debt policy on maximum long-term debt might resist a desire to use this source in time of need (though perhaps with the unstated approval of the financial officer). On the other hand, the needs of mobility and the strategy designed to meet those needs were periodically challenging the restraints of policy and at times breaking through to fashion new policies. This interaction in both directions is not surprising when financial policy is seen as an evolutionary process of feeling out new positions in a constantly changing world, positions which, it is hoped, will be both safe and successful by whatever yardstick the company sets for itself.

Part IV

A Strategy of Financial Mobility

Introduction

The purpose of Part IV is to take a step beyond a critical commentary on management behavior concerning financial mobility. It is one thing to call attention to the apparent limitations and weaknesses in current practice. It is easy to find evidence of imperfection in the way human beings respond under pressure to a highly complex problem. It is another thing to propose guidelines for action that have any assurance of producing better results. Any attempt at generalization in this regard, however sound the logic, has an inherent abstraction which reduces its relevance in the real world of individual practice. Nevertheless, the obligation remains on the critic to propose a better way and to do so in terms that have meaning for the practitioner. This is what I have attempted in Part IV.

The organization of ideas follows the sequence of Part III. Chapter 10 has something to say about making better use of the time before the unexpected funds flow deficit occurs. It is concerned with the methodology of analyzing information about the future. Chapter 11 has suggestions relating to an orderly approach to identification and measurement of the resources of mobility. Chapter 12 takes up the most difficult problem of all: the process of formulating a strategy for dealing with the unknown need for funds, a strategy that will be a guide for action over time. If these chapters are successful they will serve to open up, rather than end, a fruitful discussion of this very important dimension of financial management.

IO

Utilizing the Resource of Time

Among opportunities for improving current practice respecting financial mobility the most striking appears to occur in the methods by which management gathers information about the future. It should now be apparent to the reader, if it was not before, that the problem of uncertainty in balancing funds flows over time can be reduced to a measure of the time needed to bring about the reallocation of resources that new information indicates is required. The role of liquid reserves is to buy the time required, time that might have been provided if forecasting had correctly anticipated the event or circumstance. In this context, the old adage Time is Money is highly relevant. One can also say with equal relevance that Money is Time. Consequently, the more a business can relate its exploration of the future to a strategy of financial mobility the less it will be dependent on the financial resources outlined in this book.

BUSINESS FORECASTING: INFORMATION OR CONTROL?

I have reached the conclusion that the basic management purposes behind most current financial forecasting, including the most advanced applications, are in conflict with the information requirements of a strategy of mobility. The ultimate aim of financial planning as a quantification of management's objectives is to gain a commitment of the organization to achieve specified levels of sales and profits. In the period covering the formulation of the plan, of which a forecast is an integral part, there is an honest search for information about the future of the industry and of the company in order to establish the most probable trend of events. Given this measure of the upper boundary of what is reasonably attainable under the expected circumstances, top management negotiates a corporate goal which presumably stretches the organization to reach for the best possible outcome.

When agreement has been reached on a target for the next planning period, however, the inevitable by-product of management by objectives is for the organization to behave as if this view of the future is a certainty and all efforts must be directed toward making it come true. Of course, there is unlikely to be a protest if the company exceeds its target. On the other hand, human beings accustomed to rewards and punishments centered around sequential targets come to realize that an achieved goal becomes the reference point for new and higher goals, and therefore to exceed the accepted target is to make the next achievement more difficult.

Although this is an oversimplified and perhaps excessively harsh interpretation of corporate planning, there can be no doubt that forward planning in a large business organization develops rigidities in the perception of the future because forecasting becomes inextricably interrelated with group targets, motivation, and control. Statistically speaking, the target expectation is perhaps best described as a consensus estimate of the most probable future experience, with an upward bias which, if realistic, reflects the extent to which management believes its own behavior can influence the future outcome. The problem comes from the fact that once consensus has been achieved the admission that there may in fact be less favorable outcomes erodes organizational commitment and provides a rationale for excusing inferior performance.

By contrast the very essence of the information search leading up to a strategy of mobility is the exploration of the whole band of possible outcomes centering on the most probable event, including those outcomes that might be described as pessimistic. Expressed in numerical terms this band or range of, say, sales volume for the next year may be broad or narrow, depending on the industry, the competitive environment, and the company's skill at forecasting; and the most likely sales volume of, say, \$125 million may have only a .30 chance of occurrence. If all effort centers on this one assumption about the future, the many other possibilities as to sales volume, comprising together a .70 probability, are ignored. Of course, the problem is much more complex than this since the net cash flow is a product of many variables, one of which is sales level, with complex inter-related chances of occurrence.

The assertion that present-day forecasting and planning are unsuited to the needs of financial mobility because of their narrow focus on one set of outcomes is likely to elicit from the experienced practitioner two kinds of responses. One is to say that the full range of possible outcomes is almost without limit and to chase them all down would be to spend all one's time on planning and no time on action. The other response is likely to be that current financial planning in many companies does in fact consider a band of behavior — an optimistic and a pessimistic estimate as well as a most probable — and thus takes the whole band of likely outcomes into account.

To comment on the latter response first, in my experience the "band" concept of forecasting is confined to long-range forecasting (3 to 10 years) and to variations in the slope of the trend line. The area where financial planning and mobility planning really count is in the up-to-one-year horizon where something real is going on in the interaction of expectation and action. Here is where the commitment to a goal is strong and here is where tolerance for alternative outcomes is low. On the other hand, here is where information about financial mobility can be critical.

The customary way for dealing with uncertainty in the near-term planning phase is the moving forecast, which is updated quarterly or monthly so that deviations of actual from forecast can be spotted as early as possible as new information is received. During periods of gradual changes, when events are evolving more or less as expected, this periodic updating of the most probable future course of events is a satisfactory guide to funds flow management in the near term. However, the system of fore-casting is usually based on a direct extrapolation of current trends on the assumption that the basic cash flow relationships will continue to hold over the next 12 months. The system works reasonably well as long as this is true. But the forecast breaks down when the rate of change suddenly accelerates, or when a new set of cash-flow relationships emerges (perhaps because a new trend line is developing), or when a new force enters the picture. In other words, the forecasting system breaks down precisely when it is most needed for purposes of financial mobility.

In time, of course, the forecast will be adjusted to include the new information; and possibly without any real understanding of why the change has taken place the forecast will gradually become more reliable again, but only because stability has returned. To summarize the limitations of current forecasting for purposes of quick response to unexpected change in cash flows, the weaknesses are:

(1) the preoccupation with one set of assumptions about the future — the one best guess as to what the situation will be x periods hence;
(2) with action primarily conditioned by expectations for the near-term future, the tendency to see the future as a gradual evolution of immediate past experience;
(3) the practice of forecasting by means of aggregate balance sheet and income values, which inhibits careful examination of the basic forces affecting the key elements of cash flow.

We now return to the first of the two probable responses of the practitioner to these criticisms of current practice, namely, that they imply an alternative in terms of a greatly expanded exploration of the future, which could be exhausting as well as exhaustive and appears highly impractical. The remainder of this chapter will attempt to address itself in a realistic and practical way to the question: What is the alternative?

THE INFORMATION NEEDS OF FINANCIAL MOBILITY

From one point of view the problem of potential cash flow deficits would seem to be reducible to relatively simple terms. Although the deficit may be the result of one change or a combination of many different changes in the company or its environment, the need reduces to x thousands or millions of dollars of cash at y point in time. Thus it would appear that all the information needed is an estimate of the net amount of the need at any given point in the future and the probability of its occurrence. One may expect that at any given time there would be a range of values for a possible cash deficit with different probabilities associated with each gradation of value. Such estimates might form the basis of a determination of a cash reserve position.

However, this study has brought out that financial mobility — the reallocation of economic resources under uncertainty — is not confined to the role of a cash balance but extends to all dimensions of the cash flow system. The study has also emphasized that the particular strategy of response is substantially influenced by the nature of the specific needs at the time and by the specific environment of the time. In addition there is the linkage of present action with a specific past and an expected future. Thus in practice it is not possible to deal realistically with the problem of financial mobility without inserting this kind of specific detail of information. This makes the problem enormously complex.

It would be foolish to suggest that a solution to the problem is immediately at hand, a solution at the same time rigorous and realistic. The goal of this study is more modest: it is to observe the "state of the art" as it is and consider what the next useful improvement might be. Having concluded that the current approach to forecasting is inherently unsuited to the informational needs we have in mind, we find it necessary to strike out in a new direction. The purpose of this information search would be to provide a broader base of understanding of the cash flow consequences of a range of events lying between what the businessman might call his optimistic and pessimistic limits of expectation. Armed with more specific information on the cash flow consequences of most or all of the events likely to occur, the financial officer can act with greater confidence and speed as the specific shape of the future begins to emerge.

Thus the focus of the analysis of the future shifts from the present emphasis on what *will* happen to what *might* happen, with particular emphasis on the possible events that would create a cash deficit. To give these comments more meaning, let us become more specific by way of an illustration. Suppose a company has gone through the usual procedures of preparing a sales forecast for the coming year and has translated this forecast into operating and capital budgets, the effects of which are summarized in a pro forma income statement and balance sheet for the end of the period. Suppose further that the projection based on evidence from the sales force and market research is that sales will be up by 5% over the year just passed. Once this increase is accepted and incorporated into company plans of action, it will be for all intents and purposes a certainty until a better guess is developed or history proves it to be in error. Even if it is in error the company may still, for the duration of the planning period, behave as if it were correct, especially if the error appears modest.

As part of the planning exercise the financial office will translate a 5% sales increase, coupled with the information contained in operating and capital budgets, into a projection of cash flows and will identify the expected cash surplus or deficit for the year. It will then make plans for dealing with this surplus or deficit. This is the easy part of financial planning — developing a financial plan consistent with the company's expectations and goals for the year. But, as asserted at the outset of this study, while the financial officer may take refuge in the excuse that the shortage of funds was due not to his plan but to the judgments of other people upon which his plan was based, his basic responsibility is to maintain continuity of funds flows at all times. He has failed this responsibility if any essential corporate purpose is thwarted for lack of funds, regardless of where the blame may lie.

Thus, although the financial officer may be as convinced as anyone that a 5% growth in sales for next year is the best guess that can be made, if he is concerned about his basic responsibility he will be asking himself a variety of "what if" questions, some optimistic but also some pessimistic in their implications for the future of the business. Suppose, for example, that midway through next year there is a general business recession. What will the cash requirements of the business be then? There will be a tendency to ask this kind of question in private rather than in public because of a lack of hard evidence and a desire to avoid a label of being inherently timid or pessimistic. After all, there are all sorts of events one could worry about.

One of the practical problems facing a rational approach to mobility is the belief that it is counterproductive to spend time on pessimistic expectations with only a moderate chance of occurrence. It is, however, one of the conclusions of this study that a well-thought-out strategy of financial mobility depends on some careful analysis of a series of "what if" questions that could signal a significant cash flow problem. That which forces the financial officer to consider in private and informally questions that he should be considering explicitly and intensively is the knowledge that he will be responsible for the continuity of funds flows whatever happens.

To do this analysis of, let us say, a prospective business recession in any depth and detail would seriously strain present methods of business and financial forecasting. The information system by which these forecasts are usually assembled puts severe limits on the number and variety of alternative assumptions that can be examined with care in any reasonable period of time. There is a need therefore for an alternative tool of analysis. The one holding most promise is computer simulation.

So much has been said about computers in recent years that the word is likely to trigger a reaction on the part of the reader, which I would like to condition immediately with a few explanatory comments. The term "computer simulation" as used here is intended to convey two ideas about the character of the analysis. First, the goal of the analysis is to depict or simulate realistically the financial consequences of a set of conditions before these conditions actually occur, thereby disclosing in advance the nature of the problem to which the company may have to respond and making possible the outline of a tentative strategy. Second, the means by which this simulation takes place is a formal description or "model" of the cash flow system which, if programmed on a computer, releases the analysis from the serious time constraints imposed by conventional forecasting procedures.

The next section will consider in some detail the nature of such a computer model and its role in the generation of information for mobility analysis. A section at the end of the chapter will refer to the options for analysis where a computer is not available.

A COMPUTER MODEL OF CASH FLOWS

In order to convey the full meaning of the shift in approach to financial forecasting and analysis which this book presents as essential to an adequate information base for financial mobility, and in order to persuade the reader of its practicality, it is necessary to deal in some detail with the nature of a computer-based model of corporate cash flows. I have been involved in the construction of three such models over a span of five years and have had a chance to observe at first hand the kind of information that can be generated. Although the experience was not directly related to this research study, the coincidence of these activities has helped me to think through some of the analytical problems uncovered by the research study. The coincidence is in fact more apparent than real since the computer models were designed to apply some of the ideas growing out of the earlier study of corporate debt capacity which, as indicated in the introductory chapter, dealt with one dimension of the mobility problem.

The basic purpose of the model of cash flows is to analyze a variety of assumptions about the future and obtain an accurate description of their potential impact on cash inflows and outflows and on the conventional measures of financial performance. The word "model" has become an academic buzz-word and is rapidly becoming a business buzz-word, often used rather loosely to cover a multitude of sins. Here it is intended to signify a set of precise statements concerning the way in which various elements of the business operation (e.g., capital expenditures) affect cash flows. The flows taken as a whole can be used to calculate the change in net cash position from one period to another. These statements of the elements of cash flow are of course expressed in numerical terms and are formulated to allow for a range of values encompassing the entire span of possible future experience. Thus management is able to put into the model any assumption it wishes about, say, capital expenditures for whatever future time period is being examined.

The construction of a cash flow model designed to simulate a real company is a task requiring substantial time, ingenuity, and patience. It may surprise the reader to find that the mathematics of such a model is really very simple since all the relationships can be expressed as linear equations involving nothing more complicated than addition, subtraction, multiplication, and division. It may also be a surprise that the computer programming is not the real problem either, although this phase requires considerable skill. Here the difficulty is likely to be that the company's computer programmers have not had experience with such models and must learn as they go.

The major problem in practice lies in bridging the gap between established accounting information systems geared to measuring values according to accepted accounting conventions and what is in effect a new information system designed not to replace but to work alongside the established system of accounts.

This gap manifests itself in two ways. One is the matter of simple verbal communication with the accounting staff, who may have difficulty understanding the model and therefore may be suspicious of its role. The other aspect is the major deficiency in the kind of information necessary to specify this kind of model. To illustrate this point it is first necessary to indicate that the most expedient way of developing the cash data is to first generate the conventional accounting information — in effect, a pro forma income statement and balance sheet — and then transform this information into its cash flow equivalents. In this way the cash model can build on the existing data base and the analysis can deal with conventional financial values and ratios as well as cash position.

The problem of the information base arises in this way. Suppose our search focuses on the cost item: Factory Labor–Indirect. To date the question that has been asked of the production and accounting staffs has been: What will the expense item for indirect factory labor be *next year?* They start with the knowledge that sales last year were, say, $256 million and that total indirect factory labor was $34 million. They are given an estimate by the sales force that sales next year will be $269 million — up 5%. They will then go through calculations in some detail which indicate that the cost of indirect factory labor will be $35.1 million because of the specific plans for increase in productive capacity that the new sales volume demands. Next year there will be another specific sales estimate and another specific plan to meet the volume requirements upon which a cost estimate can be based, starting with the firm knowledge of what the cost is today and making a one-step and probably modest change.

Now more difficult questions arise: What if sales go up 10% rather than 5% or what if sales are down 5% — what then happens to Factory Labor–Indirect? Does it make any difference whether the change takes place over one year or three? (Of course it does.) What if there is a series of 5% increases or an increase of 5% followed by a decline of 7% followed by a rise of 2%? These are not academic questions, for in fact these are some of the possibilities for the future having great significance for forward planning. They are questions that the normal accounting and forecasting procedures cannot answer. Obviously what is being sought is a formula relating Factory Labor–Indirect to Sales (or some other key variable) so that whatever value for sales is inserted for a given future period a rational value for Factory Labor–Indirect is automatically generated. The conventional forecaster may be suspicious of formulas, but a cash flow model is based on the beliefs that there are logical reasons to explain how various items of cash inflow and outflow change over time and that these underlying causes of change can be discovered and expressed quantitatively — at least with sufficient accuracy to be useful for planning purposes.

Two basic sources provide the information for this simple but precise mathematical statement of how an element of cash outflow varies over a range of sales assumptions, as well as for all other such statements of how various elements of cash flow react to change. One source is the historical records of the company. The company has experienced a variety of changes in sales over that part of its past history which is still relevant to today's experience, and a judicious look at how a cost item has responded may be informative. Statistical tools are available, specifically regression analysis, which can be used to sort out which of the likely determinants of indirect factory labor can be used for future prediction of values with the greatest confidence and reliability.

Such historical analysis, however, must be viewed with caution.

When companies are undergoing rapid change, the length of past experience that is really relevant for the future may be very limited. Second, the kinds of events that we may be trying to understand may be completely missing from past experience. Third, the regression analysis may produce formulas so dominated by recent values of the variables that they are not very helpful to understanding more extensive change over longer periods of time.

This makes the use of the second source of information, management judgment, doubly important. Experienced management can of course be helpful in interpreting the record of the past and in suggesting its relevance for the future. More importantly, however, the information search of management ideas is needed in those areas where management discretion determines the behavior of cash flows and where therefore the decision rules of management must be built into the model. All of this must of course be carefully screened by common-sense analysis. For example, in the very important area of inventory management, the way in which inventory accumulation affects cash flows lies in the relationship between rate of production and rate of sales. No amount of regression analysis on inventory behavior in a period of decline can be regarded as a substitute for some investigation as to the precise procedures by which machines are shut down and men are laid off. Here the union contract may be the best source of information.

In these ways, step by step, the various elements of cash flow are tied back to the basic causal factors, primarily sales, through which the environment operates on the financial affairs of the individual business. The principal point to be emphasized is that wherever behavior is predictable for whatever reason (environmental, technological, organizational, behavioral, or contractual) that behavior will be specified. Wherever behavior is not predictable, or where prediction is unreliable, the model will be constructed so as to permit experimentation with different patterns of behavior, e.g., sales variation over time. The purpose of the model is to enable the analyst to focus on the few elements of cash flow about which he requires information and to let the rest be taken care of automatically.

It is not the purpose of this chapter to spell out how a computer model of cash flows actually works. On the other hand, any attempt to state the process in a few words runs the risk of being overly general, vague, and unpersuasive. The reader may be helped by the illustration of the output of one such model, seen in the Appendix. This particular model takes as a given the latest balance sheet and income data of the company (or any other selected starting position) and projects, quarterly for any desired period, balance sheets, income statements, cash flow statements, and any desired analysis of the accounts in operating or financial form. Before it will do this the model must be fed a sales "profile" for the period, that is, an experimental pattern of sales variation. Before each run it is possible to specify variations in the company's environment or response to change in environment, and by varying one element at a time an analyst can determine the sensitivity of the cash flows to these changes.

Those familiar with computers will recognize the model described here as a "deterministic" model, that is, essentially a complex device for rapid calculation where certain basic information such as the sales projection must be inserted from information outside the model. In effect the model must be "told" certain things about the future before it can respond. It is possible to construct the model so that these values are produced randomly by what is called a random number generator. This would make it possible to use the model to produce some measures of the probability of various events occurring, such as a cash deficit of a given magnitude. However, it is my opinion that neither the information base nor the users of the computer output are ready for this kind of refinement and that the more modest goals of analysis suggested in this section, if accepted as desirable by management, would represent a major step forward in the state of the art of generation and use of financial information.

THE USES OF SIMULATION INFORMATION

Once this heavy investment in financial analysis has been made, the company's scope for analysis has become enormously broadened and at the same time more reliable. In the process the management will learn much about the company's cash flows that it did not know before. Parenthetically, it is the discipline of constructing something that must be precise and must produce sensible results, consistently, that produces the main improvements in analytical ability. Management is now at liberty to ask any "what if" question it likes and can expect a useful answer almost instantaneously and at very little additional cost. Here are some of the questions that could be asked and answered:

(1) How do different patterns or sequences of sales variation over time affect cash flows? The common but naive assumption of a fixed percentage growth every year can be dropped and any number of fluctuations can be examined.

(2) What difference does it make whether the change in dollar volume of sales comes from a unit change or a price change? For example, what does a 2% across-the-board price cut do to cash flows?

(3) What is the financial effect of losing or gaining a major customer? If a customer accounting for 15% of sales volume decides to make rather than buy, how would he phase out and how would the expected pattern of cash inflows and outflows change as a result?

(4) What is the effect of a strike of x months' duration on the cash position of the company? The result could be a cash deficiency or a cash surplus depending on the specific events.

(5) How important is the speed of recognition of an event such as a business recession and how important is the speed of management response once the downturn has been recognized? For many companies the cash crisis of a recession period lies in the first few months or quarters when the lag of recognition and response produces sharply diverging outflow and inflow.

(6) How would the cash position be affected by changes in the various management decision rules that regulate discretionary elements of cash outflow? Where are the areas where a modest change has a major effect? For example, what are the guide lines on inventory levels — suppose they were modified by ± 5%?

(7) How would a lengthening of the collection period on receivables by 15 days affect the cash position?

(8) What is the effect of the timing of a change in the level of sales and operations? If current forecasting suggests an upturn in January rather than June as previously expected, does this make much difference?

(9) Proposals may be in motion for new financing. What are the long-term cash flow and other financial consequences of different debt-equity proportions or different contractual arrangements?

(10) How would a proposed acquisition affect the present pattern of cash flows?

If the reader has accepted the proposition that by the means indicated we can now have reliable answers to these questions, he is still entitled to ask: So what? He may feel that, now that the limitations of conventional forecasting have been overcome, he is about to be flooded with information that he is unsure how to use. How would answers to the above questions, for example, help to design or improve a strategy of financial mobility? We are in fact no closer to knowing the precise form the future will take. Once we leave the reassuring trend line of the conventional long-range forecast, the possible alternatives seem to be without limit.

In answer to this question it should be stated that the recommendations of this chapter are based on the following assumptions about the real world of business:

(1) That businessmen do not in fact make specific plans in terms of generalized trend lines but rather in terms of specific pieces of information about future events, however incomplete and fragmentary. The result of their continuing search for information is that they carve out of the limitless possibilities for the future a finite set of possible events which establish boundaries and define the circumstances to be taken seriously. As new information is received this set of events will be revised and modified in specific terms. For example, a strike may or may not be an element of this "relevant set" but is more likely to be if the planning period spans the expiration date of a labor contract. Being judgmental, these boundaries in the future may be to some extent peculiar to the person making the judgment; but there will often be general agreement among the knowledgeable management group. Where significant differences exist the differences can be explored.

(2) That with the right analytical equipment the set of possibilities relevant at any given time can be fully explored at no great cost.

(3) That when full financial information has been provided on the relevant set of possibilities, including funds flow impact, the list can be further narrowed for financial purposes to a smaller set with significant financial implications. What is judged "significant" is of course relative to the financial circumstances of the company at the time.

(4) That this information can then become a basis for one or a series of contingency strategies, which can only be developed in advance when the full financial implications are known in advance.

(5) That when a recession strategy, for example, has been thought through in advance of the kind of evidence that says a contingency is now a reality, valuable time can be gained in swinging this strategy into action. This study has stressed that time is every bit as valuable to a strategy of mobility as are cash reserves. The whole point of the analytical exercise recommended here is to move faster and with greater confidence on the steps necessary to change the flows as required.

There is a significant if unhappy parallel here between financial strategy and military strategy. Military strategists often engage in a series of war games in which different postures are assumed on behalf of the enemy and appropriate responses are then worked out. These games attempt to simulate the real world, to introduce the unexpected and force the planners to think out what they would do while there is time to refine judgment and assess alternatives without cost. The enemy for business is its unknown, unpredictable, and often hostile environment. That environment becomes less menacing when its more likely thrusts against the company have been thought out in advance.

In fact, of course, a great deal of this kind of thinking goes on right now in many businesses. Chapter 7 reported that formal forecasts show only the most probable outcome (or the most preferred outcome) and it is left to the private thought processes of the financial officer to think through possible variations on that theme. Discussions with financial officers show not only that this thinking goes on everywhere but also that alternative financing strategies in the event of unexpected change are under active consideration. The thrust of this chapter is to urge that this important area of financial planning be brought out into the open, at least within the financial office; that it be given the assistance of formal analysis and the most powerful analytical tools available; and that this information be used to minimize the lag in recognition and response when specific events begin to emerge.

AN EXAMPLE OF SIMULATION RESULTS

The following is an actual example of how a company obtained new insights into possible future events and thereby strengthened its capacity for financial mobility. The company in question is a large manufacturing business, which in recent years has gone through a period of accelerated growth. Because the rate of growth exceeded the rate of internal generation of funds, the company's long-term debt increased to levels that by conventional rules of thumb would be regarded as above average for its industry. This situation led to some concern within top management, which decided to take a closer look at the problem.

As a part of the process of analysis it was decided to build a cash flow computer model of the type described in this chapter, not merely to do this analysis but to provide a general purpose analytical tool in the financial area. The period of construction took six months from the time the active effort began. The model was tested to see whether it was generating sensible results, by going back in time and comparing machine output with actual results. Then it was used to simulate a business recession in order to observe possible problems resulting from what some members of the board considered to be excessive debt. Existing long-range forecasts were based on an industry growth trend, which was backed up by sound economic data so far as the *average* rate of growth was concerned. On the other hand, the industry was characterized by substantial cyclical swings, which were largely unpredictable as to timing, magnitude, and duration. The most confident statement that could be made about the future was that sales would *not* grow at 5% every year.

Historical evidence and the experienced judgment of marketing and production management laid out some probable boundaries on the magnitude and duration of a future recession with respect to both unit sales and price. With the use of the model it was then possible to test the effects of a variety of sales "pro-files" within these boundaries and beyond if desired. A great deal was learned from this exercise in forward analysis. The most obvious result was that the type of recession considered as a distinct possibility by management could be expected to result in a substantial deficit in cash flows. This would occur in spite of substantial cuts in capital expenditures and overhead expense when the recession reached a level considered as a "severe" de-cline.

Part of the analysis was a series of "sensitivity runs" in which all the elements of the model were held constant except one and that one was changed over a range of values considered to be the boundaries of likely variation. From these runs it was learned that the principal villains in the cash flow problem were (1) recession price policy — sharp reductions in cash inflow without compensating reductions in outflow; (2) the time lag in recogni-tion and response in the early recession period; (3) sluggish in-ventory controls, which meant that large amounts of cash were consumed in the early recession period and were slow to be released; (4) (related to #3) rigidities in the rate of plant output; (5) rigidities in discretionary expenditure categories. The com-puter runs not only identified the sources of the problem but also indicated relative significance and the potential gains from modi-fication of the practices assumed by the model.

Interestingly, the level of long-term debt did not turn out to be one of the major causes of the recession cash flow problem. Changes in the level of debt assumed within the range of 25% to 45% of capitalization resulted in very modest changes in the size of the recession deficit. This was due to the facts that the recessions considered likely were only two or three years in duration, that the long-term debt was a serial obligation over an extended period, and that other elements of cash flow had a more severe impact. The effect of having this information was clearly to shift contingency planning for recessions away from a concern with debt magnitude to a concern for such matters as inventory control as the means by which flows could be held in balance and mobility preserved.

ANALYSIS WITHOUT A COMPUTER

A persistent question, particularly in the minds of the managements of smaller companies, is whether this kind of formal mobility analysis can be done only with the aid of a computer. The answer is that it can be done without a computer but the process is necessarily much more time-consuming and therefore the range of items analyzed is much more restricted. A much greater burden is placed on those making the analysis to judge *in advance* what are likely to be the most important things to be examined. However, I have done this kind of analysis for a smaller company without the use of a computer and the gain in information was considered substantial.

There are a variety of ways in which the elaborate analysis of the Appendix can be collapsed into a simple arithmetic model which can be analyzed on paper. For example, the detailed study of costs can be reduced to a simpler breakdown of fixed and variable costs if necessary. Judgments can be made about the assumptions to which cash flows are likely to be most sensitive. Recession and other tests can be restricted to the adverse limits rather than the full range of possibilities. Assumptions about such considerations as debt levels can be limited to a few sharply contrasting values. The use of a computer greatly extends the range of exploration of future possibilities, but some useful exploration is clearly available without it. Its absence simply heightens the importance of sound judgment in advance of the analysis.

II

Taking Inventory of the Resources
of Mobility

Chapter 10 dealt with the first step in developing a strategy of mobility — a thorough search for information not only about what is likely to happen in the near future but also about what might happen to disrupt funds flows. The search includes the need for the fullest possible understanding of how these events affect the financial position of the company. Then, as the specific sequence of events clarifies to the point where they can be anticipated in action, that action can be taken as early and as accurately as possible. The resulting gain in time for response to events is a direct substitute for mobility in invested resources. It is quite unrealistic, of course, to expect a complete absence of surprises. Every company must be prepared to deal with the need that comes with little or no advance notice.

The second step therefore in developing a strategy of mobility is to take stock of the company's resources of mobility. Most companies do not attempt to do this in an open and systematic way, although unquestionably the financial officer will have in his mind rough orders of magnitude for the key resources on which he leans most heavily. The position taken in this chapter is that it would be beneficial to develop a regular procedure for identification and measurement of these resources. The purposes in so doing are (1) to focus attention on this important dimension of financial management, (2) to encourage a comprehensive look at the whole set of alternatives and their relation to each other, (3) to communicate change in the resource position on a regular basis to other members of the management team, and (4) to encourage a more careful examination of resources by an attempt to measure them quantitatively.

CURRENT APPROACHES TO MEASUREMENT OF RESOURCES

The conventional forms of financial reporting have certain well-known characteristics which are rooted in the purposes for which the reporting was designed and in accounting conventions developed over the years to improve consistency and comparability. At regular intervals the company's economic resources are identified and valued as of a date now passed, with the intent that owners, creditors, and others may know the value of the business at that time and compare it with its value on some prior date. The balance sheet reflects a view of management as the custodian of economic value and as a creator of economic value. The supplementary income statement measures change in value (profit or loss) between two dates. While these numbers have a considerable element of opinion and judgment embedded in them, they do have the advantage for objectivity of being based primarily on historical cost and reported after the fact of expenditure.

These efforts at keeping score on the innings played up to the present are important to every game, including business, and are taken seriously not only by those who have a claim on the value reported — owners and creditors — but also by management, whose performance is primarily measured in these terms. However, in recent years, with the increased emphasis on forward planning, management has shifted its attention to a formal analysis of the future rather than the past on the sound reasoning that it has a chance of influencing the future and no chance of changing the past. Balance sheets and income statements are the documents of the observer; forecasts and budgets are the documents of the participant. Understandably, management is also interested in how these plans for the future will affect the score card, and companies are now accustomed to the process of producing pro forma income statements and balance sheets to see how values will look if things work out as planned.

These documents dealing with the future will of course indicate the timing and magnitude of any gap in funds flows that is expected to follow from external events or internal action over the planning period. Specific plans will exist for covering any excess of outflows over inflows by means of reduction in cash balances, loans, or other sources. The changes will be reflected in the pro forma balance sheet for the terminal date. However, the key question for financial mobility is: Where does one find a statement of the resources available for the unexpected need? The most likely source would appear to be the latest balance sheet since this presumably lists all the assets of the company. But the left-hand side of the balance sheet answers the wrong question. It answers the question: Where have we invested funds up to now? instead of: Where can we find funds to invest in the future, say the next 12 months?

So, for example, the balance sheet tells us that the company has invested $12 million in credit to customers. That specific $12 million of accounts receivable may well become $12 million of cash over the next four months, but so long as sales volume remains at present levels the company will have around $12 million locked into accounts receivable continuously and hence quite unavailable as a resource to meet new needs. If the new need is a result of an unexpected 5% increase in sales, part of it will be an increase in accounts receivable from the new customers. The same holds true for any other earning asset standing on the books, unless it happens that the unexpected event that creates the need for funds also releases funds from use elsewhere.

Even cash, the completely unspecialized asset, often turns out to be as unavailable for use as the more tangible physical assets. Much of what appears on the balance sheet as cash is really permanently lodged in the transactions pipeline. Unless the volume of transactions changes, the commitment will not change. A check in transit through the company's collection system may be recorded at some moment in time as "cash on hand and in the banks" but may still be unavailable for spending. Companies and banks have made valiant efforts to reduce float but large amounts remain.

The unhappy fact is that there does not now exist an inventory of the resources that are critical to management action in the future — the means by which it will survive the shocks of uncertainty.

A New Kind of Financial Statement

This study proposes the creation of a new set of financial statements representing a clean break from the purposes and conventions of the traditional balance sheet and income statement. They would be forward looking, not backward looking. They would be frankly judgmental, not based on historical fact. They would be designed for a limited internal audience, not for public information. They would be concerned with funds flows, not with income and value. Thus they would be supplemental to existing financial reporting, aimed at a better "handle" on financial mobility.

The first of these two statements already exists in retrospective form — the funds flow statement. What is desired here is a pro forma funds flow statement for the planning period, say of one year. Funds flow statements take many forms ranging all the way from a simple recasting of the balance sheet plus income

EXHIBIT 11A

Pro Forma Funds Flow Statement for the Period
January 1, 19XX–December 31, 19XX

Inflows		
Collection of accounts receivable	$	
Revenue from investments	$	
New external financing		
Bank loans	$	
Term debt	$	
Sale of equity	$	
Liquidation of assets	$	
Total inflows		$
Outflows		
Expenditures dictated by planned		
production schedule	$	
Expenditures for marketing program, 19XX	$	
Research and development, 19XX	$	
Administrative overhead	$	
Capital expenditures	$	
Dividend payments	$	
Nondiscretionary outflows		
(interest, debt repayment, taxes, etc.)	$	
Total outflows		$
Net increase (decrease) in cash balance		$

statement to show major changes between two points in time to an elaborate breakdown of gross revenues and expenditures. What would be most useful here would be a grouping of inflows and outflows to reflect distinctive management choices in the allocation of funds. One example of this statement is shown in Exhibit 11A. The specifics would vary from company to company and from time to time depending on the nature of the critical choices in the allocation of resources.

EXHIBIT 11B

INVENTORY OF POTENTIAL RESOURCES OF FINANCIAL MOBILITY
AS OF JANUARY 1, 19XX, FOR THREE TIME HORIZONS

Resources	Lead Time for Release (to coincide with planning periods)		
	One Quarter	One Year	Five Years
I. Uncommitted Reserves			
A. Instant reserves			
1. Surplus cash	$		
2. Unused line of credit	$		
B. Negotiable reserves			
3. Incremental bank loan			
Unsecured	$		
Secured	$		
4. Incremental long-term debt		$	
5. Issue of new equity		$	
II. Reduction of Planned Outflows			
A. Volume-related			
6. Change in production schedule	$		
B. Scale-related			
7. Marketing program		$	
8. Research and development budget		$	
9. Administrative overhead		$	
10. Capital expenditures		$	
C. Value-related			
11. Dividend payments		$	
III. Liquidation of Earning Assets			
12. Shut-down		$	
13. Sale of unit			$
	Total→ $		
		Total→ $	
Total Resources			$

We have repeatedly emphasized that the first statement will reflect one perception of the forthcoming year at one point in time. The second financial statement, illustrated in Exhibit 11B, anticipates the possibility that when the funds flow statement for this same period is drawn up retrospectively, it will be substantially different perhaps in both the items listed and the magnitudes. The fact that the company was able to survive this change will have been thanks to the resources found in Exhibit 11B.

A statement similar to Exhibit 11B would be prepared to show the state of the reserves as of the end of the planning period and would reflect the changes anticipated in the pro forma funds flow statement of Exhibit 11A.

As said before, this statement is frankly judgmental. Every item on the list of resources represents a guess as to events, circumstances, magnitudes, and timing; and this kind of number is likely to horrify the conventional accountant. However, to action-minded management this information is far more important than the left-hand side of the balance sheet, for it is an attempt to measure as well as possible the economic muscle of the business either for seizing opportunity or for coping with adversity. Notice that in the process of transforming a balance sheet from a backward to a forward looking document liabilities become assets (unused bank debt) and assets become liabilities (plant that cannot be converted into cash). Notice also that the question of who owns the resources now is not an issue. The question is: Are they at the disposal of management?

In order to emphasize the uncertainty of some of these resources it might be helpful to have an additional column showing the probabilities assigned to each value by the person making up the statement. This would be useful only if he thought he could identify substantial differences in this respect — assigning, say, a .95 probability to an unused line of credit but a .10 probability to the sale of certain earning assets. If this were done, the dollar figures could be expected values (estimate multiplied by the probability), thus deflating resources having a very low chance of availability.

The funds expected to be available are also conditional. Under one set of circumstances one subset of the list of resources would be available and under another set of circumstances another subset would be available. This suggests that the form of Exhibit 11B is over-generalized. Perhaps the document should identify the principal uncertainty toward which it is directed. For example, if the principal concern as of January 1, 19XX, is for a possible boom during the year, then one would not expect resources to be available under item 6, whereas if the concern is for a strike this source would be a dominant one. While it would be foolish to think of a different document for every possible contingency, it may be possible to identify a few categories of contingencies into which most events would fit.

Exhibit 11C suggests one grouping of contingent events having a material effect on funds flows, each group having significantly different implications for available resources. A variety of contingencies are placed in six boxes, which are defined in two

EXHIBIT 11C

CLASSIFICATION OF EVENTS CAUSING UNBALANCED FUNDS FLOWS

Effect on Company	*Atmosphere of Change*	
	Defensive	*Aggressive*
	Unexpected Events	
Change in volume of production/sales	Strike Recession Loss of major customer	Major price change Industry boom Gain of major customer
Change in scale* of investment	Response to competitor — marketing or R & D Technological obsolescence	Expansion abroad Going national Automation
Change in nature of business	Liquidation Spin-off Phase-out of product line	Acquisition New product line

* Significant shift in level of operations or increase in dollars invested per dollar of sales.

dimensions: (a) the general atmosphere of change — whether the need for a financial response is basically defensive or aggressive; and (b) the effect on the company — its volume of operations, its scale of operations, or the nature of the business. Although the items listed in these boxes are intended to illustrate rather than exhaust the list, they contain the most common threats to balanced funds flows.

The time horizons of Exhibit 11B are of course very important. Some resources that could be available with a lead time of one year would not be available if the lead time was only one quarter. It follows from this that as the horizon is lengthened the cumulative totals at the bottom of the columns of figures should increase. Given two years, for example, a company should be able to take the liquidation of certain earning assets seriously, as an addition to the use of bank credit and other resources that can be activated in a much shorter period.

ESTIMATING INDIVIDUAL RESOURCES

Because of the judgmental nature of the numbers to be found in an inventory of financial resources of the type proposed, it is not possible to lay down precise rules for measuring amounts for any given resource. On the other hand, some comments may be useful on the subject of the process of deriving these estimates. There are four basic dimensions to each estimate:

(1) magnitude;
(2) conditions of availability, if any;
(3) certainty of availability within a given time horizon;
(4) required lead time to activate.

This section will comment on the various resources listed in Exhibit 11B with respect to these dimensions.

1. Surplus Cash

The amount of cash available to meet contingent variations from the pro forma funds flow statement will be the actual cash plus marketable securities at the beginning of the period less:

(1) the minimum transactions balance consistent with the planned level of operations;
(2) seasonal cash needs if provided internally;
(3) specific cash commitments carried over from previous periods;
(4) cash commitments required to cover a planned deficit in cash flows for the planning period, if any.

What is left, if anything, is the company's cash reserve against contingencies for which the strategy of financial mobility is to be designed. If the contingency is an event that changes the volume of transactions, then there will be a change plus or minus in the minimum transactions balance. These amounts are probably not known precisely but the purposes of this document do not require conventional accounting accuracy.

Surplus cash has been referred to in this study as an instant reserve. This implies not only that it is available without any activation lag but also that it is 100% certain, has no conditions upon which its release depends, and is usually directly accessible to the financial officer. In addition to the cash explicitly listed as such on the balance sheet, there may be pockets of cash in the organization which are reserved for specific purposes but can be made available under some circumstances. If significant, this cash may require separate classification.

It is worth noting that the estimate of surplus cash should disregard whatever rules of thumb may have been used by the company in the past for determining minimum cash balances. Such guidelines are normally generalized to cover a variety of needs, including a contingency reserve. It is more informative to deal with each major need for cash specifically and independently. When the known demands on cash have been identified, the remainder is presumably there to cope with the unknown demands. At this point the question is not what the reserve against the unknown need should be but rather what it is.

2. Unused Line of Credit

The second part of the instant reserve is the unused portion of a negotiated line of credit at the bank. Whatever the original purpose behind this loan might have been, if it is available to the company without major restrictions on its use it may be considered a part of the general mobility reserves. These are the funds to which financial officers refer as the "funds at the end of a telephone line," implying not only speed but certainty. Even though the usual arrangement does not represent a legally binding contract by the lender to deliver funds under any circumstances, for all practical purposes the source can be considered certain. However, the credit squeeze of recent experience has led some financial officers to revise their opinions on this. If a higher degree of certainty is required, a commitment fee may be involved. The rare use of such a fee suggests that most businessmen assume the risk of "default" on the line of credit is very modest.

Care should be taken not to double count this reserve in evaluation of the total credit position of the company. It may be that the bank expects the line to be converted in due course into term debt, at which time term debt capacity must be available.

3. *Incremental Bank Loan*

With or without a negotiated credit line, a financial officer will have in mind an amount of money that could be negotiated with one or more commercial banks. This information may be gained from past experience, inferences drawn from current conversations, or direct representation from banks seeking new business. While such sources are obviously open to challenge, especially if the need falls in an environment of some crisis, there are good reasons why the estimated amount can be accepted as a likely prospect. Most financial officers speak with some confidence of their commercial bank borrowing power, a confidence largely based on close personal association with bankers over the years. Normally what is referred to is an amount that can be borrowed on normal terms at reasonable rates, perhaps prime, perhaps not, and without a specific pledge of collateral.

Beyond the line of credit and the estimated limit on unsecured bank borrowing there is the prospect of additional bank debt on a secured basis. Invariably a secured bank loan is regarded by borrower and lender as a defensive move to be avoided so long as other alternatives remain. Thus it is not likely to be part of the, explicit strategy of mobility of the healthy company unless industry practices have made it acceptable. A company may not wish even to list an estimate of the incremental borrowing power attainable in this way. Nevertheless, it is there and at some time the "last resort" alternatives may become relevant.

4. *Incremental Long-Term Debt*

As in the case of short-term debt, the inventory of resources converts a potential liability of long-term debt into an asset since it is unused purchasing power available to the company in implementing future decisions. The upper limit on long-term debt is usually a more uncertain estimate because of the infrequency of such borrowing, the more impersonal atmosphere, and the greater importance of subjective data in the decisions of the lender. The outside limit is, of course, what the lender is willing to lend. Evidence on this can be obtained from generalized standards, specific guidelines in existing debt contracts, or the direct responses of specific lenders to a tentative loan request. The availability of the debt is going to be influenced by the prospective terms, including period of repayment and interest rate. In making an inventory of resources of mobility the company should be willing to consider a reasonable range of rates and not insist on prime, since the full measure of cost must include a look at the alternatives if debt is not used.

As well as being a difficult number to pin down precisely, the long-term debt limit is conditioned by the circumstances of need. It is obviously much easier to borrow in larger amounts if the need is clearly for profit-making purposes with a good chance of success. It is more difficult to borrow long term for defensive reasons. However, the terms defensive and aggressive are relative and much depends on how persuasive management can be in putting the case before the lender.

In spite of these difficulties a company can come up with a good approximate estimate of how much additional long-term borrowing can be done under reasonably normal terms. If the long-term debt is currently 10% of capitalization and this is clearly below what various sources of information indicate as a "normal" limit of debt for the industry in the minds of lenders, then the additional 15%, or whatever it is, can be listed as a reserve for many of the purposes that may arise. Only when the company approaches the 25% level will it know more precisely what the actual limit is.

The reader familiar with *Corporate Debt Capacity* may wonder why this discussion of long-term debt limits has been solely in terms of conventional rules of thumb. That book argued for an internally derived standard based on a careful analysis of the variability of cash flows. The answer is that the purpose of this inventory is not to set debt policy but merely to indicate what funds are available, which is basically a matter of the lenders' willingness to lend. At a later point, when all the alternatives are out in the open, the question of a possible reserve of long-term borrowing power must be considered as part of the general strategy of mobility. At that time, all considerations affecting future flows can be taken into account.

5. *Issue of New Equity*

A number to be placed on the inventory of resources opposite item 5 may well be the most controversial of all. Of all the sources on the list it is the one that some will argue has no measurable limit, particularly if the use of the funds is aggressive rather than defensive. This position has its greatest validity in the case of a need to acquire another business in which the transfer of ownership is accomplished by an exchange of stock. Very large amounts of assets have been acquired in this way, representing an important element of financial mobility. However, this is only one of many contingent needs and it is the only one where stock can be used as a direct substitute for cash. In other uses the stock would first have to be sold for cash on the open market.

Here we encounter a number of practical limitations on the amount likely to be issued in any given time period. One of these is the question of how recent was the previous issue of equity. It is a well-established convention that companies do not go to the equity market frequently for small amounts. A second limitation would be the current state of the equity market. A downward trend practically eliminates equity issues while the trend is in progress. A third limitation would be the circumstances of the company and the nature of the need for funds. A fourth would be the amount of equity that the underwriter can comfortably place with his clientele. A fifth, a self-imposed one, would be the amount of dilution in earnings per share that management feels it can stand while still showing growth over the planning period.

Although all these limits are vaguely defined, they add up to the prospect that in certain planning periods the amount of new equity a company can count on for strategic purposes is a finite amount which can be estimated in approximate form. Whatever number is used will of course be heavily conditional on the specific events emerging during the period. Here again, as in the case of long-term debt, the initial estimate should not be in terms of a self-imposed limit but rather in terms of the maximum imposed by the circumstances and environment of the time. This will leave open the question of whether and when equity will be employed in response to unexpected needs.

6. Reduction of Planned Outflows — Change in Production Schedule

As the classification in Exhibit 11B recognizes, certain volume-related outflows under certain circumstances can be curtailed in favor of other needs as they emerge. This package of outflows is described here in terms of those outflows paced by the production schedule. Curtailment of the production schedule is a function of (a) a decline in the rate of sales, magnitude, and duration, and (b) the size and composition of the buffer stock of inventory. If it were not for inventory, this source of funds flow adjustment would be conditional on the coincidence of the unexpected need with a decline in sales and then only to the extent of the sales decline. However, the existence of inventory may provide the possibility of a significant departure of the rate of production from the rate assumed in the pro forma funds flow statement. The problem is then one of gaining management commitment to see that the reduction takes place.

As described in Chapters 4, 5, and 6, curtailment is very difficult, even under conditions where funds flow pressure is clearly on the company. However, given the will at the top of the organization, a sum may be available from this source, particularly under conditions of declining sales volume. How much is available depends on the time period involved and the specific process by which a partial shut-down of operations can be achieved. In this situation it must be recognized that cash flow considerations may be taking preference over income considerations, short run. On the other hand, there are costs of carrying inventory as well as costs of not having it.

Regardless of how uncertain and conditional the amount, it is important to recognize this resource as an alternative and to attempt to measure its magnitude.

7. Marketing Program

I believe that an effort to measure a company's ability to cut back on certain of its scale-related expenditures forces that company to ask some searching questions about these expenditures. The basic question is one of attempting to relate the expenditure to the time period over which the benefits are assumed to accrue and in particular to distinguish those expenditures directly related to the sales and earnings of the current planning period from those expenditures designed to improve sales and earnings beyond that period.

The question is posed in very blunt terms when one asks how much can be carved out of the marketing budget, for example, without seriously reducing current sales and earnings. Of course the answer will be different depending on who is asked, but the purpose is to get an answer as objective and free of bias as possible. Generally speaking the answer breaks down into three main components: (1) expenditures explicitly tailored to serve long-range marketing goals, e.g., certain kinds of market research and image-building; (2) fat — slack in the budget that accumulates in good times when controls loosen up; (3) items the benefit from which is difficult or impossible to measure. In the latter category fall some forms of advertising which, as has been seen, are fair game when things get a bit tight.

Thus the effect of these cuts in expenditure when they come is to pull in the company's expenditure horizon and eliminate inefficiency. They may also damage some genuine effort in the fuzzy areas, but since the benefit is obscure, so is the damage. The difficult question for management is how flexible its expenditure horizon is — how much pulling in and pushing out later can be done without serious long-range effects. This question can only be answered in terms of specifics and in the form of the judgments of experienced men.

8. *The Research and Development Budget*

One of the areas of expenditure where there appears to be a remarkable degree of flexibility in the timing of expenditure is that referred to as Research and Development. In the abstract this would seem to be an area where expenditures would have to be stabilized for a number of years in order to attain the desired technological advances. It would also seem to be an area where the outcome was vital to the strategic objectives of the company. The evidence to the contrary may be explained by the facts that (1) this expense category often becomes a tent covering a variety of expenditures, including routine engineering that is not as vital as might appear; (2) the actual output from an R&D department may not be very notable; (3) in any case the accomplishments may be hard to measure at any given time. If a president is not satisfied with what is going on, he may be willing to have a shake-up, including loss of some personnel, in the hope of a better start later. Thus, once again, how flexible the expenditure horizon is in this area depends on the concept of Research and Development, the productivity of the group, and its stage of development.

9. *Administrative Overhead*

This group of expenditures usually has some degree of postponability and even some degree of simple improvement in efficiency. The extent of the potential diversion of flows to other uses depends largely on the amount of pressure that can be brought to bear. In the case histories we saw examples of the company that mounts a crusade against budget slack and charges off in all directions. A kind of collective zeal must be kindled, which is something that apparently cannot be maintained indefinitely. Thus, how much can be gained by pressure on the general scale of overhead outlays depends heavily on how recent was the last economy drive and how apparent are the needs demanding the diversion of these funds.

10. *Capital Expenditures*

Undoubtedly the area of the greatest movement in the expenditure horizon is capital expenditures. Earlier chapters stressed the need for a breakdown into subcategories, for the flexibility varies greatly. These categories were: scale-related, strategic, and value-related. Because of the considerable time lag between decision and cash outlay in this area, there is a problem of how quickly the stream of outflows can be arrested. Past commitments and partially completed programs may have to be run out, though the abruptness of the action depends on the seriousness of the new need for funds. Likewise we have seen companies facing the question of whether to break in on a budget year to revise the outlays or wait until the normal time comes up for the new capital budget.

In any case there will be a natural reaction to differentiate as to the purpose of the capital expenditure. Expenditures for expansion of capacity in time of declining sales are of course cut back sharply. Expenditures of the value-related sort, designed primarily to cut costs and improve earnings performance, will likely be subjected to a much sharper review when funds flows tighten up. The opposing interests of cash needs and income needs will come to the fore. What happens will depend on which is the greater need at the moment. Truly strategic capital expenditures will be protected from cutbacks except in very severe situations.

The expected duration of the cut will vary with circumstances. Eventually scale-related capital expenditures will begin to creep up again as it becomes apparent that they are vital to current sales and profits. Likewise value-related expenditures are likely to become increasingly pressing if earnings are clearly jeopardized. However, as we have seen, some companies cut capital outlays sharply for several years without any *apparent* damage to current sales and earnings. All the way through these areas of scale-related outlays one can see the evidence of funds flow pressure uncovering opportunities for genuine economies in operation, economies that apparently were not attainable before the pressure arose.

11. *Dividend Payments*

Practically speaking, it is a rather rare case where cash dividends to common equity holders can be cut before there has been a material decline in earnings. The option to reduce dividends as a part of a drive for funds for expansion appears open only to those companies that can clearly establish the market image of a growth company and attract a substantial majority of stockholders who have only capital gains in mind. The problem is, of course, in the danger of a serious decline in market value because stockholders see the cut as a signal of weakness.

If the need for funds coincides with a decline in earnings, then the option is open and management must decide whether item 11 will be a resource for mobility and if so, how much. The decision in this area is likely to be a highly subjective one, partly because it stirs strong emotions and partly because there is no clear evidence by which to weigh the consequences in advance. The consequences are exterior to the business itself — in the stock market and on the stockholder — but they are of concern to top management. Some managements will elect to cut dividends quickly and sharply. Some will attempt to defend the cash dividend as a fixed outlay under anything but the most extreme pressures. If the response is quick and sharp, this can be a significant source of funds in an emergency.

12/13. *Liquidation of Earning Assets*

Earlier comments on the role of liquidation in strategies of mobility indicated the considerable uncertainties surrounding the release of funds from this source and therefore the limited role to be played by the liquidation of specialized earning assets. (The liquidation of marketable securities was considered separately as the equivalent of a cash reserve). At the same time, I am convinced that existing investments should not be shielded from the competition of new opportunities and that a well-run company will decide to finance some new capital requirements as a substitution for rather than an addition to the existing capital commitment.

Without question the decision to liquidate a separable segment of the company's earning power should be a decision carefully considered over time and not under pressure when information may be incomplete and bargaining power low. On the other hand, once a company has made the decision to liquidate a unit, a product line, a market or production facility, the potential sum to be realized can become a part of the list of resources for mobility during the period when liquidation may take place. The difficulty will be in estimating the amount and timing since often the outcome will depend on a single negotiation with an outside party. In certain circumstances of a general purpose asset the amount can be estimated with reasonable accuracy, but in other circumstances the sum will be a very rough guess unless specific negotiations have already begun. The inclusion of an amount in this category of the inventory of resources would be misleading unless there was a broad market for the asset or some reasonable assurance that a given sum could be realized in the period in question.

THE MANAGERIAL USES OF AN INVENTORY OF RESOURCES OF MOBILITY

Despite all the problems of estimation and the qualifications that must be attached to the figures produced, an inventory of the resources of financial mobility can serve useful managerial purposes. Now that the inventory has been discussed in some detail, these purposes can be made more specific. The first is the simple but important task of recognizing explicitly the entire array of alternatives open to management and differentiating these from the conventional concept of balance sheet assets. The inventory places in better perspective the partial role to be played by cash balances or reserves of borrowing power. It recognizes the fact that mobility has an internal and an external dimension. It brings in the dimension of time to activate.

Of course there are some human problems to be recognized. The vice president of marketing or of production or the director of research and development may be unwilling to concede in advance of a specific need for funds that 20% of his budget could be eliminated without disastrous consequences for the business. This natural reluctance to give away internal bargaining position may make it difficult to have an open discussion of the action that might be taken. Also, the assertion by a company president that an area of expenditure could be cut if needed by some amount would be seen as a threat and could have unsettling effects on management in that area. However, these human problems do not appear to be so great as to invalidate consideration of specific action for purposes of top level financial planning.

In addition to the benefit from identification of sources of mobility there are benefits from the effort to quantify the relative magnitudes of these sources. This will reveal the dominant sources of mobility and identify gaps. It will indicate whether strategy must be dependent on internal or external negotiation, whether the dominant sources are predictable or unpredictable, whether they are subject to conditional events, whether they are quickly or slowly activated. Since the inventory of resources will be taken periodically, it will reveal changes over time and the effect of the financial plans represented by the funds flow forecast. The total at the bottom of the sheet will suggest a possible excess or deficiency on overall reserve position, which may in turn condition the financial plan.

Although the intended audience for this report on the resources of mobility may be limited to the chief executive and his financial advisor, it ought to include the operating heads as well. As this study has stressed, in most companies the implicit or explicit strategy of financial mobility involves an interplay or tradeoff between financial and other forms of mobility — production, marketing, technological, strategic. The inventory of resources clearly shows that the alternative to a cash balance may be a budget cut, which forces those who work in the area involved to absorb the shock of the unexpected need. Changes in the relative magnitudes of these alternative resources over time reveal the extent to which operations are sheltered from or exposed to those kinds of pressures.

An actual case may be helpful here. A company had been proceeding in an active program of diversification for several years in an effort to overcome the long-term weaknesses of its original basis of operation. The new acquisitions were in industries quite unrelated to the parent industry, but all had been developed vigorously to make the most of their several opportunities. The very rapid rate of diversification had placed a strain on the company's financial resources. At the same time, however, the company was making a reasonable profit and the balance sheet did not suggest any serious structural weakness. From all normal appearances the program was proceeding reasonably well.

One member of the board, however, became concerned about the vulnerability of the company to financial shock and asked for an inventory of resources developed along the general lines suggested above. This report brought out in sharp detail that the company had no surplus cash, no remaining short-term or long-term borrowing power, little in the way of forward anticipation in its budgeted outflows, and because of repeated issues of common stock in acquisitions it was most reluctant to add to its shares outstanding. Although there was no immediate crisis, it became clear that the only real alternative left open was to liquidate the parent business and use the funds to restore a better balance of resources of mobility and make possible further diversification. If this was to be done, it had to be done in an atmosphere free from pressure, for the potential purchasers were few and strong financially. Liquidation might take considerable time. Presentation of this information to the board crystallized a decision to move on this alternative immediately and vigorously. The idea of liquidation of the parent had been talked about for years, but the stark evidence of vulnerability to even a modest funds flow deficit was persuasive in a way that conventional financial reporting had never been.

Reconciling Reporting of the Past and the Future

To further clarify and consolidate the proposals of this chapter an example has been developed to illustrate the relation of the inventory of resources of mobility and the more conventional pro forma financial statements. The example is based on a real situation but the inventory of resources is in part hypothetical. We start with the case of the Mainland Company at September 30, 1968, the end of its fiscal year, and provide a projected budget of receipts and expenditures for the next fiscal year plus a pro forma balance sheet at the end of the period. The actual balance sheet for September 30, 1968, the pro forma balance sheet for September 30, 1969, and a simple funds flow statement for the coming year are shown in Exhibit 11D.

EXHIBIT 11D

MAINLAND COMPANY: SIMPLE FUNDS FLOW PROJECTION AND
RELATED BEGINNING AND ENDING BALANCE SHEETS
Projected Sales, 1968–1969 $6,000,000
Projected Profit, 1968–1969 $202,000

Opening Balance Sheet September 30, 1968		Pro Forma Uses and Sources 1968-1969		Pro Forma Balance Sheet September 30, 1969
ASSETS		Uses	Sources	
Cash	$ 300,000			$ 300,000
Accounts receivable	400,000	$200,000		600,000
Inventories				
Raw materials	400,000		$ 4,000	396,000
Finished goods	340,000	24,000		364,000
Total current assets	$1,440,000			$1,660,000
Fixed assets, net	630,000	120,000		750,000
Other assets	260,000			260,000
Total assets	$2,330,000			$2,670,000
LIABILITIES AND NET WORTH				
Accounts payable	$ 500,000	100,000		$ 400,000
Notes payable to bank	100,000		351,000	451,000
Accrued taxes	120,000	15,880		104,120
Total current liabilities	$ 720,000			$ 955,120
Long-term debt	640,000	50,000		590,000
Preferred stock	450,000	20,000		430,000
Common stock and surplus	520,000		174,880	694,880
Total liabilities and net worth	$2,330,000	$529,880	$529,880	$2,670,000

These are the conventional projections of the accounting effects of the expected demand for products and the company's planned response. As the pro forma funds flow statement shows, funds will be invested in working capital, new fixed assets, a reduction in accounts payable, and reductions in long-term debt and preferred stock outstanding. The total uses of funds are $529,880, which are to be provided by retained earnings and a substantial increase in the bank loan. All of this is positive in tone: there will be a reasonable profit for the year, $202,000, and the balance sheet at the end of the year shows a significant increase in total assets. There will be a small reduction in liquidity as measured by the current and quick asset ratios, but on the other hand there will be an improvement in the long-term debt to equity ratio.

Now compare Exhibit 11D with the revised concept of resources shown in Exhibit 11E. Instead of asking how we have invested funds up to the present moment, we ask: From what sources can we obtain funds if the projected funds flow statement turns out to be in error? If that statement is correct, then all will be well. If it is not correct, then the company's plan and its future may be in jeopardy.

The exhibit opens by summarizing the net results of a detailed month-by-month cash budget for the coming year. Gross expenditures for the year are expected to be $6,250,000 and expected receipts fall short of this sum by $350,000. The present plan is to balance the flows with an increase in the commercial bank loan. If for any reason more than this amount is needed, then we look to the sources shown in the exhibit. The cash balance is the minimum required for transactions at the projected level; so on the new statement of "assets" this item is zero. The amount available under a current line of credit is $350,000, negotiated in anticipation of the projected deficit in flows. No further funds are considered available on an unsecured basis. The total instant reserves are $350,000.

All other reserves require some negotiation with outside parties and therefore will take some time to activate and involve some uncertainty. However, it is believed that if the company would pledge its current assets, more bank funds would be available, with an upper limit estimated at 75% of accounts receivable plus 50% of inventory values. To go to this limit would add another $300,000. Because the company's long-term debt has been recently negotiated and is relatively high by conventional yardsticks, the company has a strong conviction that long-term debt cannot be increased in the near future. Hence this resource is set at zero.

The estimate of additional equity funds is based on the present policy of the company not to increase but rather to reduce outstanding preferred stock whenever possible. In spite of a reluctance to sell common stock because of the dilution of earnings per share, it is recognized that this would be the only way to break

EXHIBIT 11E

MAINLAND COMPANY: INVENTORY OF RESOURCES OF MOBILITY
AS AT SEPTEMBER 30, 1968 — ONE YEAR HORIZON

Projected Gross Expenditures	$6,250,000
(Oct. 1, 1968–Sept. 30, 1969)	
Projected Deficit of Receipts	$ 350,000
Projected Source of Funds:	
Bank Line	$ 350,000

	Sources of Mobility in Funds Flows, September 30, 1968			Pro Forma September 30, 1969	
I. Uncommitted Reserves					
Instant reserves					
Surplus cash	–0–			–0–	
Line of credit	$350,000			–0–	
Total instant reserves		$ 350,000			–0–
Negotiable reserves					
Incremental bank loan (secured)	$300,000			$450,000	
Incremental long-term debt	–0–			(50,000)	
Preferred stock	–0–			(20,000)	
Common stock	300,000			300,000	
Total negotiable reserves		600,000			$ 750,000
Total reserves		$ 950,000			$ 750,000
II. Reduction in Planned Outflows					
Volume-related (reduction in production schedule)	$ 74,000			$ 74,000	
Scale-related					
Marketing	84,000			84,000	
Admin. overhead	70,000			70,000	
Capital expenditures	100,000			50,000	
Value-related					
Common dividends	50,000			50,000	
Total reduction in outflows		378,000			328,000
III. Liquidation of Assets					
Sales of land		50,000			50,000
Total Mobility for Potential Flows Deficit		$1,378,000			$1,128,000

out of the current limitations on long-term debt. Thus at least for purposes of this exercise the company is willing to look at the equity alternative. Discussions with the company's investment banker in the past have indicated that in an upward moving equity market the underwriter could move an amount of new stock up to 25% of the company's outstanding common stock without difficulty. At current market prices this suggests a sum in the area of $300,000. Of course this resource could evaporate over night with a change in the stock market, a change that might well be associated with an unexpected need for more cash in the company.

With regard to the cash budget itself, possible modifications in planned outflows would release expected receipts for alternative use. The amounts indicated for the various categories of outflow represent a line-by-line review of the budget for reductions that could be made on the assumption that the unexpected need would be of such importance as to override the present reasons for spending this money. They are also conditional on an atmosphere of economy. In particular, the cut in dividends would demand strong, visible evidence of an overriding need. The total of such reductions is $378,000, a respectable sum compared with the "hard" reserves (borrowing power).

The final source is the liquidation of specialized assets. In this case the company does not have segments of the business that can be liquidated as earning units. It does have some individual assets that can be sold if the cash is needed. In particular, some land held for long-range expansion plans has a ready market, with an estimated value of $50,000.

Taken all together these resources standing available for the purpose of keeping flows in balance add up to $1,378,000. It is of interest to compare this sum with the balance sheet total of $2,330,000 already invested. Which is the more relevant number for management? Of course the $1,378,000 is heavily conditional on good judgment and circumstance, but whatever a conservative number might be (say, $1,078,000, with the equity issue deleted) this sum represents the real basis for corporate continuity and forward movement.

The next step in the analysis is to assess the impact of the planned funds flows on this set of resources. These are seen in the second set of columns of Exhibit 11E. If all goes as planned the line of credit will be used up by the end of next year. Since the proposed use of these funds will increase current assets substantially, it is expected that the company's secured short-term borrowing power will be increased. There will be small reductions in long-term debt and preferred stock, which theoretically might leave a little reserve in these areas, but practically speaking the difference is not great enough to be counted at this point. The actions of the year do not materially change the amount to be obtained from sale of common stock though perhaps a rise in the market value should be built into that number for the sake of consistency. The net effect in the reserve position is therefore to lower total reserves from $950,000 to $750,000 and, more significantly, to wipe out the company's instant reserves.

No great change is expected to take place in the ability to reduce budgeted outflows. This is of course open to differences of opinion, but the suggestion of no change in most items indicates that the company's expenditure horizon will be about the same at the end of the year as at the beginning. The potential reduction in capital expenditures is a function of the long-range capital budget, which happens to show 1968 as a year of unusually high planned expenditure and hence greater flexibility in the budget than usual at this point. Since the reduction in reserves is much greater than the reduction in the ability to postpone or eliminate planned outflows, a greater share of the burden for mobility is now placed on the latter alternative. The absence of instant reserves means inability for instant response and an absolute necessity for time within which to activate resources.

Indeed, one interpretation of the evidence could be this: with a reluctance or inability to sell common stock, with a reluctance to go to secured bank borrowing because it is considered a blot on the company's good credit standing, a substantial deficit of funds flows falling unexpectedly late in 1969 could force sharp and rapid cuts in budgeted expenditures as the only major alternative open. The proposed statement highlights these circumstances in a way that conventional pro forma statements fail to do.

12

Toward a Rational Strategy of
Financial Mobility

INTRODUCTORY QUALIFICATIONS

To those readers who are seeking a precise formula for the calculation of the resources to be committed to a strategy of financial mobility this chapter will be a disappointment. To those seeking a formal conceptual model it will also be a disappointment. It should be apparent that we have been dealing with an exceedingly complex problem involving a great many variables that are difficult to relate and quantify systematically. No quick and easy solution comes out of an initial study of the problem. At best what emerges is the beginning of a definition of the problem and of the variables most relevant to its solution.

Undoubtedly, a full-blown definition of the problem and of the framework for analysis would require some high-powered logic using abstraction and symbolism. When it is available this analysis will surely shed some light on the direction for improvement in practice. In the meantime, however, the practitioner must continue to deal with the problem in all its complexity using the more straightforward powers of reasoning at his command to reach a sensible solution. In the process he undoubtedly uses some method for reducing the relevant considerations to a comparatively simple framework (another form of abstraction) in order that what he would call "common sense" can be employed to extract a solution. It is the purpose of this chapter and this book to make some contribution to the current state of the financial practitioners' art in the hope that common sense reasoning in this critical area can be made both more sensible and more common. It is left to the business reader to decide whether any of the ideas presented are useful to him in his everyday affairs.

THE PROBLEM RESTATED

The first part of this book asserted that a business entity has specific operational objectives related to its economic function in society, which it is the function of financial management to serve. Ideally all the resources at the disposal of management, including the financial resources, should be committed to the achievement of these objectives whatever they may be: size, growth rate, market position, technological superiority, or whatever. However, in a world of change it is the next decision and action, not the last, which is the most critical. When change may be and often is unexpected in some degree, the process of redirecting financial as well as other resources to harmonize with a new environment can be difficult. So the problem is: Given that a business entity wishes to keep its financial resources fully committed in support of corporate objectives, how does it provide the mobility to respond to any and all essential changes in funds flows?

Clearly this is not the kind of problem that can be solved once and forgotten. On the contrary it is ever present and continuously on the mind of the responsible financial officer. The practical import of this is that management must be concerned not only with the need for mobility in the current planning period but with the need in future planning periods as well. It would be irresponsible and dangerous to act so as to leave no room for unexpected needs beyond the current planning horizon. This implies some thought for what lies beyond that horizon. The guidelines that link the practice of financial mobility in the present with the potential for mobility in the future are referred to in this chapter as *strategy*. Inevitably the discussion will concern both strategy and tactics, and no effort will be made to draw a sharp distinction in this respect.

When the problem is considered in the context of an established dynamic business entity at a moment in its history, the following elements with an important bearing on the solution may be expected to exist.

(1) A set of resources of mobility as outlined in Chapter 11. This inheritance from the past will likely be in part the result of

conscious planning and in part the result of the force of
events acting on the business. Thus with respect to the planning period there will be an initial distribution of the total
financial resources between those that must be considered
committed and therefore unavailable for new uses during the
period and those available at least under certain conditions.

(2) A Plan of Action for the company during the planning period. As previously discussed, this plan represents what is considered to be achievable within the anticipated environment
of the period and includes specific reallocation of the financial
resources being released from active use during the period
(gross revenues). These plans (budgets) may also include some
commitment of the resources of mobility as identified under
number (1).

(3) A "known" inventory of the resources of mobility at the end
of the planning period, generated as discussed in Chapter 11
from the "known" pattern of funds flows as defined by the
Plan of Action.

(4) A perception of the unknown or contingent fund requirements of the planning period — an identification of the more
likely sources of potential variation in expected funds flows
and an awareness of the nature of their financial impact as
discussed in Chapter 10.

(5) An attitude toward financial risk bearing which will ultimately determine the response to the perceived risk of being
unable to fulfill a need for funds considered essential to corporate goals.

These are the initial inputs into the decision-making process.
They form the raw material from which a strategy of mobility
will be fabricated.

In order to understand the ideas that follow regarding the
process of fabrication of strategy, the reader must be fully aware
of one key assumption that I accepted about the nature of the
real world — an assumption with which some may quarrel. This
is that practicing management does not and cannot deal with uncertainty as a generalized abstraction. Management must "know
its adversary" in order to formulate specific plans for coping with
it. It must by some means convert the unknown into a known,
particularly where responses are conditional on the specifics of
the unexpected need. This is what Chapter 10 was about.

The descriptive chapters brought out that a concern for financial mobility was not merely an undefined uneasiness in the pit of the stomach but a small list of specific threats or opportunities which were to be taken seriously in the period immediately ahead. A strike, a recession, an acquisition opportunity — such are the events that may be considered to have a probability not high enough to be treated as a certainty in the formal plan but yet high enough to demand the ability to respond should they materialize. Thus the strategy discussed in the following pages is aimed at dealing with the known unknown. Despite the difficulty of sticking to this concept in all dimensions of the problem of mobility, it is satisfactory as the dominant concept for dealing with uncertainty.

Having made this necessary digression on behavior with respect to uncertainty, we return to the definition of the problem and the statement of initial inputs by proceeding to outline what is required of a strategy of financial mobility. A company may be considered to have fulfilled its management obligation in this area of responsibility when it has met the following requirements.

(1) An evaluation of the adequacy of current resources of mobility for the needs of the period over which specific planning takes place (say, one year). This means an evaluation of the number at the bottom of Exhibit 11E (page 295) in terms of the specific contingencies of greatest concern during the period. One contingency or one set of interrelated contingencies is likely to dominate. An appraisal is also needed of the distribution of the total resources of mobility with respect to predictability and speed of activation. This evaluation will be made against the background of known pressures for investment and attitudes toward the risk of failure to make essential outflows.

(2) An evaluation of the resources of mobility at the planning horizon as predicted by the Plan of Action. This concept of strategy conceives of future time broken into two segments: (1) the period bounded by the horizon of detailed forecasting, financial plans, and specific corporate goals; (2) all time beyond that horizon. The evaluation of resources of mobility at the horizon is intended to be responsive to the needs for mobility over all relevant time beyond the period of specific planning, which is, say, one year. In order to indicate a recog-

nized limit to the ability of management either to influence or to identify the boundaries of future experience an arbitrary secondary horizon is chosen. In most cases the number is five to ten years hence. Whether it is five or ten makes very little difference.

The evaluation of resources at the planning horizon also is in terms of both the total capacity to respond to unexpected needs and the distribution of that capacity among major sources differing in predictability and activation time. Ideally, this evaluation should be done coincidentally with the formulation of the Plan of Action so that the findings can modify that plan if desired.

(3) The establishment of priorities to determine the sequence in which the several sources of mobility will be committed in the event of unexpected need, a sequence which is conditional in part on the specific need (its magnitude and distribution over time) and in part on the amount of advance notice provided by the company's intelligence system. The priorities are therefore a matching of the anticipated need and the characteristics of the source — its magnitude, certainty, and speed of activation.

The other and highly important side of this consideration is the establishment of priorities of restoration when resources become depleted. The return to the desired capacity for mobility may be more difficult than the commitment of these resources but is a highly important part of long-run strategy if sharp variations in exposure to risk are to be avoided.

(4) The process of implementation, which is related to the setting of priorities — the practical procedures by which resources are released from one use and transferred to another. Successful implementation is largely a matter of sensitivity to the need for negotiation and recognition that negotiation is a full-time job, not just something involving a few hours of hard bargaining once in a while.

We now examine these four dimensions of a strategy of mobility one at a time.

THE ADEQUACY OF RESOURCES FOR SPECIFIC CONTINGENT NEEDS

As previously indicated, a company will find itself at a point in time with a specific set of resources of mobility which is in part the result of conscious planning and in part the result of specific funds flow requirements placed on the business by its competitive environment. As likely as not therefore this resource position will not be considered optimum. The company may find itself with too large or too small an overall position and with an unbalanced distribution among resources. The most difficult question in the whole area of mobility is: How do we know when we have the right amount and composition of resources?

From the vantage point of hindsight, the right amount of mobility was the minimum amount needed to cover the maximum variation from expected flows that actually occurred. If the maximum unexpected deficit was $100,000, then the appropriate mobility derived from sources suited to the magnitude and timing of the need was $100,000. This assumes that the potential cost of not having the $100,000 when needed exceeded the cost of carrying that capacity for mobility. But of course we do not know what variations will occur with the kind of certainty that would lead us to arrive quickly and confidently at the $100,000 figure.

It should be clear from the beginning that we are dealing with two dimensions of the problem: (1) an estimate of the nature and magnitude of the variations from projected flows and (2) a judgment by someone of the appropriate amount of risk to assume of being out-of-stock of funds. A whole new area of discussion, far beyond the scope of this book, is opened up when the subject of risk preferences is introduced. At the same time, the issues are inextricably bound up with the subject of financial risks and financial mobility. Perhaps it will be sufficient to assert the assumptions on which these thoughts on mobility are based, namely:

(1) That although the penalty for mistakes in risk bearing ultimately falls in part at least on the corporate entity, the corporate entity cannot think and cannot have risk preferences.
(2) That a proxy must be found for a corporate risk preference and it is found in the attitudes toward risk bearing imbedded in the thought and experience of key members of management.
(3) That although it is possible to extract information on these risk preferences from management and give them quantitative form, most managements would not trust major decisions to a mechanical application of this information. Most managements

would have greater respect for their own ad hoc, instinctive reaction to specific events and circumstances.

On the basis of these ideas the following approach to the
adequacy of the existing resources of mobility is proposed. As
previously suggested, the corporate intelligence system has alerted
management to the existence of certain threats to the balance of
funds flows developed for the planning period. Of the threats
believed to exist one is likely to dominate the others (though
that one may in fact be a combination of related events or circumstances). Let us assume, for example, that the dominant
threat to next year's plans is a business recession. While management does not have the kind of evidence that would lead it to
make formal plans on the expectation of a recession, it believes
the possibility should be taken seriously. It wants to be in a
position to adjust if recession occurs.

The first step is the simulation suggested in Chapter 10 of the
funds flow and cash impact of a recession on the business at this
time. This requires a careful statement of the characteristics of a
business recession which derive from such factors as the nature
of the industry, the product, the production process, the customer,
the terms of trade, the behavior patterns of management. These
characteristics produce valid expectations as to the adverse limits
of the recession sales "profile" and as to the way in which the
company is likely to respond to that pattern of sales. This does
not mean that there will be only one graph of recession sales,
but that experience and judgment will place boundaries on how
far sales will decline, how fast they will decline, how long the
recession will last, how fast or slow the recovery is likely to be,
to what extent the decline is a volume decline and to what extent
a price decline, and so on.

Other matters for exploration and definition are the lead or
lag in recognition of recession conditions, the further lag in
organizing a response to such evidence, the expenditure patterns
that apply under "normal" conditions and the controls that may
be exerted in times of adversity, the significance of seasonality to
the timing of a decline in sales, and the significance of other
random circumstances at the time of a recession, such as the
timing of major capital expenditure programs.

The following information will emerge when all this information is assembled in the form of a total description or model of cash flows, capable of simulating the full range of possibilities within the limits of expectation placed on it by management.

(1) The identification of those assumptions about a recession to which the cash flow result is most sensitive. For example, small changes in price may be much more significant than larger changes in unit sales. The specific spacing of maturities on debt contracts may be much more significant than the overall debt-equity proportions. This sensitivity analysis will suggest where efforts for better information and understanding should be concentrated and where refinement of the assumptions is most needed. It also suggests the areas where the biggest pay-off will come from close supervision and control and from quick and vigorous response.

(2) The identification of the circumstances under which a recession would place the greatest burden on the company's resources of mobility and of the magnitude and timing of that burden (cash deficit).

In respect to number 2 above, the maximum deficits produced by the analysis clearly imply a limit to the severity of a recession. This is a judgment of management open to challenge. In making it management does not claim that more severe circumstances could not occur but asserts the belief that the (unspecified) probability of a more severe occurrence is so low that policy should not be influenced by it. Expressing this important point somewhat differently, management will specify those circumstances (of business recession or any other contingency) against which it wishes to be insured by conscious policy or action, specifically by its strategy for financial mobility. In so doing it rules that other risks are nonexistent *for policy purposes*.

The recommended analysis has now provided management with two basic pieces of information: (1) a quantitative measure of the *range* of cash deficits likely to result from a recession in sales and (2) a quantitative measure of the available resources of mobility by which to cover this deficit if it should occur. The relation of these two will show what particular combinations of events over which management has no control are within the present capacity for mobility as expressed by the inventory of resources. If the analysis reveals that the current resource position exposes the company to the risk of uncovered deficits under certain recession conditions previously specified as conditions to be taken seriously (insured against by policy), then management must reassess its risk preferences and its assessment of probabilities. In other words, it must reassess the chances of occurrence of these uncovered events and decide whether its subjective risk preferences will tolerate that risk or will demand protection.

The appraisal of the overall resource position in terms of specific contingencies must also extend to the composition of those resources. The simulation analysis will have revealed the likely distribution of the funds flow deficit over time. Having focused on a specific contingency it will have identified any conditions relating to the availability of certain resources. For example, if a condition for the reduction of cash dividends as a part of the balancing process is a decline in earnings of a certain magnitude for a certain period of time, that will have been identified. One of the likely problems of cash flows in a recession is the completely unexpected cash drain occurring in the period from the start of the downturn to the point when the recession is "discovered" by the company. This situation demands a certain proportion of instant reserves. Once the recession is recognized, those resources that can be released by the conscious process of internal or external negotiation can be brought into play, but only at a rate controlled by the nature of the source.

Thus a knowledge of the make-up of resources and of the timing of needs will indicate whether there is any serious disproportion among the resources for the particular contingency. A company in the condition of the example given on the right-hand side of Exhibit 11E, with no instant reserves, would be badly equipped to handle a business recession at this time regardless of the total of its resources. Unless it could accurately forecast the downturn well in advance, it would have little chance of survival. The unattractive alternative would be to respond to every slight dip in sales as if it were the beginning of a real recession.

The most critical question regarding the proportions among the several resources of mobility is the balance between instant and negotiable (time-related) reserves. Academic writers have been greatly intrigued by the challenge of determining appropriate cash balances. I have criticized such writings for their excessively narrow definition of contingency or mobility resources as being solely liquid balances. At the same time, the question they raise is an important one which puzzles many a practitioner as well as academics. Precedent or rules of thumb can provide an answer but not necessarily a rational one.

How much cash — or, more properly, instant reserves — should a company carry? The answer suggested by the line of reasoning of this chapter is: a variable amount, primarily determined by the expectations of the characteristics of specific contingencies. This study has developed the idea that the instant reserve is properly considered in terms of a time-equivalent: so many days or weeks of a cash deficit of a given magnitude. Thus the instant reserve buys a finite amount of time to cover lack of recognition plus time for activation of the negotiable resource next in line, whether that be the negotiation of additional long-term debt or the negotiation of a change in budgeted outflows. The specific characteristics of the contingent need(s) that dominate the primary planning period — their magnitude, uncertainty, and distribution over time — will suggest how much time is needed in this respect and therefore how much cash or its equivalent in instant borrowing power is needed.

This raises the question: What does a company do if it concludes that its total resources of mobility are too small or that they are badly distributed among sources? As an example of the latter problem, assume that there appears to be excessive dependence on a reserve of long-term borrowing power. The evidence is that cash reserves have been used up and also short-term commercial bank debt is at or close to its limit. Under these circumstances, the logical conclusion would be to negotiate now for an increase in long-term debt with the primary objective of paying down the bank loan and increasing the reserve of short-term bank credit, or of increasing cash reserves, or both. Similarly if there appears to be excessive dependence on control of discretionary outflows, these controls could be exercised in advance of any specific pressure of need in order to increase cash reserves.

If the balance of resources appears reasonable but the total of these resources appears undesirably low, the problem is quite different. Here we have a basic unbalance in the allocation of total economic resources between committed or immobile funds and uncommitted or mobile funds. If management has determined that this is excessively risky and must be corrected, then it has a choice between a slow but sure method of correction and a fast but uncertain method. The slow but sure method is to curtail the rate of growth of investment and gradually build up more depth in reserves. The fast but uncertain method is a partial liquidation of some of the investments of the business. The process is uncertain because the closing down or selling off of a segment of the business means an uncertain market without and resistance from within. These are hard choices to make and many companies may elect to run the greater risks of an inadequate mobility in the short run in the hope that they will not get caught. The important point is that if they do, at least they do it consciously and are more alert as a result.

The basic problem for the short range in the adjustment of resource position is, of course, time. The fact may be that in assessing the near-term contingencies the company may not be in a position to make basic changes in its resources of mobility soon enough. In that case over-exposure to the risks of the short term is unavoidable. Attention is therefore shifted to the longer run considerations — to the second item on our list of requirements in strategy development, the evaluation of resources at the planning horizon.

THE ADEQUACY OF RESOURCES AT THE PLANNING HORIZON

As suggested in the previous section, the evaluation of the resources of mobility is first in terms of specific contingencies dominating the near-term plans and actions of the company. It is also necessary to evaluate the effect on the resource position of the plans and expectations of the company as far into the future as they have taken specific form. Chapter 11 proposed that a pro forma inventory of resources be developed which measures the effect of these plans. If, for example, the plans call for the commitment of the company's entire line of credit by the end of the planning period, some thought must be given *now* to the implications of this action for corporate mobility beyond the horizon of specific planning.

It is at this point that an assumption about the real world of business practice made at the beginning of this chapter is challenged. The assumption was that businessmen do not respond to risk in the abstract but only to specific risks about which they have some information — a strike, a recession, the loss of a particular customer. The period beyond the planning horizon is by definition a period of very limited information about circumstances and events. It would appear that any judgment about the need for mobility at the planning horizon would necessarily be a judgment based on a generalized concept of the risk of financial immobility in the longer term.

However, I continue to be persuaded that as a practical matter there is no way to translate a completely unknown future into a specific allocation between mobile and immobile resources except to say that the future will continue to involve errors of forecasting and therefore *some* resources should remain mobile. *How much* cannot be defined in this manner. It would be possible to present management with a range of proportions for the future and ask it to choose in terms of subjective risk preferences. But this gives management no reference point at all by which to assess its intuitions. It has no way to separate risk magnitude from risk preference.

The one possible solution to this dilemma that has the greatest appeal as a guideline for practice is to deal with what was called earlier the secondary horizon in terms of the primary horizon. The previous section suggested a judgment on the adequacy of resources in terms of the specific contingency or set of contingencies dominating the primary planning period. This would result in a conclusion that current resources of mobility were adequate, more than adequate, or less than adequate. If they were judged adequate now but the plan of action promised to change their magnitude or distribution (for example, they were to be reduced at the planning horizon), then it would have to be decided whether this change was acceptable or whether the plan of action should itself be modified. This would be done by relating expectations concerning the secondary horizon, however vague and fragmentary, to the more specific expectations for the primary planning period. If the uncertainties were considered to be "about the same," then presumably the reduction in mobility would be unacceptable and something should be done about the plan for action during the primary planning period.

Thus the practical solution is to deal with the secondary horizon in terms of rough magnitudes relative to the first. Often some rather fragmentary ideas are known about the longer term — about such factors as product cycles, technological change, expiration of wage contracts, and so on. These will lead to impressions about the longer term being more or less uncertain than the near term, or about the same. This is the best that can be done. In the same way judgments will be made about the distribution among the various sources of mobility and how it is changing in the longer run. If specific expectations are essentially nonexistent, then it would seem sensible to have a varied bundle of resources rather than a concentration in one or two. Here the "squirrel instinct" would seem to be sound — many nuts in many places.

It should be noted that there is an inherent danger in the concept of relating near-term mobility to specific near-term contingencies and then relating longer-term mobility to near-term mobility. It is possible that the time span represented by both the primary and secondary horizons is not long enough to cover the full range of contingencies and that the current period is one of relative stability. If there is little appearance of variations from projected needs, resources may become overcommitted to immobile assets. Then there is a sudden change and a new period arrives in which much greater uncertainty enters, say, because of a sudden change in technology. The business might then be ill-prepared for the required readjustments of resource allocation. There would appear to be no real defense against the major, rapid, and completely unexpected change.

The only answer is essentially an article of faith: that major change rarely comes completely unheralded and overnight. Therefore, the company with its information antennae out to the secondary planning horizon will pick up signals and as a result begin to build in greater mobility while there is still time to readjust the distribution of resources without great internal or external strain.

Before concluding this section it is worthwhile to comment on something that appears to be a characteristic of behavior and relates to the question of changes in risk. I believe that businessmen are often willing to tolerate a considerable range of variation in observed risk without response or modification of risk posture. Thus if a plan of action calls for a considerable reduction in financial mobility in the future, the increased risk may simply be accepted and no explicit steps will follow with respect to a plan for restoration of mobility. This may be explained on the grounds that there has been no change in the basic risk posture, only a change in the expected rewards from risk bearing. Thus, in a case cited above, it may be assumed that the plan is not modified because the expected gains are above average.

On the other hand, it could be that people do not know their own risk preferences well and are not completely consistent over time. In addition, there is the tendency to be less concerned about adversity the more removed it is in time and to rely on the hope that things will work out somehow — the renowned muddling-through doctrine. We are of course dealing with one of the more obscure elements in human thought processes. The only point to be made here is to be cautious about expectations of great objectivity in decisions respecting uncertainty.

PRIORITIES IN THE COMMITMENT OF RESOURCES

Assuming that the appraisal of the resources of mobility has been completed and that both the total magnitude and the distribution of these resources are considered appropriate, the next step is to give some advance consideration to how these resources would actually be committed to use if the contingency became an actuality. This means having some rationale for setting priorities so that as a need emerges (with the total amount and timing perhaps still unknown) it will be known which source is to be used first, which second, and so on. As this study has observed, it is often the case in practice that the principle of priorities is the line of least resistance, but this has little appeal as a rational guideline for strategy. The question is: What objective or objectives *should* govern the priorities?

In order to approach this question, it is necessary to look again at the composition of the resources of mobility and consider their role in terms of the overall corporate objectives. Whatever these objectives may be, it is considered that they lead management to be interested in control over economic resources and that it is in the long-run interests of the business entity to have maximum growth in the economic resources over which management has control. This is the basis of the financial muscle behind management's power to act. (See Chapter 2.) We must therefore look at the several resources of mobility in terms of their current contribution to the growth process. In general, it would seem rational that a priority system for the commitment of resources to unexpected needs would aim to start with the resource currently contributing least to the growth process and to use last the resource contributing most to growth of economic resources. In this way any given demand on the inventory of resources would produce the least disturbance in the growth process. This concept of priority will be considered and then certain constraints added that in practice would qualify or limit its application.

For the sake of simplicity the resources listed in Exhibit 11B will be reduced to the following categories:

> A — Active   (1) liquidation of earning assets
>   Resources   (2) reduction of planned outflows
>
> B — Passive   (3) negotiable reserves
>   Resources   (4) instant reserves

According to the line of reasoning suggested above, the company in time of unexpected need would turn first to the passive resources which are not currently contributing to the achievement of corporate objectives. Whether it will be the instant or the negotiable reserves will depend on the degree of unexpectedness and on the urgency of the need. If time is available, the negotiable reserve should be used first unless the instant reserves happen to be in an overstocked position because of past events.

This brings us to a point that cannot be overemphasized: The instant reserve — cash and bank line of credit — is a very precious resource which must be guarded with great care. While the amount to be provided is a matter of judgment, which is therefore open to challenge, there is no doubt that some capacity for instant response to completely unexpected needs should be on hand *at all times.* To some people the idea of a cash reserve that you never touch is anomalous. There is, however, great validity in the idea as a goal. The parallel with the military strategist is useful. In the recent unhappy experience in Vietnam, the United States has maintained military ready reserves and refrained from committing them even though at times the pressures of the war seemed to demand it. The average citizen has a hard time understanding why, with well-trained men ready to go, the government continues to draft young civilians to meet these emergency needs. The answer appears to be that the type of emergency for which these reserves are maintained has not yet occurred, namely, the emergency that has come with such suddenness and lack of warning that no other alternative is available.

The same concept applies to the minimum instant financial reserve. When the need is urgent and there is not time enough to activate alternative resources, then the cash is committed. The cases cited in Part II showed examples of companies that did not have this concept of instant reserves and consumed all their instant reserves as the first of a series of steps to meet needs for which there was enough advance warning to provide alternative resources. A meaningful general rule would be to respond to an unplanned need by starting with those passive resources with the longest activation time permitted by the lead time on knowledge of the need. The purpose is, of course, to protect the reserves having the capacity for more speedy response for the urgent needs that come without warning.

When the passive resources of mobility begin to approach exhaustion and the cash deficit shows signs of persisting, then the next step would be to begin the involvement of the active resources of mobility — those now contributing actively to the corporate objectives. The release of these resources normally requires relatively long lead times and therefore action would have to begin well before the passive resources had actually run out. This of course incurs the risk that the resources, when released, would not actually be needed. The use of active resources will be primarily concerned with the modification of planned outflows rather than the liquidation of earning assets. As suggested previously, the liquidation of earning assets should ideally take place as a result of long-range choices and under unhurried circumstances when negotiation of sale can be most advantageous. As a practical matter this alternative would either stand as a last resort or would be activated in response to an unexpected need only when it coincided with new information modifying adversely the long-range prospects of some current investments.

The placing of the reduction of planned outflows on the priority list below the negotiable reserves depends to some extent on circumstances. It is conceivable that at the time of an unexpected need the pattern of flows would have remained relatively stable for a long period of time, leading to a relatively long expenditure horizon and probably some fat in the budget. Under those circumstances, the time might be appropriate to a reallocation of outflows as an action ahead of the use of negotiated reserves. Under such circumstances, the disturbance to the long-range strategy of the business might be minimal and the action might even be beneficial in lowering the base of outflows for future periods (wages, dividends, etc.).

This suggested priority system for the use of resources of mobility is thus: from passive to active resources; from least productive to most productive. It is subject to important constraints, some of which have already been emphasized. These constraints may now be summarized:

(1) the need to preserve the capacity for instant response;
(2) the desirability of matching the time required for activation of a resource with the time available to activate;
(3) the fact that the nature of the need determines the availability of certain conditional resources;
(4) the circumstances of the company and the past record of mobility, which bear on which resources may appropriately come into play at any particular time;
(5) the degree of uncertainty as to the magnitude and timing of availability of any given resource, leading to different priorities under varying degrees of urgency of need.

The priority system for the use of resources should be matched by a priority system for the restoration of these resources if and when they are used. This element of strategy often appears to be lacking in practice. To be consistent with what has been said previously, highest priority should be accorded to the restoration of minimum instant reserves if they have become depleted. After that has been done the active resources should be restored first and the passive resources second. Once again, constraints may exist that prevent this from being done in strictly logical order. The purpose is clear, however: to fill in those resources first that are going to contribute directly to the corporate goals.

IMPLEMENTING A STRATEGY OF MOBILITY

The earlier sections of this chapter have outlined a sort of generalized prescription of how a strategy of financial mobility *should* be developed. It is now necessary to recognize that very significant practical problems of implementation cannot be ignored. Rather than concede that the worlds of the normative and the practical are so far apart as not to influence each other — a disastrous conclusion for a professional school of business administration if not for practice itself — it is preferable to see in what ways the constraints of the real world are likely to modify what has been described as "rational" behavior.

The basic problem of implementation lies in two interrelated facts about the real world: (1) that financial resources represent only one of several resources being managed by the corporate entity and therefore financial considerations represent only one dimension of corporate strategy; (2) that decisions respecting the allocation of funds flows are frequently a collective judgment of several people, both inside and outside the business, who may have conflicting viewpoints.

It is very convenient for the financially oriented observer to look at the assets of a business in terms of their assumed monetary equivalents and to consider them as identical pawns on a business chessboard. In fact, when financial resources are committed through budgets and through expenditures to specialized uses, they change not only form but also custody. When $25,000 is spent on a machine, it is no longer a bank deposit over which the treasurer has direct control but becomes a part of the productive facility over which the vice president of production has direct control. This very obvious statement would be unnecessary except for the latent deception inherent in the accounting practice of recording the act as if the $25,000 were still intact as a financial resource but now under the heading of Plant and Equipment. It is now only a potential financial resource conditional upon its release through liquidation of the asset, an act which the vice president of production would have to approve.

It is also apparent that the balance sheet very imperfectly represents the real asset structure of a thriving business entity in terms of its full complement of human, technological, managerial as well as physical and financial resources. Management of these resources is delegated to the various functional centers of control, and top management must be concerned with the coordination and efficient use of the resources in working toward corporate goals. When a portion of the flow of funds becomes committed to maintenance and growth of human, technological, physical, and managerial resources, then a reallocation of that flow cannot realistically be considered merely a financial problem. Able and powerful spokesmen of the interests vested in existing flows may be expected to oppose change that appears to shift the balance of financial resources away from their areas of responsibility.

This means very simply that almost any major overt change in the pattern of funds flows will involve vigorous negotiation. The implications of the negotiation process, both within and without the organization, are substantial for the strategy and implementation of financial mobility, as well as for financial management generally. There is little or no recognition of this fact in current financial theory. The consideration of cost involved in the determination of priorities in the use of resources must be defined not only in financial terms but also in terms relevant to the other parties involved in the negotiation. Mobility must be defined not only in financial terms but also in terms of the other resources involved in the total corporate effort. What we are basically concerned with here — and this lies at the heart of the policy issue as viewed by top management — is the *form* in which corporate mobility will reside.

An illustration will help here. One strategy of *corporate* mobility would be to maintain large reserves of financial resources in cash or unused borrowing power so that when an unforeseen change takes place in the competitive position — new products, new technology, new moves in the market place — the company can respond quickly and with considerable economic muscle. Another strategy would be to invest financial resources fully — in aggressive marketing, in product development, in research — so that the company's mobility lies in being, and staying, out in front of its competitors, in initiating change rather than responding to it and thus in effect reducing the uncertainty for which financial mobility is designed.

Undoubtedly the various control centers that manage the different resources of the company will each see a need for mobility in its own area as a defense against uncertainty and each will be contesting with the others for the limited corporate resources available for this purpose. Since financial reserves are the least specialized or most mobile of the corporate reserves, they will be the target of all such demands. Pressures to build up inventory, to increase research expenditures, to improve production facilities, to increase advertising are all in their own way designed to provide a greater margin of protection against the unknown so far as other areas of management are concerned. The financial officer will have to fight to preserve his own form of mobility.

One thing that comes out of this recognition of mobility as a corporate problem is a recognition that the line of least resistance in negotiation, which was observed so often in case examples, is not so irrational after all. Certainly it must be recognized as a major constraint on a literal application of financial priorities based on maximizing corporate economic value. It recognizes that there must be a give and take in the practical world of decision making and that bargaining or negotiating strength does not always coincide with the priorities suggested by value maximization. It may not be rational but it is understandable when some financial officers develop a strategy based on a retreat into the world of the few resources over which they exercise direct and personal control: cash balances and bank lines of credit. This, however, is not the correct view of their corporate responsibilities.

Another way of expressing the aspect of negotiation is to say that it introduces another element of uncertainty which modifies the expected values of the negotiated resources. The more unpredictable a resource, the more uncertain the amount to be released and the time of the release, the more the personal stress involved in its release, the less will be the importance attached to that resource in the overall strategy of financial mobility. "Cost" in the sense of stress and strain on the financial officer and on his relations with his fellow executives and outside sources of funds is a highly relevant consideration and may at times outweigh economic cost. However, this should not be allowed to obscure the economic cost to the corporation as a major factor in the ranking of alternatives.

We have now covered the four basic dimensions of a strategy of mobility: an evaluation of the resources for the planning period, and at the planning horizon, a determination of priorities, and a review of the practical problems surrounding implementation. The remainder of this chapter will be directed to three questions, in part practical and in part theoretical, for which some summary comments may be useful. The first of these questions is a practical and organizational issue: Who should be responsible for securing a policy of financial mobility? The second is perhaps more theoretical: What are the possibilities for attaining what this study has called funds flow equilibrium — the state where funds flows not only are in balance but tend to remain there? The third question relates the conclusions of this study to its predecessor: How does a strategy of financial mobility relate to the theory of debt capacity expounded in *Corporate Debt Capacity*?

ORGANIZATIONAL RESPONSIBILITY FOR FINANCIAL MOBILITY

The message of this study for management should now be clear. Financial mobility is too important to a company's future to be left to the random fortunes of the business at the time of an emergency need or to the undefined value system of one man who happens to be its financial officer. In the larger company there is a possibility of real benefit to be derived from a formal and systematic approach as outlined in this last chapter of the study. The question raised in this section is: Where in the organization should the responsibility for this type of financial intelligence work rest?

In recent years many business firms in the United States have seen a strong upsurge in the responsibilities normally placed on the controller and a reduction in the traditional role of the treasurer. This can be attributed to the swing in recent decades toward internal financing and the growing importance and effectiveness of internal financial controls. Many treasurers are now primarily custodians of company cash, with the related responsibility of keeping channels open to the commercial bank. Negotiation with external sources of long-term capital has for many companies become an infrequent event. Even in large companies the treasury is almost always confined to the personality of one man, with the possible assistance of someone to manage the short-term securities portfolio and one or two staff members to maintain the cash budget.

Of course, in most companies the functions of both the controller and the treasurer are overseen by a vice president–finance, who may have come up from either branch, and the relative importance of those who hold the titles of controller and treasurer depends greatly on the men in the jobs. There is therefore no merit in trying to generalize about relative importance. However, in the context of this study of financial mobility there is reason to rethink the role of the treasurer — or, more impersonally, the role of the treasury function. While there will always be circumstances and personalities that invalidate any generalization, there are reasons for suggesting that the increased emphasis on financial mobility should reside in the office of the treasurer.

The first and most important reason is to maintain a separation between the consideration of funds flow balance on the one hand and the traditional concern for financial goals, performance measurement, and appraisal on the other. The objective is to keep a separation between cash or funds flow management and the traditional accounting system for measuring income and value. The proposed analytical approach for managing funds flows is designed not to replace but rather to complement the existing forecasting and budgeting procedures. Since the latter commonly rest in the hands of the controller and since the two analytical systems are inherently incompatible, it would seem wise not to add this responsibility to the controller's area. In addition, cash forecasting is often found in the treasurer's area, related to cash and marketable securities management. While cash flows or funds flow simulation is far from what many companies do today in the area of cash forecasting, both forecasts are concerned with the same basic variables.

In other words, forward thinking related to specific goals, commitments, and controls should be organizationally separated from the kind of forward thinking recommended here, which is related to contingency planning and funds flow management. In this way the controllership would continue to be identified with income or profit management and the treasury would develop a distinctive competence in managing funds flows both internally and externally — each having a separate information system suited to its needs.

A second and perhaps more obvious reason for locating responsibility for financial mobility in the treasurer's office is that he is custodian of the company's cash and short-term borrowing position, which are the key resources of mobility. Typically, he is the first to feel the impact of a lack of balance in cash flows. Long-term contracts also have potential importance to mobility. The action respecting these resources should be closely integrated with the whole strategy of financial mobility. It would appear logical therefore to expect the treasurer to assume a dominant role in shaping this strategy. The general thrust of this emphasis would be to change the concept of the treasurer from that of the relatively passive custodian of liquid resources, as it has been developing in recent years, to that of the active manager or coordinator of mobile resources in the broad sense of that term used in this study.

To center the initiative for financial mobility in the treasurer's office would place demands on that office for information assembly and analysis that may be beyond its present capacity, since a research staff capable of doing the kind of analysis described in Chapter 10 would be needed. The overhead burden of the treasurer's office would be likely to increase to some extent as it geared up to the demands of active surveillance of funds flows.

Of course, the full implications of financial mobility can only be appreciated and evaluated at the very top of the organization. The ultimate trade-offs between maximum growth and the ability to respond to the unexpected opportunity or need are presidential considerations. The choice involved in allocating mobility between reassignment of budgeted flows and idle reserves has the same company-wide implications. In this the chief financial officer must function as an extension of the chief executive. Ideally, the values he imposes through the choices he makes should be the values of the company as a whole as seen by top management as a team.

THE STATE OF FINANCIAL EQUILIBRIUM

Early in this study a state of financial equilibrium was defined in terms of a pattern of funds flows in which inflows and outflows not only were approximately in balance but also tended to remain in balance without overt action by management. It is worth raising this concept again in the light of what has been said about a strategy of financial mobility. Is there such a thing as financial equilibrium in the real world? Is it a desirable goal of financial policy?

Observation suggests that there are periods in the history of some companies when, for a number of years, inflows and outflows of funds remain more or less equal to each other and there are no major financial shocks to upset this happy state of affairs. Undoubtedly this state is related to the nature of the industry, technological maturity, stability of competitive relationships, and other external conditions as well as to the attitudes and policies of management. Some managements deliberately pace the growth in investment to the rate of internal generation of funds. In the absence of major external demands on the financial system, funds would necessarily remain in balance. Further, some companies have by accident or design accumulated a substantial reserve of unused resources inside or outside the company, which serves to insulate the organization from such irregularities as do occur in the stream of inflows and outflows.

The picture this presents of a company in a steady state of funds flow balance, called equilibrium, although undoubtedly attractive to a certain kind of financial officer (one who likes to sleep well) is not necessarily a picture of a company achieving its full economic potential. Such stability can result from inactivity or excessive conservatism as well as from perceptive long-range planning or a stable environment. For purposes of discussion here we can rule out the former pair of causal factors and consider only the latter. Fundamental to the possibility of equilibrium in funds flows would appear to be the matter of environmental stability: customers' tastes and expenditure patterns, competitors' share of the market, technology of product and productive process, general economic conditions, to name some of the more obvious aspects. These are largely if not entirely beyond the individual company's control. Further, the ability to do the kind of forecasting on which sound long-range planning is based depends on and is made much easier by stability in the environment.

Consequently, while the possibility is not ruled out of shrewd judgments made in an unstable environment, it would appear that equilibrium in funds flows may be something that "happens" and not something that is managed or planned (except at the expense of maximum utilization of the company's resources). On the other hand, equilibrium would appear to be a legitimate objective of a strategy of financial mobility. That is to say, the objective of the strategy would be to achieve a balance of funds flows under conditions where the resources of mobility were in their desired amounts and proportions and where financial policies designed to promote the growth of the economic power of the firm were intact. If, as is likely, these conditions do not obtain at the moment, then long-term financial planning should aim at restoring the resource position and at achieving the desired adjustment of financial policy. For the aggressive, dynamic company working in an unstable environment, equilibrium in funds flows is an ideal position attained perhaps only momentarily, with the more normal condition being that of moving, like the pendulum, toward equilibrium or away from it.

As just stated, funds flow equilibrium requires at the same time the conditions of balance in the resources of mobility *and* maximum support to growth in corporate economic power. These conditions, taken together, necessarily represent a compromise position since a company cannot have the maximum growth rate in economic resources and maximum mobility at the same time. As previously stated, the only companies observed to have a financial officer in single-minded pursuit of maximum profit were those with clearly abundant mobility reserves — in other words, in single-minded pursuit of maximum profit on *part* of the investment.

However, the need for compromise between mobility and

growth rate does not mean that this compromise will exist at all times. Observation suggests that there will be stages when growth appears to management to be particularly opportune. At such times mobility may be cut back sharply in order to have the full benefit of available resources. At other times, the emphasis may shift. A period of uncertainty means hesitation on investment alternatives and a need for holding resources more in reserve. Thus long-term judgments about investment opportunities and about the stability of the environment will influence the current balance between active and passive resources.

DEBT RESERVES AND DEBT CAPACITY

Although debt reserves have been considered here as a part of the total strategy of mobility, some summary comments may be helpful for those readers who have attempted to relate the conclusions of this study with my earlier work, *Corporate Debt Capacity*. In the latter work, the capacity of a business to sustain the fixed cash commitments of a debt contract was defined in terms of a study of the variability of the company's pattern of cash inflows and outflows and the risk of running out of cash. The analysis was in terms of simulated recession conditions and the likely stresses put by declining sales volume on the company's cash position — on its ability to service not only contractual commitments but also outflows for which continuity was essential for policy reasons.

Up to a point, this approach to the setting of debt limits was and is consistent with the approach of the present study to financial mobility. They both deal with debt in terms of the uncertainty in future funds or cash flows and they both use simulation of probable future experience as a means of assessing the magnitude of the provision to be made. Both approaches require some sort of model of cash flows as a tool of analysis. However, there are important differences. This study of mobility deals with the whole set of uncertainties, of which business recession is only one. It deals with the whole range of alternative resources, of which unused debt capacity is only one.

What the debt capacity study did was to treat the priority of all other sources of mobility as given and to assume that the residual control was what was exercised over the *level* of debt servicing. In contrast, this study of mobility takes the level of *existing* debt servicing as given and opens up the choice of priorities among alternative sources of mobility, including any available unused borrowing power. In terms of the phenomenon of uncertainty, the debt capacity study took a generalized view of one important aspect of uncertainty, the business recession; and as a result, the analytical approach lent itself to the possibility of quantitative estimates of the risk of running out of cash. In contrast, this study leans toward a more specific identification of near-term risks and places more reliance on managerial judgments respecting the magnitude and timing of the related need for funds.

As indicated at the outset, this study shifts attention from the question of the debt that is in use to the debt that remains to be used in the form of a debt reserve. It places particular emphasis on the instant reserve — the capacity to buy time in order to bring about the desired reallocation of working resources in response to new information. In this respect the reserve of borrowing power at the commercial bank, which by specific prearrangement or by firm custom is an assured and instantly available source, is a key element of strategy. The study places special emphasis on the importance of close and continuous relations with the commercial banks, an aspect of financial policy that has come under considerable pressure in this age when it is fashionable to keep funds fully invested and to be "hard nosed" about bank relations.

The reserve of long-term borrowing is also a part of the total capacity to respond to unexpected need, but a part requiring time to activate and involving some uncertainty. Whether the company makes full use of this long-term borrowing power at any given time is now seen not simply in terms of one resource (debt) but in terms of all resources of mobility. If the debt capacity is fully utilized, then it is obvious that for the near future the responsibility for financial mobility is shifted to other resources, including the reallocation of budgeted flows, and this may be quite rational under the circumstances. In other words, while a reserve of long-term borrowing power is useful, it may not be essential for any given time period. The ideal of insisting that there *always* be a long-term debt reserve appears to place excessive emphasis on long-term debt in the total strategy of mobility.

A LAST WORD

In its annual report for 1967 Philips, the large and well-managed European manufacturer of electrical and electronic products, recorded the retirement of its chief financial officer who had served the company in various capacities for more than forty years. The report of the supervisory board expressed "sincere appreciation . . . for the very important work he has done, particularly with regard to the financing of our Company. Even for large transactions, the funds needed were always available. During all the years of his management the financial basis of the Company has remained sound. We are most grateful to him." What financial officer would not trade his 40-years-of-service diamond lapel pin for such praise at the time of his retirement?

"Even for large transactions, the funds needed were always available." This is the goal of a strategy of financial mobility. Despite continuing uncertainties the essential needs of the business have always been met. The skeptic is entitled to a raised eyebrow: *Always?* Have there not been *some* occasions when the company had to scramble for funds to meet an unexpected and urgent need, or alternatively had to postpone important action because the resources were fully committed? Have there not been occasions when, in order to balance funds flows, the company was temporarily exposed to excessive risk with respect to future funds flows and hence, in that sense, temporarily "unsound"? The answer is probably yes, even in the case of Philips; and the financial officer would probably be the first to admit it.

In the last analysis the year-to-year implementation of a strategy of financial mobility involves a continuous three-way compromise between the tangible goals set by corporate strategy, growth in the economic and financial power of the corporate entity, and risk posture. In the long run, both the corporate objectives and the financial goals must be achievable within the limits of a tolerable risk level. In the short run, one consideration or another may dominate. Adequate financial mobility is designed to assure that there will be a long run.

Appendix
Example of a Computer Simulation Model

This computer simulation model was developed for a large, rapidly growing company, which was looking forward to a continuing sequence of financing decisions under circumstances that were anything but predictable. It was a general purpose model for simulating cash flow and related accounting data to enable the management to explore a variety of decisions.

The model itself was developed by a team comprising two consultants, a member of the staff of the financial vice president who was responsible for long-range planning, and a second company man who was on the computer staff and was to program the model. Thus the group consisted of those who knew what outputs would aid the ultimate financing decisions, the finance staff man who was familiar with existing data flows and could assemble the relevant inputs, and the computer expert who was to specify the relationships to translate inputs into useful outputs.

Initial efforts to develop directly the essential cash receipts and payments associated with various levels of corporate activity were ultimately frustrated by a lack of historical data and of judgmental experience on the part of management. Although the company had a highly modern accounting system, it was unaccustomed to operating in terms of cash payments per se and did not generate cash flow data directly. Furthermore, as in most companies, the management showed a remarkable indifference to historical patterns representing a period it could no longer influence. This experience resulted in the decision to shift to a

This example is based on consulting work from which the author prepared Harvard Business School case No. EA-F 315, entitled Alpha Equipment Corporation. Copyright © 1968 by the President and Fellows of Harvard College.

model constructed in terms of the accrual accounting procedures familiar to the company, which generated in the first instance pro forma income statements and balance sheets and produced a cash flow statement as a by-product of the pro forma statements (see Exhibit 4).

As a part of its work the group produced a 150-page Financial Simulation Model Manual. The memorandum presenting the model and excerpts from the manual follow.

INTEROFFICE MEMORANDUM

Subject: Financial Simulation Model

Attached is the manual for the Financial Simulation Model that is now programmed for our 7070 Computer. The manual covers the concepts and specifications employed in building the model; major assumptions; input requirements; operating features; and explanation of the output.

The Financial Simulation Model was constructed to represent the Company, in financial aspects, as it now exists. To allow for changing policies, operating characteristics, and environment of the Company utmost flexibility has been incorporated in specifying and programming the model.

The model offers the Company the ability to approximate future results, in both accounting and cash flow terms, given management's assumptions about growth potential, key policy decisions, and their reactions to likely events. Furthermore, the operating speed of the computerized model permits considering a large number of these assumptions to ascertain the range of alternatives and the best decision.

The model has a wide range of potential uses in the areas of financial analysis and simulation, forecasting, and control. The following are some specific applications:

> *Debt Capacity:* The model's determination of cash available under a variety of adverse conditions can be used to test our limits of debt servicing for given levels of risk.
> *Dividend Policy:* The ability to sustain a given dividend policy, even under severe economic conditions, can be tested via the model.

Capital Expenditures: Specific expenditure programs and trends of capital expenditures can be evaluated in terms of financial effect and trade-offs required with other payouts, like dividends.

Downturn Policies: The model can be used to study the cyclical downturn and upswing effects of given policies as a basis for formulating reactions that minimize the adverse effects on the Company.

Policy vs. Behavior: The development of the model and its subsequent uses should serve to spotlight differences of actual behavior from stated policies.

Major Programs: The model can be used to generate the effects of major programs into the future, e.g. merchandising programs, revised warranties, cost reduction, etc.

Pricing: In a limited manner the model can simulate the financial consequences of price changes (the present model is company oriented and cannot simulate market reactions; but these actions can be given the model to interpret in terms of effect on our operations).

The model is of further use as a general analytical base from which it becomes feasible to refine and automate the determination of such items as book and tax depreciation, investment credit, original equipment population, etc.

The advantages of the Financial Simulation Model stem from its immediate availability to quickly generate a large number of financial items for our total operation, in a consistent manner. The construction of the model has brought about a consideration of individual financial aspects of the Company in context of total operations and has produced new analytical and programming techniques.

The present model is limited in several areas. It does not consider subsidiaries and international operations in detail but on a basis of net cash flows. Domestic Operations are treated as producing only two parts — original equipment and parts — rather than dealing with families having different cost relationships. Furthermore, the construction of the model was limited by our ability to perceive certain cause and effect relationships, a general lack of historical cash flow data, and the absence of experience with some adverse situations that may occur in the future.

Section I. Introduction

FINANCIAL SIMULATION MODEL

Purpose: The initial purpose for developing the Financial Simulation Model was to generate cash flows available for servicing debt under a variety of economic, competitive, and operating conditions as a means to *generally define debt capacity and explore the risks attached to various debt policies.*

During the development work it was found that the model could feasibly be constructed for a broader range of financial simulation and financial analysis activities. Consequently, the model can be viewed as a general purpose analytical tool that can consider most conditions affecting Company Operations that can be quantified.

Scope: The model considers all Company activities to fall into one of these categories: (1) Domestic Operations (including manufacturing activities carried on domestically), Corporate, and Research and Engineering; (2) Domestic Subsidiaries; and (3) International Operations (including subsidiary companies, affiliated companies, and joint ventures). The first category, Domestic Operations, is dealt with in detail and all elements are determined within the model. Domestic Subsidiaries and International Operations are only considered when the model is dealing with total company considerations (such as debt position) and then certain data are to be given the model for these operations on a net basis.

Consolidated Data: The Financial Simulation Model deals with a total company position in regard to debt, equity, investments in subsidiaries and foreign companies, net cash flows, profits, and in developing the majority of the statistics available on the output. The output given for the total company is so indicated on the print-out.

To generate data on these consolidated positions, the model requires net profits of Domestic Subsidiaries and of International Operations be given for each quarter as well as the net cash inflows or outflows for both Subsidiaries and International.

The profits data are to be given less eliminations required to consolidate with Domestic Operations so when added to Domestic, the sum yields consolidated net profits. The required net cash flows for International consider all borrowings and repayments for International to be undertaken by the consolidated company except that joint ventures undertake and support their own debt resulting in their cash flows being only the Company's share of equity investments or dividends.

Specification of Model: The core of the model is the manner in which each element is determined (specifications for each element are given in Section II).

In most cases, the elements are developed from a linear relationship to one or more other elements (often related to sales in the manner suggested by historical company data). In some instances, the model considers a prescribed number of alternatives and then decides upon the one giving a value that fits certain criteria.

It is a characteristic of the model that it does not know in advance future conditions or assumptions. Therefore, when a future value is needed for a current quarter calculation, it must make an estimate of the prospective value (and its ability to do so accurately is quite limited), as is the case in reality.

The model has been refined to where some of its normal relationships are varied during the course of a cyclical downturn. However, the historical and subjective information available on a variety of downturns and the present company's reactions to these, as an aid for constructing the model, were very limited.

Major Assumptions: The Financial Simulation Model has been constructed to represent the Company as it presently exists or is known to become. Changes in the characteristics of the company that may occur can be simulated by making changes in the specified relationships of Section II. To allow for this, the utmost flexibility has been sought in building and programming the model — see "Operating Inputs."

Specifying the determinative relationships for some elements embodies certain major assumptions as follows (as expressed in the original design of the model):

(1) Capital Expenditures — to be the capital expenditures budgeted for the next two years, then a four-year gradual movement toward 6.0% of sales trend, and then a constant 6.0% of sales trend for the remaining years. The resulting values are only modified by a downturn that is fairly severe.

(2) Dividend Policy — to be a steadily increasing (15% annually) dividend rate that is unaffected by the business cycle.

(3) Debt or Capital Structure Policy — to be the debt to equity ratio that is given as input to each run.

(4) Merchandising Programs — to be maintained in the approximate relative proportion to sales as presently exists.

(5) Warranty — to be based on a condition of equipment population similar to that of the last three years.

(6) Subsidiaries and International Profits and Cash Flows — to be given to the model as inputs.

Operating Concept: The logic of the model employs three phases:

Phase I encompasses the inputs, starting conditions, and sets the relationships that are to be used in Phase II.

Phase II develops all information requested by Phase III.

Phase III contains the output requested, edits the work of Phase II, and is the controlling unit for what the model does.

The model is designed to consider sequentially a number of different sales assumptions and/or a series of assumptions for one other item to be varied (in the original design, this one other item was debt policy, but debt policy could be fixed and, say, capital expenditures varied successively over a series of runs). Consequently the model can be operated to make a single run or to make several runs (each under different sales assumptions and/or a different relationship for a major item) for the period being studied.

Inputs: Three types of inputs are required:

Sales Inputs — Each run or series of runs on the model requires the following inputs to be given:

(1) The various sales trends to be used. These trend values are expressed as quarterly growth rates (+ or —) for original equipment sales and for parts sales (the two can differ) and the trend growth rates can change as many as three times during one run. As many sets of trend values can be used as desired to give successive runs by the model.

(2) Seasonal adjustment factors for original equipment sales and for parts sales (more than one set of seasonal factors can be used per period).

(3) The sequences of given cycle patterns.

(4) Cycle patterns to be used. The cycles are expressed as quarterly index numbers and can cover any number of quarters. As many cycle patterns and cycle sequences can be used as desired to give successive runs by the model.

(5) The number of quarters the model is to run and the starting point in the first cycle pattern to be considered.

Debt Policy Inputs — Each run requires that the debt policy (expressed as a debt to equity ratio, e.g., 125.0%) be given. A number of debt policies can be specified for a series of runs and then each debt policy will be applied to each different sales assumption. (For example, with 8 sales assumptions, specifying 6 different debt policies will yield 48 runs by the model.) Debt policy could be fixed and some other relationship, such as dividend policy, could be varied, thus requiring Dividend Policy Inputs for each run or series of runs.

Operating Inputs encompass the four following categories of data:

(1) *Starting Values* — In developing values for any quarter, the model takes into consideration conditions existing in the previous four quarters. Consequently, certain actual, historical data must be given the model as the starting conditions. The starting values required for any quarter starting point are given in

Section III. These may be drawn from the latest
actual balance sheet and income statement at the
time of the analysis.

(2) *Forecast Values* — The model is set up to take advantage of the future values that are known or
planned on at present. This is accomplished by
feeding in forecast values as input. Also, the necessary Subsidiaries and International data are given
the model via forecast values. In addition, forecast
values can be used to override the amount normally
determined by the model for any element in any
single or group of future quarters. The forecast
values required are given in Section IV.

(3) *Normal Relationships* — In Section II, all elements
have a normal determinative relationship specified.
However, these so-called normal relationships can
be changed for any run or series of runs. If changes
are to be made, the new relationships have to be
given as part of the operating inputs.

(4) *Downturn Adjustments* — In Section II, relationships for some elements have had a cyclical adjustment specified. The model applies this adjustment
during a downturn to whatever relationship has
been given for that element. (Note, a run without
cycles will not invoke these adjustment factors.) If
these adjustments are to be changed or eliminated
or additional ones added, they must be given as
part of the operating inputs.

Operating inputs may or may not be given for each
operation of the model. If they are not given, the model
will start with the first quarter after the last quarter of
actual data supplied and use the latest version of normal
and cyclical relationships it has been given together with
the latest forecast values (i.e., the operating inputs will
be the same as those used on the last run of the model).

Outputs: Internally, the Financial Simulation Model gen-
erates all elements for each calendar quarter and a complete set of annual data for as many years as requested.
From this, two types of output are available: (1) a summary

report giving each quarter and annual value in columnar form for from one to twenty-four elements, and (2) a detailed report covering all elements in the P/L statement, cash flow statement, and balance sheet for each quarter and year-end included in the period being studied. Both reports are printed in thousands of dollars.

The summary report is printed out on from one to four sheets per run and can be generated separately or in addition to the detail report.

The detail report requires five sheets per year to print out (e.g., six runs over a ten-year period will produce 300 sheets of print-out — 6 x 5 x 10). Section V includes samples of report print-outs and further explanations.

SECTION II of the manual, which covered some 112 pages, presented in detail the specifications of each of the financial elements (how the number was to be generated) so that a complete and continuous series of financial statements could be built up. There were 103 such elements separately defined, some of which were balance sheet and other ratios that were to be produced for purposes of analysis. As indicated in the Introduction, many of the elements were tied back to the initial assumption about sales level in any given quarter or year. Two sample pages from this detailed description follow as Exhibits 1 and 2.

SECTION III of the manual presented a detailed schedule of all starting values required for the calculation of each of the elements of the analysis. For example, it was indicated that for the Key Variable "Total Sales," the value for the first quarter to be run by the model required the values for the four quarters preceding the initial run by the model. These would be found in the records of the company — the income statements published for the preceding year.

SECTION IV outlined the forecast values required for the calculation of certain of the elements. For example, the items "Interest Payments" and "Repayments on Initial Debt" required that the model be provided with a schedule of maturities and interest due on outstanding debt for all future quarters over which the runs were to be made.

Some of the most interesting and critical aspects of model speci-

EXHIBIT 1

Financial Simulation Model

Element: Inventories Balance

I. Inventories Balance
  A. Quarter Value (INVAB)
    1. Normal
      (1) INVAB = 45% KTSAQ (1)
      (2) INVAB = 45% KTSAQ (1)
      (3) INVAB = 45% KTSAQ (1)
      (4) INVAB = 48% KTSAQ (1)
    2. Cycle
    During a downturn the above percentages are increased by the following percentage points for the indicated quarter of the downturn:

1st qtr.: 0	4th qtr.: +5.0%
2nd qtr.: +5.0%	5th qtr.: +4.0%
3rd qtr.: +5.0%	6th qtr.: +2.0%

  B. Annual Value (INVAB)
  Same as 4th quarter value.
  C. Comments

Code:
  INVAB — Inventories Balance
  KTSAQ — Key Variable Total Sales

fication related to the manner in which the model runs dealt with deficiencies and excesses of cash resulting from the assumed level of operations for any given quarter or year. Excesses of cash presented the simpler of the two problems because such surpluses could merely be accumulated and invested in the short-term securities market at some assumed rate of return until needed again. Deficiencies were a different matter. They were dealt with as follows.

It was first assumed that there was a minimum cash balance required for the transactions pipeline of the company and unavailable for other uses. This minimum was defined as a fixed percentage of sales, which was varied by quarters on the basis of past experience. In any quarter when net cash flow from all company activities was negative, the model would first test to see whether this sum was available from surplus cash in excess of the minimum balance.

If surplus cash in this amount did not exist, the model next checked to see whether the deficiency could be found in unused short-term borrowing power from banks. The model had been

EXHIBIT 2

FINANCIAL SIMULATION MODEL

Element: Research and Engineering Expenses

I. Research and Engineering Expenses
  A. Quarter Value (REEAQ)
    1. Normal
      (1) REEAQ = 2.8% KTSAQ
      (2) REEAQ = 2.6% KTSAQ
      (3) REEAQ = 3.4% KTSAQ
      (4) REEAQ = 3.8% KTSAQ
    2. Cycle
      During a downturn, the above percentages are altered by the following percentage points for the indicated quarter of the downturn:

1st qtr.: +.2%	5th qtr.: +.1%
2nd qtr.: +.4%	6th qtr.: 0
3rd qtr.: +.4%	7th qtr.: −.2%
4th qtr.: +.2%	8th qtr.: −.2%
	9th qtr.: −.1%

  B. Annual Value (REEAY)
      REEAY = sum of REEAQ from (0) thru (3)

  C. Comments
      The salary and wages included in the research and engineering expenses consider applied fringes.

Code:

  REEAQ — Research and Engineering Expenses (Quarter)
  REEAY — Research and Engineering Expenses (Year)
  KTSAQ — Key Variable Total Sales

given an upper limit on short-term borrowing power based on current knowledge of bank attitudes, to be increased over the forecast period (10 years) on a simple linear growth trend consistent with expected growth in the size of the company. Thus for any future quarter a bank loan limit was specified.

If in any quarter cash needs exceeded surplus cash plus unused bank borrowing capacity, the model then tested for unused long-term debt capacity. Since this was the focus of the particular analysis to be done when the model was completed, a considerable range of long-term debt limits was specified. For any given run any level could be assumed. Debt limits ranged from a low of 25% of equity to a high of 150% of equity. If short-term borrowing proved to be at its limit but unused long-term debt capacity existed, then the model would float a new long-term loan in the amount of the existing short-term debt plus the extra funds needed, thus restoring the short-term borrowing capacity. A simplifying assumption was made as to the interest rate and maturity schedule on all new long-term debt.

If, as sometimes happened, particularly when low debt limits were set, the short-term and long-term borrowing power proved inadequate for current cash needs, the model then took action to raise the funds needed by an issue of common stock of a prescribed minimum amount. Obviously this necessitated the determination of a market value for the common stock at that time — what is called a Market Price Generator. The market price generator used was one based on a statistical study of the market price behavior of the company's stock in the past as interpreted by those who designed the model. It represented a weighted average of recent Earnings per Share and Dividends per Share. The model did not relate market price to the debt level then current as some experts would insist that it should.

Thus, by means of one or a combination of prior cash surplus, short-term debt, long-term debt, and common stock the model always provided the funds required for company growth related to any sales assumption including both working capital and fixed asset needs. Unlike the real world, the model did not force a reconsideration and possible reduction in planned expenditures if, for example, the current market value of the common stock did not appear attractive.

Thus the model involved not only a statement of historical relationships among the various elements of funds flows but also an explicit and consistent statement of financial policies relating to such matters as dividends, corporate borrowing, and new stock issues. In addition, it was clear that a number of key assumptions about the company's economic and financial environment, including stock market behavior, also had to be made explicit in order for the model to work at all. While these judgments were often crude and open to challenge, they were necessarily implicit in any financial forecast and there was great educational value in getting them out into the open where they could be examined systematically and tested for consistency with other related assumptions about the future.

The FINAL SECTION of the manual provided samples of the outputs of the model of corporate cash flows. The starting point of these outputs for any given run was an assumption made about the specific sales pattern of the next 10 years, quarter by quarter. This involved a combination of a trend assumption, a pattern of cyclical movements superimposed on that trend, and a seasonal index. An infinite number of combinations were possible here; but an examination of the company's past history, modified by the future expectations of management as necessary, narrowed down the test runs to eight different trend assumptions, twelve cycle sequences, and one seasonal pattern. These are summarized in Exhibit 3.

Given any one combination of sales trend, cycle, and seasonal and given a set of starting values for cash balance, inventory, etc., the model then proceeded to generate quarterly balance sheets and income statements for the next 10 years. An example is shown in Exhibit 4. These were then converted by the computer into a cash flow statement quarter by quarter, also illustrated in Exhibit 4. From these basic statements an analyst could determine the expected impact of a wide variety of changes, external or internal, on the cash position, reported income, and balance sheet relationships of the company. Depending on the particular purposes of the analysis, it was a simple matter to program the computer to generate additional exhibits to analyze and compare these data in any way desired.

EXHIBIT 3

SALES INPUT IDENTIFICATION FOR CAPITALIZATION STUDY RUNS

I. ASSUMED GROWTH CONDITIONS

	Original Equipment	Parts
A. Maximum Likely	$r = 2.9\%$ $n = 42$ $g = $ n.a.	$r = 2.6\%$ $n = 22$ $g = 2.9\%$
B. Most Probable	$r = 2.4$ $n = 42$ $g = $ n.a.	$r = 2.4$ $n = 42$ $g = $ n.a.
C. Minimum Likely	$r = 1.9$ $n = 42$ $g = $ n.a.	$r = 2.2$ $n = 22$ $g = 1.9$
D. Maximum Adverse Trend	$r = 1.4$ $n = 42$ $g = $ n.a.	$r = 2.2$ $n = 18$ $g = 1.4$
E. Lose Major Customer; Otherwise Normal Growth	$r = 2.4$ $n = 18$ $g = 1.0\%$	$r = 2.4$ $n = 32$ $g = 1.0$
F. Lose Major Customer; Otherwise Slower Growth	$r = 1.9$ $n = 18$ $g = 0.8$	$r = 2.2$ $n = 26$ $g = 1.0$
G. Growth Slow Down	$r = 2.7$ $n = 22$ $g = 1.6$	$r = 2.4$ $n = 34$ $g = 1.6$
H. Maximum Slow Down from Normal	$r = 2.4$ $n = 18$ $g = 1.5$	$r = 2.4$ $n = 30$ $g = -1.5$

r = quarterly growth rate for the first "n" quarters
g = quarterly growth rate for the last "$42-n$" quarters
n = number of quarters to which "r" applies

II. SEASONAL FACTORS

	O.E.	Parts
1st calendar quarter	1.008	1.014
2nd calendar quarter	1.115	1.009
3rd calendar quarter	.941	.908
4th calendar quarter	.939	1.068

III. CYCLE SEQUENCES

1. A, A, A, A	A. G, G, C, C
2. A, B, C, A	B. G, E, C, C
3. A, D, A, A	C. E, G, C, C
4. C, D, C, D	
5. A, E, A, A	
6. A, F, A, A	
7. A, G, A, A	
8. C, G, C, A	
9. H, H, H, H	

IV. DEBT POLICIES

Ratio	Debt/Total Capital	Debt/Equity Ratio
150%	60%	150.0%
122%	55%	122.2%
100%	50%	100.0%
82%	45%	81.8%
67%	40%	66.7%
54%	35%	53.8%
43%	30%	42.8%
25%	20%	25.0%

V. CYCLE PATTERNS

Quarter	A Normal		B Moderate		C Adverse: Short & Sharp		D Adverse: Protracted		E Serious: Short & Sharp		F Serious: Protracted		G Serious Sharp & Protracted		H No Cycle Effects	
	O.E.	Pts.	O.E.	Pts.	O.E.	Pts.	O.E.	Pts.	O.E.	Pts.	O.E.	Pts.	O.E.	Pts.	O.E.	Pts.
1	100	98	100	98	100	96	100	95	100	90	100	95	100	95	100	100
2	110	100	105	100	105	100	104	100	110	100	110	100	110	100	100	100
3	114	103	108	102	110	105	108	105	120	105	118	105	118	105	100	100
4	116	106	111	104	115	108	110	109	125	109	125	109	125	109	100	100
5	117	109	113	106	120	110	116	112	130	112	128	112	128	113	100	100
6*	118	111	115	108	125	112	120	114	135	114	134	114	132	118	100	100
7	119	113	115	109	130	114	122	116	140	116	135	116	136	120	100	100
8	120	114	115	110	130	116	124	118	140	118	135	118	140	122	100	100
9	120	115	100	110	120	118	125	119	110	119	135	119	140	124	100	100
10	115	115	96	108	100	120	116	120	60	120	125	120	100	125	100	100
11	105	108	92	106	70	112	106	115	60	105	100	110	65	105	100	100
12	90	100	89	102	70	100	100	108	75	85	75	95	60	85	100	100
13	80	92	87	95	75	83	85	100	90	75	65	80	60	75	100	100
14	80	85	85	90	85	80	75	88		80	65	75	60	75	100	100
15	85	85	96	90		90	75	80			65	75	65	75	100	100
16	92	93					77	80			70	75	70	77	100	100
17							80	85			85	80	80	80		
18							95	90			95	90	85	84		
19													90	89		
20																

* assumed to relate to 1965, 3rd quarter, conditions

EXHIBIT 4

FINANCIAL SIMULATION MODEL — DETAIL REPORT

CALENDAR QTR 1 — YEAR 1971 — FORECAST QTR 23 — KEY VARIABLES — ORIGINAL EQUIPMENT SALES $49,268 PARTS SALES $29,176 TOTAL SALES $78,444

— Balance Sheet Items —

U.S. Only Unless*

Cash Balance	4,042	
Receivables	40,006	
Inventories	34,005	
Prepayments	3,062	
Total Current Assets		81,116
Bank Loans*	757	
Accts Payable	19,219	
Merch Reserves	11,716	
Other Reserves	6,509	
Fed Tax Reserve	8,889	
Total Current Lia		47,091
Net Working Capital		34,025
Gross Fixed Assets	167,891	
Depreciation Res	51,173	
Net Fixed Assets		116,718
Invest in Subs/Intl*		135,488
Initial Term Debt*	26,140	
Subseqt Term Debt*	128,536	
Total Long Term Dbt*		154,676
Common Stock*	12,394	
Number of Shares*	4,958	
Surplus and Earnings*	119,159	
Total Equity*		131,553
Balancing Figure		1

— Profit and Loss Statement —

Gross O.E. Sales	46,804	
Gross Parts Sales	29,176	
Returns and Allowances		1,900
Total Net Sales		74,081
Material Costs	29,809	
Labor Costs	5,334	
Mfg. Expenses	11,767	
Total Depreciation	3,329	
Cost of Sales		50,238
Warranty and Other Expense	7,484	
Commissions	4,079	
Wholesale Comp	1,122	
Bonus/Insp Fees	613	
Merchandising Plan	887	
Merchandising Accruals	1,177	7,878
Outbound Freight	471	
P Taxes & Insurance	624	
State Income Tax	190	
Donations	426	
Other Income, Net	200	
Year-End/Inventory Adj	1,748	
Other Expenses		3,259
Interest Expense		2,166
Profit Before Taxes		3,056
Federal Tax Provision		1,467
U.S. Profit After Tax		1,589
Profits from Subsidiaries	880	
Profits from Internatl	1,431	
Total Profit After Tax		3,900

— Cash Flow Statement —

Total Gross Sales	75,981	
Change in Receivables	4,490	
Returns and Allowances	1,900	
Cash Inflow		69,591
Cost of Sales		46,909
Marketing Expenses	2,432	
Research & Engr Exp	2,856	
Other Div Controllables	2,196	
Controllable Expenses		7,484
Warranty and Other Expense	3,116	
Commissions	1,122	
Wholesale Comp	613	
Bonus/Insp Fees	716	
Merchandising Plan	1,014	
Merchandising Payments		6,581
Outbound Freight	471	
P Taxes & Insurance	207	
State Income Tax	13	
Donations	178	
Other Income, Net	200	
Other Payments		669
Interest Expense		3,585
Federal Tax Payments		3,188
Cash Profit		7,551
Change in Inventories	337	
Change in Payables	429	
Change in Prepayments	69	
Capital Expenditures	5,146	
Repymts of Initial Debt	36	
Repymts of Subseqt Debt	0	
Cash Dividends	1,720	
Net Subsidiary Transfers	455	

Statistics — U.S. Only

Return on Sales	2.1%
Sales Per $ Tot Asset	$.374
Sales Per $ Fix Asset	$.635
Current Ratio	1.7:1
Equity	$107,536
Return on Equity	1.5%
U.S. Profit/Tot Profit	40.7%
Capital Needs/Excess	$43,964 —
D 9H Ratio 150% Cycle Series	
100 100 100 100 100	

* includes foreign

Statistics — Total Co

	C Qtr	4 Qtrs
Earnings Per Share	$.787	$3.283
Dividends Per Share	$.347	$1.253
Per Cent Payout	44.1%	38.2%
Market Price of Stock	$80.680	$76.384
Return on Equity	3.0%	12.8%
Return on Capital	1.8%	7.5%
Unutilized Liq Resources	$41,896	$129,293
Flexibility Ratio	14.6%	54.2%
Debt-Equity/Capital Ratio	118.2%	54.2%
Interest Coverage	4.5x	4.9x
Burden Coverage	4.3x	4.2x
Cash Flow Burden Cover	7.2x	6.9x
Debt Retirement Period	7.7 Yrs	7.6 Yrs

Net Internatl Transfers	1,000 —	
Preliminary Cash Flow		1,641 —
Preliminary Cash Bal		3,285
Change in Bank Loans	757	
New Debt Inflows	0	
New Stock Inflows	0	
Increase in Shares		757
New Capital Inflows		
Net Cash Flow		884 —
Ending Cash Balance		4,042
Minimum Cash Bal Needed		4,042

INDEX